LEVEL III PRACTICE EXAMS – VOLUME

SCHWESER 2017 LEVEL III CFA® PRACTICE EXAMS VOLUME 1

©2016 Kaplan, Inc. All rights reserved.

Published in 2016 by Kaplan, Inc.

Printed in the United States of America.

ISBN: 978-1-4754-4122-2

HOW TO USE THESE PRACTICE EXAMS

Save practice exams until last. Just do not wait too long. Complete the readings and other practice questions before the practice exams. Your final four to six weeks of preparation should focus on practice exams. You will need ample time to take, review, and retake these exams. We at Schweser provide you with six complete, six-hour exams. They are designed like the actual exam. The first three hours are constructed response, and the second three hours are 10, six-question vignettes. The CFA Institute provides the actual morning sessions of the past three years as practice. *Online in the Candidate Resource Library, we provide you full, question-by-question coverage of these past morning exams. We review the relevant taught material, but our focus shifts to extracting the key case facts and how to use them to write an effective answer in the allotted time. This is a critical exam (and career) skill.* The Institute also has item-set practice tests on its website. You will want to complete these exams and tests at least one week before the actual test so you have time to learn from your mistakes and improve. One of the worst things you can do is wait to take a practice exam just before the real exam, leaving no time to learn anything from the experience.

A good strategy is to take the CFA Institute practice tests and then take the Schweser practice exams, finishing one to two weeks before exam day. Then retake the Institute's constructed response questions and several Schweser practice exams. In particular, take the time to write out and improve your constructed response answers. Each year, we hear from candidates who did well on the afternoon session but terrible in the morning session and flunked the exam as a result. It is much harder to write a reasonable constructed response answer in the time allotted and under exam conditions than you think. The good news is it gets better with more practice, and practice the item sets as well.

Time management is critical in practice and, even more so, on the exam. Plan to work in three-hour blocks of time and not peek at the solutions. Initially the most important thing is to work carefully and don't worry how long you spend on a single question. You are learning the material and good technique. As the exam becomes closer and certainly on your second try, answer the questions in the allotted time. Some candidates say our practice exams are easier than the real exam, while others say our exams are harder. It largely comes down to how well you prepare. The CFA Institute has made it clear that the Level III exam requires more judgment and perspective than is required on Level I or II. Count on there being questions that do not look like what you studied. Think about the concepts that were repeatedly stressed in the curriculum. Give the most logical answer you can in the time and space provided for the question. Remember, others around you feel the same stress too.

Be ready for the Level III exam format. The morning session (three hours and 50% of the exam) is entirely constructed response essay format. The afternoon session (three hours and 50% of the exam) is 10 selected-response, six-question item sets, each worth 18 points. The Level III topic area weights, as presented by CFA Institute, are shown here. You will notice these guidelines are vague. *The Level III exam is very "lumpy" in terms of what specific items make it into the exam in any one year. Do not expect an even distribution of topics.*

Topic Area Weights for the Level III CFA Exam	
Topic Area	*Level III Weight*
Ethical and Professional Standards	10–15%
Economics	5–15%
Fixed Income	10–20%
Equity Investments	5–15%
Alternative Investments	5–15%
Derivatives	5–15%
Portfolio Management	40–55%

The only things you can count on at Level III are surprises. The CFA Institute has specifically stated that all areas except ethics can (and have been) tested in combined fashion. Historically:

- There have been two item sets for ethics in the afternoon. In 2015 the ethics exam weight was changed to 10–15%, so do not be surprised if there are three item sets or even some constructed response questions.
- It is more accurate to think of the exam as 100% portfolio management in orientation.
- GIPS has been 0–5% with 0 or 1 item set. It is part of the portfolio management exam weight, not ethics.

Answering constructed response questions. Follow the specific directions for each question. The question will direct "use the template provided" or "answer on the blank pages provided." It may ask you to give one, two, or three reasons; or, it may state nothing and you must give the best answer you can in the time and space allowed. If you do not read and follow the directions given, expect to fail. The CFA Institute has said it gives no points for a general display of knowledge.

Give the CFA answer. Graders use an answer key and don't give points for creative thought. The correct exam answer is the one that best reflects what was prominently taught in the assigned material and is relevant to the case facts. Creative or personal views do not receive credit. Graders are not allowed to read anything into your answer, so you must be precise. Also, organize your work and think before you write. If the graders can't find or decipher your work, you will receive no credit. Constructed response questions are typically designed to have a range of acceptable as well as unacceptable answers. Most answers receive partial credit based on how close to the acceptable they come, so show and explain your work. In constructed response, you are being graded on your work process, not just the final answer.

Don't forget to prepare for item set questions as well. These tend to be more comfortable and technical, in other words, like Level II. The practice exams will prepare you for both types of questions.

Be prepared. Get plenty of sleep the night before the exam. Bring all necessary items (including snacks) with you and arrive early enough at the test site to get a decent parking space. In fact, I recommend thoroughly checking out the site before exam day. Important! Be sure to read the CFA Institute testing policies, which can be found on the CFA Institute website. All CFA candidates are expected to know and abide by all CFA Institute testing policies and procedures as well as the CFA Institute Code of Ethics and Standards of Professional Conduct.

My thanks to the Schweser team. I would like to thank all of my colleagues at Schweser, especially Kurt Schuldes, CFA, CAIA, and Jared Heintz, Production Project Manager, for their incredible work ethic and commitment to quality. Schweser would not be the company it is, nor could it provide the quality products you see, without all the Schweser content and editing professionals.

Best Regards,

David Hetherington

David Hetherington,
CFA Vice President and Level III Manager
Kaplan Schweser

2017 Practice Exam Answers and Explanations are Online at www.schweser.com

Answers and explanations for self-grading all practice exam essays and item sets are included at the end of this book. Explanations and calculations for the *item sets* are also available online at schweser.com. They also contain embedded links to supporting curriculum material for the relevant Learning Outcome Statements. In addition, you can access Performance Tracker, a tool that will provide you with exam diagnostics to target your review effort and allow you to compare your scores to those of other candidates.

Use Your Schweser *Online Access* Account

You should have received an email with login information for Online Access. This is your login to view "How to Pass the Level III CFA® Exam" and the two videos on answering constructed response questions in the Candidate Resource Library. You can also access other videos in the Candidate Resource Library, use the Schweser Study Planner and Performance Tracker, and (if you purchased any package) ask us questions regarding our material. Simply log in at www.schweser.com and select Online Access to use any of these features. You can access practice exam answers and explanations with the Practice Exams Vol. 1 left-hand menu item. If you need password help, go to www.schweser.com/password or use the Password Help link that appears if your login is unsuccessful.

Practice Exam Online Features at a Glance

Answer Explanations
Our answer format contains explanations to help you understand why one answer is the best of all the choices. When using Performance Tracker, you can choose to get detailed explanations for only those item set questions you missed or for all item set questions.

Links to Curriculum
Within the answer explanations, we have embedded links to the relevant content for review. This can include multiple Learning Outcome Statements, concepts, definitions, or formulas.

Exam Diagnostics
When you access Performance Tracker, you can request a breakdown of your overall score on the afternoon session of any exam. You can even get the LOS references for questions you answered incorrectly to facilitate your review efforts.

Performance Comparison
Log in today and enjoy the benefits of the Candidate Resource Library*, Office Hours**, the Schweser Study Planner, expanded Practice Exam item set answers, and Performance Tracker.

* Included with the Premium and Premium Plus study packages.

** Included with the Essential study package.

PRACTICE EXAM 1 MORNING SESSION QUESTION BREAKDOWN

MORNING SESSION		
Question	Topic	Minutes
1	Portfolio Management – Behavioral	15
2	Portfolio Management – Individual	18
3	Asset Allocation and Alternative Investments	21
4	Portfolio Management – Institutional	8
5	Alternative Investments	25
6	Equity Portfolio Management	17
7	Portfolio Management – Individual	23
8	Alternative Investments	14
9	Asset Allocation	15
10	Performance Evaluation	12
11	Asset Allocation	12
	Total	180

PRACTICE EXAM 1 SCORE SHEET

MORNING SESSION		
Question	Maximum Points	Your Approximate Score
1A	4	
1B	3	
1C	4	
1D	4	
2A	8	
2B	6	
2C	4	
3A	4	
3B	3	
3C	3	
3D	3	
3E	3	
3F	5	
4	8	
5A	2	
5B	5	
5C	3	
5D	3	
5E	4	
5F	3	
5G	3	
5H	2	
6A	5	
6B	3	
6C	4	
6D	5	
7A	4	
7B	6	
7C	5	
7D	2	
7E	6	

MORNING SESSION (CONTINUED)		
Question	Maximum Points	Your Approximate Score
8A	6	
8B	6	
8C	2	
9A	4	
9B	3	
9C	2	
9D	2	
9E	4	
10	12	
11A	9	
11B	3	
Total	180	

AFTERNOON SESSION		
Questions	Maximum Points	Your Approximate Score
1–6	18	
7–12	18	
13–18	18	
19–24	18	
25–30	18	
31–36	18	
37–42	18	
43–48	18	
49–54	18	
55–60	18	
Total	180	

PRACTICE EXAM 1
MORNING SESSION

QUESTIONS 1 HAS 4 PARTS (A, B, C, D) FOR A TOTAL OF 15 MINUTES.

Joe and Sara Finnegan are both 62 years old and live in Kerrville, Texas. They are retired and have a combined investable net worth of $2 million, the bulk of which was inherited from Sara's father's estate. Included in their total wealth is Joe's $500,000 defined-contribution retirement plan that is managed separately in a 401(k) retirement plan. Joe makes the investment decisions for his 401(k) plan, but Sara makes the investment decisions for their other portfolio. The Finnegans home in Kerrville is valued at $750,000. The Finnegans do not have a mortgage on their home.

Mr. Finnegan's 401(k) plan is administered by a local bank trust department. The trust department offers its clients a range of portfolio allocations from aggressive to conservative as shown in Exhibit 1. Without regard for asset class characteristics or his own risk and return objectives, Mr. Finnegan selected a portfolio that is equally weighted in each asset class and has made no changes to the portfolio allocation or to the allocation of new deposits to the plan portfolio. Mr. Finnegan is primarily concerned about potential losses in his account and prefers not to make investment decisions. He is often fearful and anxious about what may happen in his portfolio.

Exhibit 1: Alternative Portfolios

Asset Class	Current Yield	Aggressive Asset Mix	Conservative Asset Mix
Domestic Equity Stocks—Income	4.0%	40%	15%
International Stocks	3.0%	25%	5%
Domestic Bonds	4.0%	5%	50%
International Bonds	4.0%	5%	25%
Alternative Investments	2.0%	25%	5%

A.   **Identify** and **support** your identification of *two* behavioral characteristics that are evident in Joe Finnegan's allocation of his 401(k) retirement account. Make your identification from the following list: myopic loss aversion, conservatism, 1/n diversification, home bias, status-quo bias, and reference dependence.

(4 minutes)

B.   Based solely on his 401(k) investment portfolio, **select** the investor behavioral type (BIT) *most likely* exhibited by Joe and **justify** your selection with one reason.

(3 minutes)

Answer Question 1B in the template provided.

Template for Question 1B

Behavioral Type (circle one)	Justification
Adventurer	
Individualist	
Guardian	

After several years, the Finnegans become dissatisfied with managing their own portfolio and approach Tim Smith in the bank trust department for advice. Smith conducts detailed interviews with the Finnegans and identifies three sets of goals with varying priority. He uses a client questionnaire and determines that their biases are mainly emotional. Because of their lack of investment success, he concludes that meeting their primary goals will be difficult. He then develops both a goals-based investment plan and one based on traditional financial concepts.

C. **Explain** both how Smith would structure a goals-based investment plan for the Finnegans and the advantage of such a plan for them.

(4 minutes)

D. **Explain** one reason Smith would and one reason Smith would not deviate from the traditional plan asset allocations. Each reason must be based directly on the information provided regarding the Finnegans.

(4 minutes)

ANSWER QUESTIONS 2 AND 3 IN ORDER.

QUESTION 2 HAS THREE PARTS (A, B, C) FOR A TOTAL OF 18 MINUTES

Lachlan Martin and his wife Chloe are both 50 years old, have no children, and live in Sydney, Australia. Lachlan's father, Liam Martin, recently died and left his entire estate to Lachlan. Lachlan expects to receive his after-tax inheritance of 9.0 million Australian dollars (AUD) in one year. The Martins both plan to retire at that time, and are meeting with Zoe White to help them establish an investment plan.

The Martins currently own a home valued at AUD 3.9 million, do not have a portfolio of investable assets, and do not consider their home as part of their investable assets. In one year, the Martins' outstanding debt will be AUD 3.7 million (home mortgage) and AUD 160,000 (other debts). The Martins will pay off their mortgage and their other debts once the inheritance is received.

The Martins currently have a combined after-tax salary of AUD 500,000, current-year living expenses of AUD 263,000, plus annual mortgage payments (principal + interest) of AUD 237,000. Lachlan's company will pay him an after-tax pension of AUD 51,000 starting in one year when he retires, with the payments increasing by the rate of inflation, which is expected to be 3% annually. His employer will continue to pay all of the Martins' medical costs until death. Both the pension and health benefits will continue to accrue to Lachlan's wife, if he dies first. The Martins expect their living expenses will also continue to grow at the rate of inflation until one of them dies. At that time, they expect the survivor's living expenses will decrease to 75% of their combined expenses and then continue to grow at the rate of inflation.

The Martins intend to fund their living expenses during retirement with Lachlan's pension and the investment income generated from the assets invested in from the inheritance. The Martins consider their investment base to be large given the inheritance, want their portfolio to be invested conservatively, and want to maintain the real value of their investable assets over time. They plan to leave any assets left in their estate to charity. All income and realized capital gains are taxed at 25%. The assumed annual effective tax rate is 20%.

A.   **Calculate** the before-tax nominal rate of return required for the Martins' first year of retirement. **Show** your calculations. Do not assume any tax effects related to the mortgage.

(8 minutes)

B.   **Discuss** *two* factors that decrease and *one* factor that increases the Martins' risk tolerance.

(6 minutes)

C.   **Formulate** *each* of the following constraints for the Martins' investment policy statement (IPS):

    i.   Liquidity.

    ii.   Time horizon.

(4 minutes)

QUESTION 3 HAS SIX PARTS (A, B, C, D, E, F) FOR A TOTAL OF 21 MINUTES

The Martins have approached Steve Perry, a charterholder, for asset allocation advice. The Martins have read about the benefits of diversification and how it will allow them to take less risk but earn a higher return. They bring in articles on three investments that they have seen regularly discussed in the press and want to know if they will help the portfolio return. The portfolio is currently invested in domestic (Australian) stocks and bonds. Perry agrees to look into it and get back to them.

As a first step, Perry compiles the following historical data:

	Standard Deviation	E(R)	Correlation to Existing Portfolio	Sharpe Ratio
Current Portfolio	7.8%	6.5%	1.0	
Additions:				
International Equity	12.5%	8.7%	0.4	0.50
Real Estate	6.4%	7.1%	0.1	0.72
Managed Futures	13.9%	9.2%	-0.2	0.48

Risk-free rate 2.5%

A.   **Determine** which addition(s) will improve the portfolio's excess return to risk ratio and **show** the calculations to support the analysis. Use only the historical data Perry collected.

(4 minutes)

B.   **State** which proposed asset class's Sharpe ratio, based on the historical data, is *most likely* overstated and **explain** why.

(3 minutes)

C.   **State** which Sharpe ratio, based on the historical data, is *least likely* to persist in the future and **explain** why.

(3 minutes)

Before meeting with the Martins, Perry asks his assistant to review the characteristics of a valid asset class and the issues of adding international assets. The assistant gathers the following data.

	Correlation:	
Asset Class:	Within Asset Class	To Other Asset Classes
Global equity	0.63	0.51
International equity	0.87	0.49
Asset class "Z"	0.91	0.33
Small cap domestic equity	0.88	0.27

Global includes domestic and international

D.   **Determine** whether it is more likely international bond or equity currency exposure should be hedged and **support** your answer with one reason.

(3 minutes)

E.   **Explain** how contagion can be a problem if emerging market securities are added to the Martins' portfolio and what tool Perry would use to manage the problem.

(3 minutes)

Perry also asks the assistant to analyze the effect on the Martins' portfolio of adding French stocks to the portfolio if the currency risk is hedged or not hedged, based on the following assumptions:

Stock market from the French investor perspective:
      Return: 12%   Standard deviation: 29%

Risk-free rates:
      French: 2%   Australian: 5%

Standard deviation of the EUR:	14%
Expected change in value of the EUR:	+2%
Correlation of French stock and EUR return:	0.30

F.   **Compute** the return and standard deviation of a currency hedged and unhedged investment in the French stocks for the Martins. There are *four* items to calculate. Approximate calculations are acceptable.

(5 minutes)

QUESTION 4 HAS ONE PART FOR A TOTAL OF 8 MINUTES

Martina Edwards is retiring and stepping down from her position as portfolio manager at the Huron Foundation, which funds undergraduate and graduate environmental science research. She is currently training her replacement, Greg Matlock, who previously worked as the portfolio manager for the defined benefit pension plan of a large corporation.

During training, Edwards makes the following statements to compare a typical foundation to a typical defined benefit plan:

1. Both have perpetual time horizons.

2. Both should consider the effects of future inflation on return by compounding (or adding) real return and inflation to determine nominal return needs.

3. Foundations consider the correlation between return and dependence of the recipient on distributions. DB plans consider correlation of return and plan sponsor business results. In both cases, high correlation reduces risk tolerance.

4. Both have high needs for cash equivalents to fund large payouts.

Determine whether you agree or disagree with *each* statement made by Edwards. **Support** your decision. *Note: supporting your opinion by simply reversing an incorrect statement will receive no credit.*

(8 minutes)

QUESTION 5 HAS EIGHT (A, B, C, D, E, F, G, H) PARTS FOR A TOTAL OF 25 MINUTES

Vincent Scavuzzo is a CFA charterholder and was recently hired as a director of high net worth clients for an investment firm. One of his goals is to move the firm into alternative investments. In preparation for this move, the firm's board has raised several issues he must address.

A.   **Explain** why the firm will need legal and tax advisors to invest in private equity and other partnerships when this is not needed for existing stock and bond portfolios.

(2 minutes)

B.   **State** whether direct real estate or REITs will be more expensive to invest in. **Support** your decision with one reason it will be more expensive for the firm and one reason it will be more expensive for clients.

(5 minutes)

C.   **State** whether direct real estate or REITs should provide the largest diversification benefit and explain why. Do not base your answer on return data for any specific historical time period.

(3 minutes)

D.   **Explain** *decision risk* and whether it is a more serious problem for private equity (PE) or for commodity futures contracts.

(3 minutes)

E.   **Discuss** how venture capital (VC) and buyout funds (BO) differ in regard to using leverage, riskiness of the underlying securities, consistency of returns, and cash flow pattern to the investors over the life of the fund.

(4 minutes)

F.   **Explain** what vintage year means and the implication for selecting private equity benchmarks.

(3 minutes)

Scavuzzo asks his assistant to prepare examples he can use to discuss commodity investing. The assistant collects the following data for the June gold contract:

	Contract price	Spot price
March	1,289	1,244
April	1,132	1,101
May	1,215	1,195

Assume all prices and contract expiration are at month's end and the risk-free rate is 2%.

G.   **Compute** the roll return for May of a fully collateralized long position and **estimate** the roll return for June. **Show** your work. Your answers should be in dollar amount, not percentages.

(3 minutes)

H.   **Recommend** whether gold or wheat futures are more likely to have positive correlation with future inflation changes and **explain** why.

(2 minutes)

QUESTION 6 HAS FOUR PARTS (A, B, C, D) FOR A TOTAL OF 17 MINUTES

Jens Gustave is a senior portfolio manager with BAM Asset Management. He is reviewing the manager asset allocation for the High Grove Foundation, one of BAM's larger accounts. The foundation has carved out a 10% allocation, which employs aggressive techniques to enhance returns. Gustave has gathered data on three equity sub-managers to be employed and collected the following data.

	Manager A	Manager B	Manager C	Market Index
P/E	15.2	18.4	22.8	18.5
Beta	0.86	1.0	1.15	1.0
Dividend Yield	4.7%	3.1%	1.5%	3.2%
Active Return	0.9%	0.0%	1.5%	0
Active Risk	1.3%	0.1%	2.7%	0
Fees	0.40%	0.05%	0.60%	n.a.

Carl Johnson is a new board member for High Grove and also a money manager. Johnson has contacted Gustave and proposed an allocation between manager A and C of 100% and 100% with a 100% short position in B to fund the allocation. Manager B allows short positions in their fund.

Johnson says that the alpha of the equity sub-managers in this strategy can (1) be transported to other asset classes and (2) transporting alpha would be desirable during periods of poor relative equity performance. Gustave has promised to consider the idea and get back to Johnson before the next board meeting.

A.   **Calculate** the true information ratio for the allocation proposal. **Show** your work.

(5 minutes)

B.   **Identify** the approach being proposed and **support** your identification.

(3 minutes)

C.   **State** and **explain** whether each of Johnson's statements are correct or incorrect. "The alpha of the equity sub-managers in this strategy can be (1) transported to other asset classes and (2) transporting alpha would be desirable during periods of poor relative equity performance." Treat each statement in isolation and be specific to the Foundation's situation.

(4 minutes)

Gustave later has his staff gather additional information on Manager A and C. From this he concludes A invests in inefficient small-cap value stocks while C invests in efficient large-cap growth stocks. Despite this, he believes they both have an equal number of unique investment insights.

D.   **Determine** which manager (A or C) *most likely* has better information content in their decisions. **Support** your conclusion with two reasons based on the information provided.

(5 minutes)

QUESTION 7 HAS FIVE PARTS (A, B, C, D, E) FOR A TOTAL OF 23 MINUTES

Johan and Andrea Kraus are both 85 years old. Their spending over the coming year should be $128,750, and they expect to increase real spending at a rate of 3% annually. Their current portfolio contains $600,000 of cash equivalents, a $300,000 position in a diversified bond fund, and a $300,000 position in a diversified equity fund.

The Krauses have decided that they would like to gift a substantial portion of their wealth, so they are going to meet with financial planner, Jens Schultz, CFA, to update their investment policy statement. Schultz has constructed the mortality table in Exhibit 1 for the Krauses given a three-year planning horizon.

Exhibit 1: Mortality Table

Years	Johan		Andrea	
	Age	Prob.	Age	Prob.
1	86	0.8882	86	0.9171
2	87	0.7644	87	0.8244
3	88	0.6277	88	0.7208

Schultz plans on computing the Kraus's core capital and excess capital based on the probabilities in Exhibit 1. He estimates inflation will be 2%. The real and nominal risk-free rates are 4% and 6.08%.

A. **Compute** the core capital required for year 2 based on the information provided. **Show** your work.

(4 minutes)

B. Schultz has decided that Monte Carlo simulation (MCS) is more appropriate and determines $450,000 of core capital is required. **Explain** three advantages of MCS over using mortality tables.

(6 minutes)

C.   **Compute** the excess capital and **explain** two reasons Schultz would not recommend distributing the entire excess capital now.

(5 minutes)

Schultz believes the Krauses have not been taking advantage of available methods to avoid double taxation on their income. The Krauses are U.S. citizens and residents. The United States taxes their income, regardless of where it is earned, at 30%. The Krauses will receive income of $60,000 next year on overseas investments from Country X, which taxes all income generated within its borders at 25%. The United States and Country X have a tax treaty to reduce the effects of dual taxation.

D.   In the template provided, **identify** the *most likely* tax jurisdiction claimed on the Krauses' income by the United States and by Country X.

(2 minutes)

Template for Question 7D

Country	Tax Jurisdiction (circle one)
United States	Source Jurisdiction Residence Jurisdiction
Country X	Source Jurisdiction Residence Jurisdiction

E.   **Determine** the Kraus's *total* income tax liability on the income received from Country X assets under the credit method, the exemption method, and the deduction method.

(6 minutes)

QUESTION 8 HAS THREE PARTS (A, B, C) FOR A TOTAL OF 14 MINUTES

Helen Baker, CFA, invests in distressed securities. Specifically, she creates an arbitrage position in the underlying company equity and the company's distressed debt. Baker's strategy is based on the premise the bonds of bankrupt companies are excessively depressed by forced selling.

A.   i.   **State** the arbitrage positions *most likely* utilized by Baker.

      ii.   Assuming the company's prospects improve, **explain** how the strategy will perform with respect to prices of the stocks and bonds as well as coupon interest and dividends paid and/or received.

(6 minutes)

B.　**Describe** the following three sources of risk in distressed debt investing and the relative importance of each.

　　i.　Event risk.
　　ii.　Market liquidity risk.
　　iii.　Market risk.

(6 minutes)

C.　**Describe** J factor risk as it relates to distressed debt investing.

(2 minutes)

QUESTION 9 HAS FIVE PARTS (A, B, C, D, E) FOR A TOTAL OF 15 MINUTES

Heather Ramberg, a consultant to the board of directors of Reins Foundation, has been asked to analyze and recommend an asset allocation for Reins. Ramberg has read Reins's investment policy statement and found the following information:

Return objective: 8.5%.

Risk objective: Maximum standard deviation 10%.

To analyze the appropriate asset allocation, Ramberg produced data on the 5 corner portfolios shown in Exhibit 1.

Exhibit 1: Data on Five Corner Portfolios

Corner Portfolio	Expected Return (%)	Expected Standard Deviation (%)	Sharpe Ratio	Portfolio Weights, in %			
				U.S. Equities	Foreign Equities	Global Bonds	U.S. Real Estate
1	10.2	14.1	0.5106	0.0	100.0	0.0	0.0
2	10.1	13.6	0.5221	42.7	57.3	0.0	0.0
3	9.7	12.1	0.5537	41.3	38.7	20.0	0.0
4	8.2	9.0	0.5778	38.4	12.9	36.7	12.0
5	7.8	8.9	0.5506	37.4	11.9	39.7	11.0

Risk-free rate = 3.0%

A.   **Calculate** the *most appropriate* weight for U.S. equity for the foundation based on the corner portfolio theory and meeting the required return target. **Show** your work.

(4 minutes)

B.   **Estimate** the standard deviation of the *most appropriate* portfolio for the foundation, based on the corner portfolio theory. **Show** your work. **State** whether the actual sigma will be higher or lower than the estimate.

(3 minutes)

C.   Using data from Exhibit 1 and assuming that short selling (leverage) or investing at the risk-free rate is appropriate, **determine** which corner portfolio or portfolios would *most likely* be selected. Provide one reason to support your selection.

(2 minutes)

D.   **Explain** whether it is *most appropriate* for the foundation to construct its portfolio from two corner portfolios or from one corner portfolio plus leverage or borrowing.

(2 minutes)

Ramberg wants to present alternative approaches to traditional mean variance optimization and to using corner portfolios at the next board meeting. In preparation, he gathers information on alternatives.

E.   **Explain** the *most serious* problem with MVO and **explain** how resampling is used to address this problem.

(4 minutes)

QUESTION 10 HAS ONE PART FOR A TOTAL OF 12 MINUTES

Nick Richards is a pension consultant and is asked to evaluate the following portfolios:

- Portfolio 1 is highly concentrated, with five stocks representing 75% of the total portfolio.
- Portfolio 2 is highly diversified with over 400 stocks, none of which represents more than 1% of the total portfolio.
- Portfolio 3 is a diversified portfolio of 70 stocks, with the top ten names representing 30% of the total portfolio.

The following investment results were recorded during 2010:

	Portfolio 1	Portfolio 2	Portfolio 3	S&P 500
Return	42.0%	25.0%	16.0%	20.0%
Standard deviation	120%	40%	20%	50%
Beta	1.80	1.20	0.50	1.00

Risk-free rate: 6%

Calculate the Sharpe, Treynor, M^2, and Jensen measures for each portfolio.

Answer Question 10 in the template provided.

(12 minutes)

Template for Question 10

Performance Measure	Portfolio	Calculation	Value
Sharpe	1		
	2		
	3		
Treynor	1		
	2		
	3		
M^2	1		
	2		
	3		

Jensen	1		
	2		
	3		

QUESTION 11 HAS TWO PARTS (A, B) FOR A TOTAL OF 12 MINUTES

Beaver Dam Lumber (BDL) is one of the largest lumber companies in the United States, and the Beaver Dam Lumber Defined Benefit Pension Plan (BDLP) currently has a funding surplus. Slumping building starts in both the residential and commercial sectors, however, have led to declining sales. In response, BDL has offered early retirement to some employees, and the BDLP investment committee has decided to restructure the plan's portfolio more conservatively.

As a result of the early retirement offer, BDLP will have to make lump-sum payments totaling $20,000,000 over the next year. The BDLP investment committee has met and adopted a required return objective for their portfolio of 8.5% with a minimum acceptable return of –8.0%, coinciding with a Roy's Safety First ratio of 2.0.

The BDLP investment committee instructs Stephen Shamley, CFA, to evaluate the plan's $200,000,000 portfolio allocation and recommend changes. Shamley presents the five alternative allocations shown in Exhibit 1 for the committee's consideration.

Exhibit 1: Alternative Asset Allocations and Return/Risk Measures

Asset Class	Allocations (%)				
	A	B	C	D	E
Cash & equivalents*	5	5	10	4	10
Global fixed income**	35	30	30	40	35
Domestic fixed income	15	5	5	20	10
U.S. equities	30	30	30	16	35
Non-U.S. equities***	15	15	13	20	10
Lumber industry equities	0	15	12	0	0
	Risk and Return (%)				
Expected total return	8.65	9.25	9.06	8.29	9.04
Expected standard deviation	8.53	8.43	8.83	8.35	8.19

*   Maturities less than 6 months
** Domestic and international
*** Europe and Asia

A. Of the allocations shown in Exhibit 1, **select** the *most appropriate* allocation for BDLP. **Support** your decision with *three* reasons, other than meeting the return requirement.

(9 minutes)

B. Shamley also decides to look more closely at the proposed asset allocation mixes and believes one of the asset classes is not well specified. **State** which asset class is *least likely* to meet the conditions of an asset class and **explain** why.

(3 minutes)

END OF MORNING SESSION

EXAM 1 AFTERNOON SESSION TOPIC BREAKDOWN

Questions	Topic	Minutes
1–6	Ethics and Standards	18
7–12	Ethics and Standards	18
13–18	Economic Concepts	18
19–24	Risk Management Applications of Derivatives	18
25–30	Fixed Income Portfolio Management	18
31–36	Fixed Income Portfolio Management	18
37–42	Execution of Portfolio Decisions	18
43–48	Risk Management Applications of Derivatives	18
49–54	Risk Management	18
55–60	Global Investing/GIPS	18
	Total	180

EXAM 1 SELECTED RESPONSE ITEM SET ANSWER SHEET

The afternoon session of the Level III exam contains 10 Selected Response Item Sets, each with six questions, and you must answer them by filling in a bubble sheet with a number 2 or HB pencil. For realism, we suggest that you use this answer sheet and darken the bubbles corresponding to your answers. This sheet will also facilitate entering your answers into our online Performance Tracker. You have 180 minutes for this session of the exam. That equates to 3 minutes per item set question, so budget your time well.

1.	Ⓐ Ⓑ Ⓒ		31.	Ⓐ Ⓑ Ⓒ
2.	Ⓐ Ⓑ Ⓒ		32.	Ⓐ Ⓑ Ⓒ
3.	Ⓐ Ⓑ Ⓒ		33.	Ⓐ Ⓑ Ⓒ
4.	Ⓐ Ⓑ Ⓒ		34.	Ⓐ Ⓑ Ⓒ
5.	Ⓐ Ⓑ Ⓒ		35.	Ⓐ Ⓑ Ⓒ
6.	Ⓐ Ⓑ Ⓒ		36.	Ⓐ Ⓑ Ⓒ
7.	Ⓐ Ⓑ Ⓒ		37.	Ⓐ Ⓑ Ⓒ
8.	Ⓐ Ⓑ Ⓒ		38.	Ⓐ Ⓑ Ⓒ
9.	Ⓐ Ⓑ Ⓒ		39.	Ⓐ Ⓑ Ⓒ
10.	Ⓐ Ⓑ Ⓒ		40.	Ⓐ Ⓑ Ⓒ
11.	Ⓐ Ⓑ Ⓒ		41.	Ⓐ Ⓑ Ⓒ
12.	Ⓐ Ⓑ Ⓒ		42.	Ⓐ Ⓑ Ⓒ
13.	Ⓐ Ⓑ Ⓒ		43.	Ⓐ Ⓑ Ⓒ
14.	Ⓐ Ⓑ Ⓒ		44.	Ⓐ Ⓑ Ⓒ
15.	Ⓐ Ⓑ Ⓒ		45.	Ⓐ Ⓑ Ⓒ
16.	Ⓐ Ⓑ Ⓒ		46.	Ⓐ Ⓑ Ⓒ
17.	Ⓐ Ⓑ Ⓒ		47.	Ⓐ Ⓑ Ⓒ
18.	Ⓐ Ⓑ Ⓒ		48.	Ⓐ Ⓑ Ⓒ
19.	Ⓐ Ⓑ Ⓒ		49.	Ⓐ Ⓑ Ⓒ
20.	Ⓐ Ⓑ Ⓒ		50.	Ⓐ Ⓑ Ⓒ
21.	Ⓐ Ⓑ Ⓒ		51.	Ⓐ Ⓑ Ⓒ
22.	Ⓐ Ⓑ Ⓒ		52.	Ⓐ Ⓑ Ⓒ
23.	Ⓐ Ⓑ Ⓒ		53.	Ⓐ Ⓑ Ⓒ
24.	Ⓐ Ⓑ Ⓒ		54.	Ⓐ Ⓑ Ⓒ
25.	Ⓐ Ⓑ Ⓒ		55.	Ⓐ Ⓑ Ⓒ
26.	Ⓐ Ⓑ Ⓒ		56.	Ⓐ Ⓑ Ⓒ
27.	Ⓐ Ⓑ Ⓒ		57.	Ⓐ Ⓑ Ⓒ
28.	Ⓐ Ⓑ Ⓒ		58.	Ⓐ Ⓑ Ⓒ
29.	Ⓐ Ⓑ Ⓒ		59.	Ⓐ Ⓑ Ⓒ
30.	Ⓐ Ⓑ Ⓒ		60.	Ⓐ Ⓑ Ⓒ

PRACTICE EXAM 1
AFTERNOON SESSION

Questions 1–6 relate to Jamie Blackmore.

Jamie Blackmore, CFA, works for a portfolio management firm. Blackmore is a partner of the firm and is primarily responsible for managing the accounts of several large pension plans. She is also in a supervisory position with several research analysts reporting directly to her. Dave Lange is a research analyst who has worked under Blackmore for the last six years. Lange recently completed the Level III CFA exam and is anxiously awaiting the results. As a display of confidence, Blackmore shows Lange a box of business cards that have already been printed up for Lange with the initials "CFA" after his name. She locks them away in a filing cabinet and promises to deliver them on the day they get the news of his passing the exam and receiving his charter.

Blackmore and Lange have been working closely to service a number of clients. Lange knows that Blackmore recently met with a prospect named Johnnie Stangle. Based on his investment policy statement, Blackmore made a recommendation to Stangle to which he agreed. Blackmore then tells Lange to execute the trade. Lange has not seen the final paperwork outlining the account, but from what he knows the trade is congruent with Stangle's situation. Lange also knows the recommendation is generally a sound one.

Blackmore has been asked to write a research report on the 7MOD7 Corporation, where she is a member of the board of directors. Because of her relationship with 7MOD7, she assigned Lange to write the report instead. Blackmore is Lange's supervisor and requires Lange to show all of his work to her for final approval. As Lange begins writing the report, he remembers that the trust fund for his children, left to them by the parents of his wife, has a sizable investment in 7MOD7.

Blackmore also manages a defined benefit (DB) pension fund for Green International. The management of Green International has just requested that Blackmore increase the portion in international equity funds to 30% of total assets from its current position of 10% of total assets. The management of Green International believes the potential for growth in international markets is much greater than the domestic market and would like to see the pension fund managed more aggressively. Lange watches as Blackmore immediately acts upon the recommendation of Green International. Blackmore allocates some of the fund's assets to a few stocks in foreign countries. One of the stocks immediately goes up in price and volatility, and Blackmore sees an opportunity to earn some extra income for the fund by selling covered calls on that particular stock. Lange asks Blackmore if the pension fund's charter allows derivative strategies. Blackmore says she does not know but only sells covered calls when she sees a really good opportunity and none of her clients has ever complained. Blackmore points out to Lange that covered calls don't cost a client anything and they earn income for the client.

Despite his close relationship with Blackmore, Lange has been preparing to start his own money management firm. He has turned a spare bedroom in his house into an office with new furniture and a computer, has had the room wired with the latest internet service upgrades, has subscribed to financial news services, and has opened a trading account in the name of his proposed company. Lange told an old friend, who has a large portfolio being managed at another brokerage firm, about his plans. The friend knows Blackmore and told Lange that he did not like her and could not let Blackmore's firm handle his portfolio. If Lange was on his own, however, the friend would want Lange to manage his portfolio. Lange also contacts a cousin who has recently inherited a large portfolio. The cousin says that he would like to get some help managing the portfolio as soon as possible. Lange instructs his cousin to use futures contracts to hedge the value of the portfolio cost-free until Lange sets up his business and can take his cousin on as a client. He sends each of them a copy of his resume where he places "CFA (expected 2016)" after his name.

1. With respect to Blackmore's instruction to execute the trade for Stangle, according to the standards, Lange should:
    A. execute the trade immediately.
    B. not execute the trade because he has not met Stangle himself.
    C. execute the trade only after consulting the firm's legal counsel.

2. With respect to the report on the 7MOD7 Corporation that Blackmore asked Lange to write, which of the following must Lange include in the report?
    A. Blackmore is on the board of 7MOD7.
    B. The position of 7MOD7 in the trust fund of Lange's children.
    C. Blackmore is on the board of 7MOD7 and the position of 7MOD7 in the trust fund of Lange's children.

3. With respect to the DB pension fund for Green International, Blackmore's fiduciary duty is:
    A. owed primarily to the management and stockholders of Green International. Blackmore should follow management's direction to potentially increase the value of the company.
    B. owed to the participants and beneficiaries of the Green International pension fund. Therefore, Blackmore should continue to manage the fund in their best interest, regardless of the management's request.
    C. owed equally to the participants and beneficiaries of the fund, and to management of Green International. Therefore, Blackmore should increase the portion in international equities as long as it is within policy statement guidelines.

4. With respect to the pension fund for Green International, after Lange becomes aware of Blackmore's actions in response to management's instructions and the sale of the call options, he should:
    A. disassociate from Blackmore's activities.
    B. report Blackmore's activities to the appropriate regulatory authority.
    C. do nothing, because he knows what Blackmore said about the covered call strategy is true.

5. With respect to Lange preparing to set up his own business, Lange violated the standards:
    A. in his communication with his friend.
    B. in his communication with his cousin.
    C. by setting up trading accounts in the name of his company.

6. Violations, with respect to the use of the CFA designation, occurred with:
    A. the printing of the business cards by Blackmore, but not the letters sent by Lange to his friend and cousin.
    B. both the printing of the business cards by Blackmore and the letters sent by Lange to his friend and cousin.
    C. the letters sent by Lange to his friend and cousin, but not with the printing of the business cards by Blackmore.

Questions 7–12 relate to Lewis Smithers.

Lewis Smithers, CFA, is the lead portfolio manager for Fundamental Investments Corp., a money manager serving individual investors. He has researched Pineda Canyon Development (PCD), an owner of mountainside real estate perfect for the development of ski resorts. However, he concludes PCD lacks the cash to build the resorts.

Smithers has lunch with a friend, Judith Carson. Carson is managing partner of a land-developer that owns thousands of acres of prime real estate. During the course of their conversation, Carson asked Smithers to invest in one of their limited partnerships, which is about to buy a land developer and its acreage near Sassy River.

Smithers talks with Liam O'Toole, his largest client. O'Toole is a knowledgeable real estate investor. When asked, O'Toole mentions that he saw in a newsletter that a large Arizona real estate developer is expected to soon sell property in the Sassy River Valley. The article only mentions the amount of acreage and rumored sale price, not the buyer and seller. O'Toole offers to make Smithers a participant in the deal. O'Toole also mentions he would like to use Smithers' condo for a week this summer.

Smithers suspects these are the same transaction and PCD is the seller. He calls Carson and asks if this is true. Carson will neither confirm nor deny it. Later Smithers sees Carson having dinner at a public restaurant with two PCD senior executives. From public records he determines PCD is the only plausible large land seller in Sassy River and Carson's firm is the only plausible buyer.

That afternoon, Smithers prepares a purchase recommendation for PCD stock. He cites the expected sale of Sassy River Valley land for a very attractive price. He includes projected revenue and profit numbers and details the location of the property. As required by firm policy, he submits the report to his supervisor for approval before issuance.

7. In gathering information for the PCD purchase recommendation and in regard to the Code and Standards, Smithers *most likely*:
   A. committed no violations.
   B. violated his obligations of Loyalty, Prudence, and Care.
   C. violated his obligations for a Diligent and Reasonable Basis.

8. After submitting his stock recommendation to his boss and before receiving a response, Smithers takes three actions. The action *least likely* to violate the Code and Standards is:
    A. advising a few family and friends to purchase Pineda stock.
    B. downgrading two other related stocks on the basis of general industry trends.
    C. discussing his views and information with Fundamental Investment's bond department.

9. When Carson asks Smithers to personally invest in a partnership, it is *most accurate* to say Smithers may:
    A. invest.
    B. not invest.
    C. may invest if it is not detrimental to his clients.

10. Regarding Smithers' discussion with O'Toole, it is *most likely* that:
    A. Smithers may not participate in the deal O'Toole offers.
    B. Smithers may not let O'Toole use Smithers' condo.
    C. both actions could be acceptable with sufficient disclosures.

11. Smithers' boss realizes that unpublished research Smithers used in reaching his recommendation on PCD would be useful to other divisions of Fundamental Investments (outside the investment management division). To control such information flows, it is recommended the firm:
    A. establish firewalls between and physically separate the divisions.
    B. designate a compliance or other officer to review such information before it is shared.
    C. both actions are recommended.

12. Assuming that Fundamental Investments (FI) has adopted the Asset Manager Code (AMC), the *most* significant differences between the AMC and the Code and Standards are *most likely* in the sections detailing:
    A. Loyalty to Clients.
    B. Investment Process and Actions.
    C. Risk Management, Compliance, and Support.

Questions 13–18 relate to GloboFunds.

Joe Lipscomb is a junior economist for GloboFunds, a large investment management company. He has been asked to develop economic forecasts for several developing and developed markets to support a few of the global funds that the firm manages.

Lipscomb is aware that many of his colleagues use the Cobb-Douglas production function to forecast real GDP growth, but he is not familiar with it. He asks Donald Prater, one of his senior colleagues, to explain the function. While discussing the Cobb-Douglas production function, Prater makes the following statements:

Statement 1: An optimal Cobb-Douglas production function recognizes diminishing marginal utility of labor and capital but assumes a constant change in total factor productivity.

Statement 2: The Solow residual is the portion of the percentage change in real output that is not explained by the percentage change in total factor productivity, the percentage change in capital stock, and the percentage change in labor.

After gaining a basic understanding of the Cobb-Douglas production function, Lipscomb is ready to evaluate the growth of a few countries. Prater asks Lipscomb to analyze three countries and determine which has the highest expected real GDP growth rate. Lipscomb has gathered the estimates for the three countries in Figure 1:

Figure 1: Growth Expectations for Countries 1, 2, and 3				
Country	Growth in Total Factor Productivity	Growth in Capital Stock	Growth in Labor Input	Output Elasticity of Capital (α)
1	2.0%	4.0%	9.0%	0.7
2	4.0%	4.5%	7.5%	0.4
3	3.0%	8.5%	5.5%	0.3

After determining which country has the highest expected growth rate, Prater asks Lipscomb to assist him by determining the intrinsic value of the equity market for a fourth developing country. The country is expected to have high growth next year that will then decline linearly over the next 20 years to a sustainable growth rate. The estimated real required rate of return is 12%, and the most recent dividend was $15. Data regarding country four are shown in Figure 2:

Figure 2: Growth Expectations for Country 4				
Year	Growth in Total Factor Productivity	Growth in Capital Stock	Growth in Labor Input	Output Elasticity of Capital(α)
1	5.2%	6.9%	8.9%	0.4
21	0.5%	1.7%	2.0%	0.7

GloboFunds has placed a significant bet on a developed country (Country 5) in Western Europe. There is some fear internally that this equity market is becoming overvalued. Lipscomb decides to evaluate the intrinsic value of this market using the Yardeni model. The yield on A-rated corporate bonds is 7.5%, the long-term sustainable earnings growth rate is estimated to be 5%, and the current trailing P/E ratio is 15. Lipscomb has estimated that the weighting factor for the importance of earnings growth is 0.15 for this country.

GloboFunds is looking at expanding into alternative investments by managing a global macro hedge fund, but the portfolio managers are unsure as to the best forecasting approach to implement. They have asked Lipscomb to identify the best method. The fund will place bets on the direction of equity markets and currencies using exchange traded funds, forwards, and futures.

13. Is Prater's first statement regarding the Cobb-Douglas production function correct?
   A. Yes.
   B. No, the function assumes a simple linear relationship between labor and capital inputs to real economic output.
   C. No, it applies a log normal function to TFP to reflect diminishing returns to scale.

14. Is Prater's second statement regarding the Solow residual correct?
   A. Yes.
   B. No, the Solow residual is equal to the percentage change in capital stock.
   C. No, the Solow residual is equal to the percentage change in total factor productivity.

15. Based on the growth and elasticity data compiled by Lipscomb, which country has the highest expected real GDP growth rate?
   A. Country 1.
   B. Country 2.
   C. Country 3.

16. The intrinsic value of the equity market in Country 4 is *closest* to:
    A. 154.
    B. 328.
    C. 345.

17. Based on the Yardeni Model, Lipscomb would *most likely* conclude that the equity index is:
    A. overvalued.
    B. undervalued.
    C. fairly valued.

18. Regarding the forecasting approach that would be *best* suited for the global macro hedge fund, Lipscomb would *most likely* select:
    A. the top-down approach.
    B. the bottom-up approach.
    C. both the top-down and bottom-up approaches.

Questions 19–24 relate to Garrison Investments.

Garrison Investments is a money management firm focusing on endowment management for small colleges and universities. Over the past 20 years, the firm has primarily invested in U.S. securities with small allocations to high quality long-term foreign government bonds. Garrison's largest account, Point University, has a market value of $800 million and an asset allocation as detailed in Figure 1.

Figure 1: Point University Asset Allocation

Asset Class	Allocation	Dividend/Coupon*	Beta
Large cap equities	40%	2.0%	1.0
Mid cap equities	25%	1.2%	1.3
Small cap equities	15%	0.9%	1.5
U.S. Bonds	10%	5.0%	0
U.K. Bonds	5%	4.7%	0
German Bonds	5%	4.0%	0
European Index	0%	1.8%	1.2

*Bond coupon payments are all semiannual.

Managers at Garrison are concerned that expectations for a strengthening U.S. dollar relative to the British pound could negatively impact returns to Point University's U.K. bond allocation. Therefore, managers have collected information on swap and exchange rates. Currently, the swap rates in the United States and the United Kingdom are 4.9% and 5.3%, respectively. The spot exchange rate is 0.45 GBP/USD. The U.K. bonds are currently trading at face value.

Garrison recently convinced the board of trustees at Point University that the endowment should allocate a portion of the portfolio to European equities. The board has agreed to the plan but wants the allocation to international equities to be a short-term tactical move. Managers at Garrison have put together the following proposal for the reallocation:

> To minimize trading costs while gaining exposure to international equities, the portfolio can use futures contracts on the domestic 12-month mid-cap equity index and on the 12-month European equity index. This strategy will temporarily exchange $80 million of U.S. mid-cap exposure for European equity index exposure. Relevant data on the futures contracts are provided in Figure 2.

Figure 2: Mid-cap Index and European Index Futures Data

Futures Contract	Price	Beta	Multiplier
Mid-cap Index	$908	1.10	250
European Index	$2,351	1.05	50

Three months after proposing the international diversification plan, Garrison was able to persuade Point University to make a direct short-term investment in Haikuza International (HI), a Japanese electronics firm. Analysts at Garrison have regressed the historical returns of the HI stock with changes in value of the yen. When the HI returns are measured in U.S. dollars, the regression slope coefficient is +0.80.

The managers at Garrison are discussing other factors that may be considered if they continue to diversify into foreign markets. The following statements are made:

Statement 1: The minimum variance hedge ratio is riskier than a simple direct one-for-one hedge ratio because it depends on the correlation between asset and currency returns.

Statement 2: An alternative to selling the yen forward to implement the HI currency hedge would be to buy calls on the USD. This would protect the portfolio from currency risk while still retaining potential currency upside. Unfortunately, it will have a higher initial cost.

19. Which of the following is *closest* to the notional principal on a swap that would allow Point University to hedge the currency risk of the interest payments from their U.K. bond holdings?
    A. GBP 16,000,000.
    B. USD 38,000,000.
    C. GBP 18,000,000.

20. With regard to Garrison's proposal to generate temporary exposure to European equities in the Point University portfolio, **determine** the appropriate position in the mid-cap equity index futures.
    A. Buy 417 contracts.
    B. Sell 298 contracts.
    C. Sell 417 contracts.

21. With regard to Garrison's proposal to generate temporary exposure to European equities in the Point University portfolio, **determine** the appropriate position in the European equity index futures.
    A. Buy 778 contracts.
    B. Sell 595 contracts.
    C. Sell 778 contracts.

22. Garrison's analysis to determine a hedge ratio for the HI exposure is *best* described as producing a:
    A. cross hedge.
    B. transaction hedge.
    C. minimum variance hedge.

23. Which of the following is the correct short position in yen the managers at Garrison will execute to implement a minimum variance hedge for a JPY 200,000,000 currency exposure?
    A. 40 million.
    B. 160 million.
    C. 240 million.

24. Which of the statements regarding diversifying into foreign markets is true?
    A. Statement 1.
    B. Statement 2.
    C. Both statements.

Questions 25–30 relate to Northern Capital Advisors.

Dakota Watson and Anthony Smith are bond portfolio managers with Northern Capital Investment Advisors (NCIA). NCIA is based in the United States and has $2,000 million under management, including $950 million in global bond markets. NCIA's clients are primarily institutional investors such as insurance companies, foundations, and endowments. Because most of their clients insist on margins over relevant fixed-income benchmarks, Watson and Smith actively manage their bond portfolios to generate excess returns while minimizing tracking error.

One of the funds that Northern Capital offers invests in emerging market bonds. An excerpt from its prospectus reveals the following fund objectives and strategies:

> "The fund generates a return by constructing a portfolio using all major fixed-income sectors within the Asian region (except Japan) with a bias toward non-government bonds. The fund makes opportunistic investments in both investment grade and high yield bonds. Northern Capital analysts seek bond issues that are expected to outperform U.S. bonds that have similar credit risk, interest rate risk, and liquidity risk. Value is added by finding bonds that have been overlooked by other developed world bond funds. The fund favors non-dollar, local currency-denominated securities to avoid the default risk associated with a lack of hard currency on the part of foreign issuers."

Although Northern Capital examines the availability of excess returns in foreign markets by investing outside the index in those markets, many of its strategies involve spread analysis on U.S. bonds. Discussing the analysis of spreads in the U.S. bond market, Watson makes the following statements about the option-adjusted and swap spreads:

Statement 1: "Due to changes in the structure of the primary bond market in the U.S., the option-adjusted spread is becoming increasingly valuable for analyzing the attractiveness of bond investments."

Statement 2: "One advantage of the swap spread framework is that it provides investors with the tools to compare the relative attractiveness of fixed- and floating-rate bonds."

Watson's view of the U.S. economy is somewhat bearish. She forecasts that interest rates in the U.S. could fall as a result of a decline in the demand for loanable funds. Although she feels yields might decline, she believes strongly that market uncertainty will drive up interest rate volatility and has reallocated a portion of her bond portfolio to investment grade bonds.

Smith is even less decided about the economy, but his bond trading strategy has been quite successful in the past. As one example, he recently sold at par a 20-year, AA-rated $50,000 Mahan Corporation bond with a 7.75% coupon that he also purchased at par. With the proceeds, he bought a newly issued A-rated Quincy Corporation bond with an 8.25% coupon. By swapping the first bond for the second, he enhanced his annual income, which he considers quite favorable if interest rates fall as he expects.

Watson has become quite interested in the mortgage-backed security (MBS) market lately. In addition to an increased allocation to investment grade bonds, she has reallocated a portion of the corporate bond portfolio to MBS. She argues that, although a moderate drop in rates could move their prices slightly higher, corporate bonds on net could fall in value because of increased uncertainty in yields. MBS, on the other hand, should experience a net increase in value. She identifies this strategy as a structure trade.

Smith is examining the liquidity of three bonds. Their characteristics are listed in the table below:

	Issue Size	Coupon Rate	Term	Market
Bond A	$720 million	5.85%	10 years	Public Market
Bond B	$1,600 million	6.13%	7 years	Public Market
Bond C	$380 million	5.95%	20 years	Private Placement

25. Which of the following *best* describes the relative value analysis used in the Northern Capital emerging market bond fund? It is a:
    A. top-down approach.
    B. bottom-up approach.
    C. combination of a top-down approach and a bottom-up approach.

26. Regarding the statements made by Watson on the usefulness of the option adjusted spread and the swap spread, are both statements correct?
    A. Yes.
    B. No, only statement 2 is correct.
    C. No, both statements are incorrect.

27. Which of the following *best* describes Watson's increased allocation to investment grade bonds?
    A. Credit-defense trade.
    B. Pure yield pickup trade.
    C. Yield curve adjustment trade.

28. Which of the following *best* describes a primary shortcoming of Smith's strategy?
    A. The yields on the Mahan Corporation bond could increase.
    B. The yields on the Quincy Corporation bond could increase.
    C. The liquidity of the Mahan Corporation bond is likely lower.

29. Based solely on Watson's expectations, determine whether she has properly identified and executed her strategy.
    A. It is executed correctly, but she identifies it incorrectly.
    B. It is executed incorrectly, but she identifies it correctly.
    C. It is executed correctly, and she identifies it correctly.

30. Regarding the bonds Smith is examining, which of the following is *most likely* to have the greatest liquidity?
    A. Bond A.
    B. Bond B.
    C. Bond C.

Questions 31–36 relate to Andre Hickock.

Andre Hickock, CFA, is a newly hired fixed income portfolio manager for Candlewood Investments, LLC. Hickock is reviewing the portfolios of several pension clients that have been assigned to him. The first portfolio, Montana Hardware, Inc., has the characteristics shown in Figure 1.

Figure 1: Asset Allocation of Montana Hardware, Inc.

Sector	% of Portfolio	Duration
U.S. Treasury	14.6%	7.54
U.S. agencies	23.7%	9.02
U.S. corporates	31.8%	4.52
U.S. mortgages (MBS)	11.4%	1.33
Non-U.S. governments	18.5%	3.22
	100.0%	

Hickock is attempting to assess the risk of the Montana Hardware portfolio. The benchmark bond index that Candlewood uses for pension accounts similar to that of Montana Hardware has an effective duration of 5.25. His supervisor, Carla Mity, has discussed bond risk measurement with Hickock. Mity is most familiar with equity risk measures and is not convinced of the validity of duration as a portfolio risk measure. Mity told Hickock, "I have always believed that standard deviation is the best measure of bond portfolio risk. You want to know the volatility, and standard deviation is the most direct measure of volatility."

Hickock is also reviewing the bond portfolio of Buffalo Sports, Inc., which is comprised of the following assets shown in Figure 2.

Figure 2: Asset Allocation of Buffalo Sports, Inc.

Sector	% of Portfolio	Duration
U.S. Treasury	10.1%	6.15
U.S. agencies	14.5%	7.20
U.S. corporates	20.9%	5.80
U.S. mortgages (MBS)	33.7%	4.65
U.S. ABS	8.2%	3.67
Non-U.S. governments	12.6%	2.50
	100.0%	

The trustees of the Buffalo Sports pension plan have expressed concern that interest rates are low and likely to rise but agree with an assertion Hickock made at a recent meeting when he stated that interest rate spreads are likely to contract. Hickock assures the trustees the portfolio can be managed to benefit from both of these views.

The trustees also request Hickock review an immunized portfolio that was set up last year to meet an expected lump sum distribution. The dedicated portfolio has a market value of $20,100,000. The distribution will be $24,000,000 and occur in five years. The trustees ask Hickock to review the performance of the portfolio and recommend an appropriate duration management strategy consistent with the goals of the portfolio and their expectations for changes in interest rates. The portfolio was initially funded with a $1,250,000 surplus and the current five-year immunization rate is 4.0%.

31.   Mity's comment regarding the use of standard deviation instead of duration to measure bond portfolio risk is:
        A. correct because duration does not directly address volatility.
        B. incorrect because standard deviation does not address interest rate risk.
        C. incorrect because historical variance measures for specific bonds are not meaningful predictors of future volatility.

32.   **Calculate** the duration of the Montana Hardware pension portfolio and assess the interest rate risk of the portfolio versus Hickock's benchmark index. The interest rate risk of the Montana Hardware portfolio is:
        A. less than the benchmark.
        B. greater than the benchmark.
        C. the same as the benchmark.

33.   Hickock is reviewing other risk measures for the Montana Hardware portfolio. He has estimated the static spread duration for the portfolio to be 6.25. Which of the following statements regarding the Montana Hardware pension bond portfolio is *most* accurate?
        A. The value of the portfolio will change more for a 50 basis point shift in interest rates than for a 50 basis point change in spread.
        B. The portfolio spread duration could be decreased by adding Treasury securities to the portfolio.
        C. A 50 basis point change in the zero volatility spread would lead to an approximately 6.25% change in the value of the portfolio.

34.   In order for the portfolio to benefit from both his own and the Buffalo Sports trustees market views, Hickock would:
        A. buy bond and credit spread forwards.
        B. sell bond and credit spread forwards.
        C. sell bond and buy credit spread forwards.

©2016 Kaplan, Inc.

35. Assuming semiannual compounding, has the Buffalo Sports immunized portfolio performed above or below expectations up to now?
    A. Performed above expectations.
    B. Performed below expectations.
    C. It is meeting expectations.

36. To meet the goals of the immunized portfolio and the trustees interest rate views, Hickock would *most likely*:
    A. sell bond futures.
    B. adjust the portfolio duration to 5.0.
    C. purchase securities with a spread duration in excess of 5.0.

Questions 37–42 relate to Kim Simpson and Janet Long.

Kim Simpson, CFA, manages a $75 million multi-cap growth portfolio. Simpson follows a growth investment strategy and her investment universe consists of small, medium, and large capitalization stocks. She turns the entire portfolio over once each year. Simpson is concerned about the amount of trading costs she has generated through the implementation of her investment strategy and decides to conduct a trade cost analysis with the cooperation of her trader, Janet Long, CFA. The first trade they examine is a leveraged purchase of 2,000 shares of Technology Company that was completed in a single day using a market order. The order was split into two trades as shown in Figure 1.

Figure 1: Technology Company buy order for 2,000 shares

Shares Purchased	Purchase Price	Ask Size	Ask Price	Bid Size	Bid Price
700	$79.25	700	$79.25	900	$79.00
1,300	$80.00	800	$80.10	1,100	$79.75

In conducting a comprehensive analysis of the trading markets, Simpson states that she is most concerned about market liquidity. Simpson defines a market with good liquidity as one with diversity of opinion, many buyers/sellers, and relatively wide bid-ask spreads. In addition to reviewing market liquidity, Simpson believes that, in order to assess market quality, both the ease with which investors can obtain accurate information and the certainty that a trade will be completed must be evaluated.

Simpson and Long review their trade of Nano Corporation, a small biotechnology company. Simpson used a limit order because her analyst had established a specific buy target and she wanted to hold down transaction costs. To handle both explicit and implicit trading costs, Simpson measures execution costs using implementation shortfall. The buy order for 100,000 shares of Nano stock has the following timeline:

- Nano stock price closes at $35.00 per share.
- *Day one*: Simpson places a limit order for 100,000 shares of Nano stock at $34.75 per share or better before the opening of trading. Nano's stock never falls below $35.00 per share and closes at $36.50 per share.
- *Day two*: Simpson adjusts her limit order price to $37.00 per share or better. Long is able to fill 50,000 shares of the order at $36.75 per share. Nano's stock climbs to $38.00 per share during the day and Simpson moves the limit price to $40.00 per share or better. Long completes the purchase of the remaining 50,000 shares of Nano at $40.00 per share, which is also the closing price of Nano's stock.
- The commission paid for each block trade is $2,500.

Long suggests implementing the Best Execution concept as established by the CFA Institute in its Trade Management Guidelines. Long states best execution would accept a high portfolio turnover strategy provided the overall portfolio value is greater after trading costs. Long asserts that her professional relationships are integral to best execution.

37. The buy order for the Technology Company shares has an average effective spread *closest* to:
    A. $0.10.
    B. $0.15.
    C. $0.20.

38. Which one of the following trader motivations *best* describes the Technology Company trade?
    A. Information-motivated.
    B. Value-motivated.
    C. Liquidity-motivated.

39. Simpson discusses both the definition of market liquidity and how to assess market quality. Are her statements *correct*?
    A. Only the market liquidity statement is correct.
    B. Only the market quality statement is correct.
    C. Both statements are correct.

40. The explicit cost component of the total implementation shortfall for the Nano Corporation trade is *closest* to:
    A. 0.15%.
    B. 0.25%.
    C. 0.35%.

41. The total implementation shortfall for the Nano Corporation trade is *closest* to:
    A. 4%.
    B. 7%.
    C. 10%.

42. Regarding Long's statements on best execution, determine whether her mention of professional relationships and high portfolio turnover are *most likely* correct or incorrect.
    A. Only the statement about business relationships is correct.
    B. Only the statement about high portfolio turnover is correct.
    C. Both statements are correct.

Questions 43–48 relate to Donaghy Management Company.

Donaghy Management Company (DMC) manages several funds only available to high net worth individuals. In preparation for an upcoming meeting, the firm has circulated among its managers the information in Figure 1 on strategies and market expectations relevant to each of three funds.

Figure 1: Fund Strategies and Market Expectations

	Fund A	Fund B	Fund C
Strategy	Predict and profit from volatility in the equity market using options on a broad equity index.	Market neutral fund with offsetting long and short equity positions. The fund utilizes leverage to enhance returns.	Long-only international equity fund. Individual securities may be delta-hedged using call options to reduce exposure to the position without selling it.
Market Expectations	Volatility in the equity market is expected to increase in the near future. However, the direction of the volatility is uncertain.	Credit markets are expected to tighten in the near future. Increased interest rates are expected across all credit qualities.	International equity markets are forecast to rise in general. Certain securities are forecast to decline in value temporarily.

The manager of Fund A has collected data on put and call options on the broad market index underlying his strategy. The option data are presented in Figure 2. All options presented have the same expiration date.

Figure 2: Option Data for the Broad Market Index

Call Price	Strike Price	Put Price
35.40	1,475	6.80
18.10	1,500	17.00
7.90	1,515	24.60

During the meeting, the manager of Fund B states that in order to enhance returns for the fund, he intends to implement a box-spread strategy. The manager explains the strategy by stating, "The ending price of the asset underlying the box-spread strategy has no impact on the payoff of the strategy.

©2016 Kaplan, Inc.

Thus, if the market price of the strategy implies a rate of return greater than the risk-free rate, an arbitrage opportunity exists."

Also during the meeting, DMC's president questioned the manager of Fund C about the mechanics of his hedging strategy. The manager explained the strategy with the following comments:

Comment 1:   "The hedge position is established to reduce the exposure to certain equity positions by writing call options on those equity positions. The necessary number of short option positions per share of stock held is calculated as the inverse of the option delta."

Comment 2:   "The hedge position only requires adjusting in the event of a price or volatility change in the underlying and is effective for small changes in the price of the underlying security."

43.   Which of the following option strategies would provide the greatest upside for Fund A given its objectives and market expectations?
       A. Straddle.
       B. Bull spread using puts.
       C. Reverse butterfly spread using calls and puts.

44.   Using the data in Figure 2, **determine** which of the following is *closest* to the maximum profit from a butterfly strategy using only call options.
       A. 7.1.
       B. 13.0.
       C. 17.9.

45.   In 110 days, the manager of Fund B expects to borrow $50,000,000 for 180 days at a rate of 180-day LIBOR plus 150 bp to pursue a leveraged strategy. LIBOR is currently 6.5%. The manager purchases an interest rate call on 180-day LIBOR that expires in 110 days with a premium of $120,000 and exercise rate of 6%. If LIBOR at the option expiration is 7.3%, **calculate** the effective annual rate on the loan.
       A. 7.30%.
       B. 8.29%.
       C. 8.80%.

46.   **Evaluate** the comment made by the manager of Fund B with respect to the box-spread strategy. The manager is:
       A. correct.
       B. incorrect, because the payoff of the box-spread is sensitive to the ending price of the asset underlying the options.
       C. incorrect, because an arbitrage opportunity only exists if the market price of the box-spread strategy implies a rate of return less than the risk-free rate.

47. **Determine** whether the comments made by the manager of Fund C with respect to determining the hedge position and adjusting the hedge position are *correct*.
    A. Only Comment 1 is correct.
    B. Only Comment 2 is correct.
    C. Both Comment 1 and Comment 2 are correct.

48. Under which of the following scenarios will Fund C be *most* exposed to the gamma effect resulting from delta hedged equity positions? When the option used to delta hedge is:
    A. at-the-money and close to expiration.
    B. at-the-money and not close to expiration.
    C. deep in-the-money and close to expiration.

Questions 49–54 relate to Joan Nicholson and Kim Fluellen.

Joan Nicholson, CFA, and Kim Fluellen, CFA, sit on the risk management committee for Thomasville Asset Management. Although Thomasville manages the majority of its investable assets, it also utilizes outside firms for special situations such as market neutral and convertible arbitrage strategies. Thomasville has hired a hedge fund manager, Boston Advisors, for both of these strategies. The managers for the Boston Advisors funds are Frank Amato, CFA, and Joseph Garvin, CFA. Amato uses a market neutral strategy and has generated a return of $20 million this year on the $100 million Thomasville has invested with him. Garvin uses a convertible arbitrage strategy and has lost $15 million this year on the $200 million Thomasville has invested with him, with most of the loss coming in the last quarter of the year. Thomasville pays each outside manager an incentive fee of 20% on profits. During the risk management committee meeting Nicholson evaluates the characteristics of the arrangement with Boston Advisors. Nicholson states that the asymmetric nature of Thomasville's contract with Boston Advisors creates adverse consequences for Thomasville's net profits and that the compensation contract resembles a put option owned by Boston Advisors.

Upon request, Fluellen provides a risk assessment for the firm's large cap growth portfolio using a monthly dollar VAR. To do so, Fluellen obtains the following statistics from the fund manager. The value of the fund is $80 million and has an annual expected return of 14.4%. The annual standard deviation of returns is 21.50%. Assuming a standard normal distribution, 5% of the potential portfolio values are 1.65 standard deviations below the expected return.

Thomasville periodically engages in options trading for hedging purposes or when they believe that options are mispriced. One of their positions is a long position in a call option for Moffett Corporation. The option is a European option with a 3-month maturity. The underlying stock price is $27 and the strike price of the option is $25. The option sells for $2.86. Thomasville has also sold a put on the stock of the McNeill Corporation. The option is an American option with a 2-month maturity. The underlying stock price is $52 and the strike price of the option is $55. The option sells for $3.82. Fluellen assesses the credit risk of these options to Thomasville and states that the current credit risk of the Moffett option is $2.86 and the current credit risk of the McNeill option is $3.82.

Thomasville also uses options quite heavily in their Special Strategies Portfolio. This portfolio seeks to exploit mispriced assets using the leverage provided by options contracts. Although this fund has achieved some spectacular returns, it has also produced some rather large losses on days of high market volatility. Nicholson has calculated a 5% 1-day VAR for the fund at $13.9 million. On average, the fund has produced losses exceeding $13.9 million in 13 of the 250 trading days in a year. Nicholson is concerned about the accuracy of the estimated VAR because when daily losses exceed $13.9 million, they are typically much greater than $13.9 million.

In addition to using options, Thomasville also uses swap contracts for hedging interest rate risk and currency exposures. Fluellen has been assigned the task of evaluating the credit risk of these contracts. The characteristics of the swap contracts Thomasville uses are shown in Figure 1.

Figure 1: Thomasville Swap Contracts

	Contract A	Contract B	Contract C
Swap Type	Currency	Interest Rate	Currency
Original maturity	3 years	4 years	4 years
Swap Terms	Yen-dollar	Plain vanilla	Euro-dollar
Time to Maturity	2.5 years	3.75 years	1.0 years

Fluellen later is asked to describe credit risk in general to the risk management committee. She states:

Statement 1:   Cross default provisions prevent a party that defaults on obligations to one counterparty from immediately declaring default on obligations to other counterparties.

Statement 2:   Credit VaR is particularly useful because it can be aggregated with other forms of VaR to determine total risk.

49.   **Evaluate** Nicholson's comments regarding Thomasville's compensation contract with Boston Advisors. Nicholson is:
A. correct.
B. incorrect, because Thomasville's contract is actually beneficial to the firm's net profits.
C. incorrect, because Thomasville's contract does not resemble a put option owned by Boston Advisors.

50.   Which of the following is *closest* to the monthly VAR Fluellen will calculate for the large cap growth portfolio?
A. $4 million.
B. $7 million.
C. $17 million.

51.   Regarding Fluellen's comments on the credit risk of the Moffett and McNeill options:
A. Fluellen is only correct regarding the Moffett option.
B. Fluellen is only correct regarding the McNeill option.
C. Fluellen is incorrect regarding both the Moffett and McNeill options.

52. Which of the following *best* describes the accuracy of the VAR measure calculated for the Special Strategies Portfolio?
    A. It is accurate but should be supplemented with scenario analysis.
    B. It is accurate and provides a complete measure of the fund's risk.
    C. It is inaccurate and should be supplemented with comprehensive stress testing.

53. Which of the following swap contracts *likely* has the highest credit risk?
    A. Contract A.
    B. Contract B.
    C. Contract C.

54. **Evaluate** Fluellen's comments to the risk management committee on cross default and CVaR. Fluellen is:
    A. incorrect.
    B. only correct regarding cross-default provisions.
    C. only correct regarding aggregating credit and other forms of VaR.

Questions 55–60 relate to Barth Group.

Sue Gano and Tony Cismesia are performance analysts for the Barth Group (BG). BG provides consulting and compliance verification for investment firms wishing to adhere to the Global Investment Performance Standards (GIPS®). The firm also provides global performance evaluation and attribution services for portfolio managers. BG recommends the use of GIPS to its clients due to its prominence as the standard for investment performance presentation.

One of BG's clients, Nigel Investment Advisors (NIA), has a composite that specializes in exploiting trends in stock prices. This Contrarian composite goes long "loser" stocks and short "winner" stocks. The "loser" stocks are those that have experienced severe price declines over the past three years, while the "winner" stocks are those that have had a tremendous surge in price over the past three years. The Contrarian composite has a mixed record of success and is rather small. It contains only four portfolios. Gano and Cismesia debate the requirements for the Contrarian composite under the Global Investment Performance Standards.

NIA's Global Equity Growth composite invests in growth stocks internationally and is tilted when appropriate to small cap stocks. One of NIA's clients in the Global Equity Growth composite is Cypress University. The university has recently decided that it would like to implement ethical investing criteria in its endowment holdings. Specifically, Cypress does not want to hold the stocks from any countries that are deemed human rights violators. Cypress has notified NIA of the change, but NIA does not hold any stocks in these countries. Gano is concerned, however, that this restriction may limit investment manager freedom going forward.

Gano and Cismesia are discussing the valuation and return calculation principles for portfolios and composites, which they believe have changed over time. In order to comply with GIPS, Gano states the firm will:

Statement 1: "Value portfolios at least monthly and on the dates of large external cash flows. The valuations are based on market value and not book value or cost."

Statement 2: "Composites are groups of portfolios that represent a specific investment strategy or objective, and a definition must be made available upon request. Only accounts for which the firm has investment discretion are included in the composite. If account cash flows are large enough to disrupt the ability of the firm to implement the intended style for even a portion of a month, that account's performance is exclude from the composite for the year."

The manager of the Global Equity Growth composite has a benchmark that is fully hedged against currency risk. Because the manager is confident in his forecasting of currency values, the manager does not hedge to the extent that the benchmark does. In addition to the Global Equity Growth composite, NIA has a second investment manager who specializes in global equity. The funds under her management constitute the Emerging Markets Equity composite. The benchmark for the Emerging Markets Equity composite is not hedged against currency risk. The manager of the Emerging Markets Equity composite does not hedge due to the difficulty in finding currency hedges for thinly traded emerging market currencies. The manager focuses on security selection in these markets and does not weight the country markets differently from the benchmark.

The managers of the Emerging Markets Equity composite would like to add frontier markets such as Bulgaria, Kenya, Oman, and Vietnam to their composite, with a 20% weight. They are attracted to frontier markets because, compared to emerging markets, frontier markets have much higher expected returns and lower correlations with each other and with developed markets. Frontier markets, however, also have lower liquidity and higher risk. As a result, the manager proposes that the benchmark be changed from one reflecting only emerging markets to one that reflects both emerging and frontier markets. The date of the change and the reason for the change will be provided in the footnotes to the performance presentation. The manager reasons that by doing so, the potential investor can accurately assess the relative performance of the composite over time.

Historically, BG has not provided services to managers of real estate portfolios; however, the firm is considering an expansion of services into this area. Gano and Cismesia have also been asked to review the GIPS provisions regarding real estate. They have prepared the following summary points:

Statement 3: GIPS contains special provisions that go beyond the basic provisions of GIPS and these special provisions exclude publicly traded real estate such as REITs and mortgage-backed securities. Instead, they apply to private real estate such as direct holdings of real estate property, limited partnerships, and private debt financing.

Statement 4: Verifying real estate fair value is likely to be more difficult than it is for marketable securities. Valuation will often depend on appraisals. In addition to internal valuation estimates, firms must have an external valuation done every 36 months.

Statement 5: GIPS real estate provisions require a minimum of quarterly return calculations reporting both total return and component returns (typically income and capital return).

55. What are the GIPS requirements for the Contrarian composite of Nigel Investment Advisors?
    A. The composite can be formed and the composite must report all performance statistics.
    B. The composite can be formed; however, the number of portfolios and dispersion does not have to be reported.
    C. The composite cannot be formed because it has less than six portfolios in it, so there are no presentation requirements.

56. What are the GIPS requirements for the Cypress University portfolio in the Global Equity Growth composite of Nigel Investment Advisors?
    A. The historical and future record of performance of the Cypress University portfolio should be kept in the Global Equity Growth composite.
    B. Because the Cypress University portfolio is nondiscretionary, its future record of performance must be removed from the Global Equity Growth composite.
    C. Because the Cypress University portfolio is nondiscretionary, its historical and future record of performance must be removed from the Global Equity Growth composite.

57. Are the statements made by Gano consistent with the requirements of GIPS?
    A. Yes.
    B. No, only statement 1 is correct.
    C. No, both statements are incorrect.

58. Which of the following *best* describes the currency management of the managers of the Global Equity Growth and the Emerging Markets Equity composites?
    A. Both managers are using active currency management.
    B. Both managers are using passive currency management.
    C. The manager of the Global Equity Growth composite is using active currency management and the manager of the Emerging Markets Equity composite is using passive currency management.

59. Regarding the Emerging Markets Equity composite, which of the following *best* describes the manager's incorporation of frontier markets?
    A. The treatment is consistent with GIPS requirements.
    B. The treatment is inconsistent with GIPS requirements because the benchmark should not be changed.
    C. The treatment is inconsistent with GIPS requirements because of the manner in which the composite is formed.

60.	Which of the summary points regarding real estate provisions is correct?
	A.	Statement 3.
	B.	Statement 4.
	C.	Statement 5.

END OF AFTERNOON SESSION

PRACTICE EXAM 2 MORNING SESSION QUESTION BREAKDOWN

MORNING SESSION		
Question	Topic	Minutes
1	Portfolio Management – Individual	30
2	Asset Allocation	15
3	Monitoring/Rebalancing	19
4	Portfolio Management – Institutional	26
5	Portfolio Management – Institutional	10
6	Portfolio Management – Individual	17
7	Portfolio Management – Individual	9
8	Fixed Income	15
9	GIPS	15
10	Economics and Asset Allocation	14
11	Risk Management	10
	Total	180

PRACTICE EXAM 2 SCORE SHEET

MORNING SESSION		
Question	Maximum Points	Your Estimated Score
1A	15	
1B	5	
1C	10	
2	15	
3A	10	
3B	9	
4A	9	
4B	8	
4C	9	
5A	6	
5B	4	
6A	3	
6B	7	
6C	4	
6D	3	
7A	6	
7B	3	
8A	6	
8B	9	
9	15	
10A	6	
10B	4	
10C	4	
11A	4	
11B	6	
Total	**180**	

AFTERNOON SESSION		
Questions	Maximum Points	Your Score
1–6	18	
7–12	18	
13–18	18	
19–24	18	
25–30	18	
31–36	18	
37–42	18	
43–48	18	
49–54	18	
55–60	18	
Total	**180**	

Practice Exam 2
Morning Session

QUESTIONS 1 AND 2 ARE TO BE ANSWERED IN SEQUENCE.

QUESTION 1 HAS THREE PARTS (A, B, C) FOR A TOTAL OF 30 MINUTES

Helen Jackson, a single mother, has just won the Big Jackpot Lottery in her state. She has chosen a lump-sum payout and, after taxes, will receive $3.7 million (with all lottery winners required to submit an annual information disclosure document to the state over the next 20 years). At the urging of state lottery officials and family members, including an uncle who is an experienced accountant, she is seeking professional investment counsel. After several initial interviews with various firms, she has chosen John Medford, CFA.

Jackson is a 29-year-old mother of three. Following her divorce last year, she won a lengthy court battle to obtain full custody of her three children, Frank (age 13), John (age 10), and Ben (age 8). She owes $158,000 in legal bills that the law firm is financing at 12.5 percent annually. She also owes $57,000 in credit card debt at an annual interest rate of 23.9 percent. Jackson lives with her children and her mother in a rented unit within a mobile home park in a small rural community. She works at the local Super Box-Mart store as a stock clerk earning $21,500 per year. She has been a valued employee for eight years and receives full health insurance benefits for herself and her children. Comparable insurance is available for $1,250 per month (not tax deductible) and is estimated to increase in cost at the same rate as overall inflation. She has no assets other than the lottery proceeds and no other sources of income.

Jackson's mother accompanies her to the first planning meeting. Jackson tells Medford that her first goal is to improve her family's quality of life. She and her mother have found a home in a neighborhood they like for a total cost of $385,000. Her uncle (the accountant) suggested that the family could live comfortably on a $125,000 after-tax income per year, assuming they have no mortgage payments or health insurance costs. Second, Jackson wants to ensure that her children get an education and other opportunities that she never had. Third, she wants to have enough money left over for a comfortable retirement in about 35 years. Finally, as soon as she is financially able, Jackson would also love to leave the Super Box-Mart and go back to school to earn a college degree herself, assuming the other goals can be accomplished.

Jackson and her mother tell Medford that they "never again want to owe anyone anything," and that "the money must be managed so as never to risk losing anything."

Medford's firm, Medford Associates, Inc., expects 3.5 percent annual inflation into the indefinite future. He also estimates that Jackson's combined federal and state tax liability will be 25 percent of income, and 15 percent of any realized long-term (assets held at least one year) capital gains. Short-term capital gains are taxed at her ordinary income tax rate. Jackson expects all three of her children to attend college, with costs expected to increase at the inflation rate. Total annual college expenses (tuition, books and other costs) are now $15,500 at the nearby state university. For calculation purposes, Medford decides to be conservative and use a 25 percent tax rate for all calculations as well as to assume 100 percent of all investment returns will be taxed. Medford also discusses the concept of human capital with Jackson and points out that if Jackson goes ahead and attends college now, her total wealth is likely to increase.

A.   **Determine** and **justify** an appropriate return objective for the Jackson portfolio. **Calculate** the required pre-tax nominal return for the coming year.

(15 minutes)

B.   **Evaluate** Jackson's risk tolerance and **state** a qualitative risk objective for her portfolio.

(5 minutes)

C. **State** and **justify** the five constraints for the Jackson portfolio.

(10 minutes)

QUESTION 2 HAS ONE PART FOR A TOTAL OF 15 MINUTES.

One year later, Jackson has met her immediate objectives, is enrolled in the local university, and has taken a couple of introductory finance classes. While she still considers herself to be a conservative investor, she has developed a more realistic understanding of the relationship between risk and return. To help guide Jackson, Medford Associates, Inc. has developed the following capital market expectations that are used to structure strategic asset allocations for all clients.

EXHIBIT 2-1: Medford Associates, Inc. Capital Market Expectations

Asset Class	Current Yield	Projected Annualized Pre-Tax Total Return	Expected Standard Deviation
Cash Equivalents	4.5%	4.5%	0.25%
Investment-Grade U.S. Bonds	6.0	7.5	5.0
U.S. Stocks	3.0	8.5	20.0
REITs	7.5	13.5	27.0
Diversified Interational (non-U.S.) Stocks	4.6	15.0	30.0

Assume Jackson has a below-average risk tolerance and a modest return objective. Using the Medford Associates, Inc. capital market expectations, **recommend** the *most appropriate* allocation range for *each* of the asset classes for the Jackson portfolio. **Justify** your recommendations with *one* reason from the objectives and constraints developed in the previous question. Do not compute or use portfolio return as a factor. Answer Question 2 in the template provided.

(15 Minutes)

Template for Question 2

Asset Class	Recommend the most appropriate asset allocation range for each of the asset classes in Exhibit 2-1. (Circle one for each asset class.)	Justify your recommendations with one reason from the objectives and constraints developed in the previous question.
Cash Equivalents	0.0% to 5.0% 5.0% to 10.0% 10.0% to 20.0%	
Investment-grade U.S. Bonds	10.0% to 20.0% 20.0% to 30.0% 30.0% to 40.0%	
U.S. Stocks	20.0% to 40.0% 40.0% to 60.0% 60.0% to 80.0%	
REITs	0.0% to 10.0% 10.0% to 15.0% 15.0% to 20.0%	
Diversified International (non-U.S.) Stocks	0.0% to 10.0% 10.0% to 20.0% 20.0% to 30.0%	

QUESTION 3 HAS TWO PARTS (A, B) FOR A TOTAL OF 19 MINUTES.

Mike Reynolds, a portfolio manager/trader made the following transactions in CMS shares for a portfolio he manages:

Day 1: At market close, CMS shares are priced at $75.

Day 2: Before the market opens, Reynolds decides to buy 8,000 shares at $74 per share by placing a limit order that will expire at the end of day 2. The limit order does not fill and the CMS shares close at $75.75. After the market closes, the company announces it has entered into a joint venture which will expand its international presence. Reynolds assumes the news could move the stock up or down no more than 1 point.

Day 3: Reynolds submits a new limit order to buy 8,000 shares of CMS at a price of $77. As the trading nears day end, 4,000 shares fill at $77 per share plus $1,500 in commission. CMS shares close at $79 and the remaining 4,000 shares are never purchased.

A.   Answer the following questions:

    i. **Calculate** the total dollar amount of implementation shortfall for the CMS transactions. **Show** your work.

(4 minutes)

ii. **Compare** and **contrast** implementation shortfall with volume-weighted average price for measuring transaction costs. Your answer must include *one* advantage and *one* disadvantage of each measure.

(6 minutes)

B.   Reynolds has used several rebalancing strategies for his portfolios that combine a risk-free asset with risky assets, depending on the client's risk tolerance/concerns and existing capital market expectations. Answer Question 3, Part B in the template provided.

i.   Briefly **describe** *each* of the three asset-class rebalancing strategies; Buy-and-Hold, Constant Mix, and Constant-Proportion Portfolio Insurance (CPPI).

ii. **Determine** under which market conditions (Rising trend, Falling trend, Flat) *each* strategy would *outperform* relative to the Buy-and-Hold strategy. Circle *all* that apply. Assume that a flat market means a volatile market with no trend in either direction.

iii. **Identify** (circle) the shape of the payoff diagram (Concave, Convex, Linear) for each of the rebalancing strategies.

(9 minutes)

Template for Question 3, Part B

Strategy	Briefly describe each of the three asset class rebalancing strategies; Buy-and-Hold, Constant Mix, and Constant-Proportion Portfolio Insurance (CPPI).	Determine under which market conditions (Rising trend, Falling trend, Flat) each strategy would outperform relative to the Buy-and-Hold strategy. (Circle all that apply.*)	Identify (circle) the shape of the payoff diagram (Concave, Convex, Linear) for each of the rebalancing strategies.
Buy-and-Hold			Concave Convex Linear
Constant Mix		Rising Falling Flat	Concave Convex Linear
CPPI		Rising Falling Flat	Concave Convex Linear

*Assume that a "flat" market is a volatile market with no trend in either direction

ANSWER QUESTIONS 4 AND 5 IN SEQUENCE.

QUESTION 4 HAS THREE PARTS (A, B, C) FOR A TOTAL OF 26 MINUTES.

Heavy Equipment Manufacturing, Inc. (HEMI) is the leader in construction and mining equipment. The company has several major competitors, but maintains a leadership role through brand recognition and customer loyalty. Profits doubled in 2015 over the 2014 period and the firm's market capitalization now stands at $46 billion. HEMI has both U.S. and non-U.S. defined-benefit pension plans covering substantially all of its U.S. employees and a portion of its non-U.S. employees, primarily in European facilities.

HEMI has recently hired Rosemary Thorn, CFA, to manage the U.S. portion of HEMI's pension plan (HEMI-PP). Her initial research on the plan sponsor concludes that HEMI is financially sound with a higher return on equity and a lower debt-to-equity ratio than the industry averages. Thorn also learns that HEMI has added 8,000 new hires to the company over the last two years. These new hires have primarily been entry-level administrative, technical, and manufacturing workers; this has resulted in lowering the average age of the workforce. The active labor force now stands at slightly over 80,000. There are no early retirement buyouts planned.

Thorn holds a meeting with Richard Thayer, HEMI's CFO. Thayer indicates that the plan's investment objective is to be fully funded within five years without any contributions from the fund sponsor. He believes this goal is attainable without assuming more risk than the plan is willing and able to take. He also indicates his confidence that the current construction boom will continue for at least five years, and would like to increase plan assets invested in the industrials sector from its current 10 percent level to 15 percent of equity assets.

Thorn constructs the following exhibits to analyze the plan's objectives and risk tolerance.

EXHIBIT 4-1: 2015 Selected Pension Plan Information (USD Millions)

Market value of plan assets	$ 9,441
Projected benefit obligation	$10,697
Discount rate	5.6%
Duration of pension liability	17 years

EXHIBIT 4-2: Comparison of HEMI to the Heavy Equipment Industry

	HEMI	Industry Avg.
Active/retired employees	75%/25%	70%/30%
Average active employee age	31	42
Percentage of employees age > 50	11%	19%

As a first step, Thorn must prepare an investment policy statement (IPS) for the plan.

A. **Formulate** *each* of the following investment policy statement (IPS) items for HEMI-PP:

i. Return requirement

ii. Liquidity requirement

iii. Time horizon

Justify *each* response with *one* reason. Note: Show your calculations for the formulation of the return requirement. Your responses for each IPS item should *specifically* address HEMI-PP's circumstances.

Answer Question 4, Part A in the template provided.

(9 minutes)

Template for Question 4, Part A

IPS Item	Formulate each of the following investment policy statement (IPS) items for HEMI-PP. Justify each response with one reason. Note: Your answer should specifically address HEMI's circumstances.
i. Return requirement	
ii. Liquidity requirement	
iii. Time Horizon	

B. **Determine** whether each of the following factors increases or decreases HEMI-PP's ability to take risk:

  i. Risk exposures that are common to both the plan sponsor and stocks in the industrials sector

  ii. Increasing the workforce with younger workers

  Justify *each* response with *one* reason.

  Answer Question 4, Part B in the template provided.

  (8 minutes)

Template for Question 4, Part B

Risk factor	Determine whether each of the following factors increases or decreases HEMI-PP's ability to take risk. (circle one)	Justify each response with one reason.
i. Risk exposures that are common to both the plan sponsor and stocks in the industrials sector.	Increases Decreases	
ii. Increasing the workforce with younger workers.	Increases Decreases	

C.   **Determine** whether HEMI-PP has below-average, average, or above-average ability to assume risk relative to the average firm in the industry for each of the following factors:

      i. HEMI's financial condition

      ii. Workforce age

      iii. Retired employees

      Justify each response with one reason.

      Answer Question 4, Part C in the template provided.

(9 minutes)

Template for Question 4, Part C

Risk factor	Determine whether HEMI-PP has a below-average, average, or above-average ability to assume risk relative to the average firm in the industry for each of the following factors. (circle one)	Justify each response with one reason.
i. HEMI's financial condition	Below-average Average Above-average	
ii. Workforce age	Below-average Average Above-average	
iii. Retired employees	Below-average Average Above-average	

QUESTION 5 HAS TWO PARTS (A, B) FOR A TOTAL OF 10 MINUTES.

After five years of successfully managing the HEMI Pension Plan (PP), Thorn notes that astute planning and some luck with the business cycle have resulted in a small plan surplus. Plan assets now stand at $14.2 billion and the projected benefit obligation is $14.0 billion.

As the result of slowing construction growth, HEMI intends to downsize its workforce by offering early retirement options to selected employees. HEMI-PP will make lump-sum payments averaging $300,000 to each of the 2,500 early retirees over the next year.

The HEMI-PP investment policy committee (IPC) has adopted the following policy recommendations to accommodate current market conditions and business objectives:

- An 8.5 percent return requirement
- A shortfall risk objective (expected return minus two standard deviations) of –8.3 percent
- Asset and liability matching in both the short and long term
- Underweight U.S. Equities allocation to industrials (S&P 500 allocation to industrials is 10 percent)

Exhibit 5-1 displays Thorn's analysis of asset allocation alternatives based upon her reassessment of the portfolio's current allocation, the desired return requirements, and constraints.

EXHIBIT 5-1: Asset Allocation Options

	Portfolios and Allocations (%)				
Asset Class	A	B	C	D	E
Cash equivalents	5.0	10.0	7.5	5.0	7.5
Global fixed income	40.0	25.0	20.0	20.0	17.5
U.S. equities*	30.0	30.0	30.0	30.0	30.0
Non-U.S. equities	20.0	20.0	25.0	30.0	30.0
Real estate	5.0	15.0	17.5	15.0	15.0
Total	**100.0**	**100.0**	**100.0**	**100.0**	**100.0**
	Return and Risk (%)				
Portfolio Measures	A	B	C	D	E
Expected total return	9.5	9.2	9.0	8.0	8.6
Expected standard deviation	8.9	8.8	7.8	8.2	8.4

*U.S. Equities include the following sector allocations to industrials: Portfolio A 20%, Portfolio B 15%, Portfolio C 10%, Portfolio D 10%, Portfolio E 5%

A. **Select** the *most appropriate* portfolio for HEMI-PP. **Justify** your
    selection on the basis of *two* investment policy committee objectives
    other than return requirement.

(6 minutes)

B. **State** for each portfolio not selected *one* reason why it was not the
    most appropriate (again, do not use return as a reason).

(4 minutes)

QUESTION 6 HAS FOUR PARTS (A, B, C, D) FOR A TOTAL OF 17 MINUTES.

Janet Lowell is a financial advisor meeting with a new client, Jim Harris. Harris is specifically interested in the tax implications of his investment strategies. Lowell collected the following information concerning tax rates in his governing jurisdiction. All investment income except long-term gains is taxed on an accrual basis and paid out of the investment account.

Marginal Tax Rate Table			
Ordinary Income		**Investment Income**	
$0 – 30,000	0%	Interest	25%
30,001– 60,000	15%	Dividends	15%
60,001 – 100,000	25%	Short-Term Gains*	25%
100,001 – 250,000	35%	Long-Term Gains	20%
250,001 +	40%		

*Short-term capital gains include realized capital gains on investments held for less than one year.

Harris earns $175,000 per year in wages and has a $750,000 investment portfolio funded from an inheritance at a cost basis equal to its current market value.

Based on her recommended asset allocation with annual rebalancing, Lowell estimates average annual portfolio return of 8 percent on a pretax basis, to be distributed according to the following table. The relative percentage distributions are expected to persist for the foreseeable future.

Harris Portfolio Expected Return Distribution		
Source	*First Year*	*Annual Proportion*
Taxable Interest	$18,000	30.00%
Dividends	5,000	8.33%
Short-Term Capital Gains	12,000	20.00%
Deferred Capital Gains	25,000	41.67%
Total	$60,000	100.00%

Lowell also addresses the tax implications of asset location. Harris's tax jurisdiction allows contributions up to a specified limit to go into tax deferred accounts, either tax deferred (TDA) or tax exempt accounts (TEA). Harris is considering saving more than the limit amount. TDA withdrawals are taxed at 30%.

A.   Excluding any investment income, **compute** the average tax rate that Harris should expect to pay on ordinary wage income at the end of the first year. **Show** your work.

(3 minutes)

B.   **Compute** the future value of the $750,000 portfolio over a 5-year investment horizon, assuming all deferred gains are realized at the end of the horizon. **Show** your work.

(7 minutes)

C.   Assuming that Harris will invest more than the specified limit and will invest about 50/50 in stocks and bonds, **state** whether Lowell will advise the stock investments primarily go into the tax deferred accounts or a fully taxable account. **Explain** why.

(4 minutes)

D.   Assuming that tax rates are expected to generally increase, **state** and **explain** why savings should go to the TDA or TEA account.

(3 minutes)

QUESTION 7 HAS TWO PARTS (A, B) FOR A TOTAL OF 9 MINUTES.

Rine Ruby is 55 years old and resides in the UK, a Common Law jurisdiction. He is a widower with two grown children, Albert and Johanna. Ruby is working with his financial advisor to develop an estate plan. The advisor estimates his core capital to be £1,000,000 and excess capital to be £4,000,000. He would like to provide each of his children a relatively equal share of his accumulated wealth. Selected additional information was collected by the advisor and is summarized in the following table.

Rine Ruby Tax Data	
Inheritance and Estate Tax Rate	60%
Gift Tax Rate	30%
Marginal Tax Rate	45%

Johanna, 25, is a married college graduate with a secure job in public service. Ruby considers her to be a very stable and reliable person. Johanna's salary places her investment income in the 25 percent marginal tax bracket.

Albert is 27 years old, single, and has held a variety of jobs. Ruby considers him to be rather reckless and irresponsible with money. Albert has been involved in two failed businesses over the last several years and is regularly pursued by creditors. His wages place his investment income in the 25 percent income tax bracket.

Ruby is considering a gifting program to his children. There is an annual tax-free exclusion of £15,000 on gifts to individuals. The tax code requires that gift taxes be paid by the recipient unless the gift is placed in an irrevocable trust. Gifts to irrevocable trusts allow the grantor to pay the gift tax. The trust would be subject to a 25 percent income tax rate. The expected real return on investments over the next 25 years is 5.50 percent.

Ai.   Assuming Ruby gifts the allowable maximum to his children this year that will qualify for the tax-free exclusion, **compute** the value of his gift in 25 years. **Show** your work.

(3 minutes)

Aii.   **Compute** the relative value over 25 years of a bequest versus a gift made this year directly to Ruby's children that will qualify for the tax-free exclusion. **Show** your work.

(3 minutes)

B.   Assuming Ruby decides to place Albert's inheritance in a trust, **recommend** using either a fixed trust or a discretionary trust and **justify** your recommendation with one reason.

(3 minutes)

QUESTION 8 HAS TWO PARTS (A, B) FOR A TOTAL OF 15 MINUTES.

Emmanuel Foppiano, CFA, has been hired by Catapult Systems to manage the bond portfolio portion of the company's pension fund. His charge is to increase the interest income and to add high-yield bond funds to the pension plan. After exhaustive research, Foppiano selects two bond funds for Catapult's pension fund, each of which will have a 5 percent allocation:

> **Tuscany High-Yield Index Fund**—Fund tracks the Merrill Lynch U.S. High-Yield BB-B Rated Index. This fund has a management fee of 2.5 basis points quarterly.

> **Feliciano High-Yield Fund**—Fund aims at high (relative) current yield from fixed income securities, has no quality or maturity restrictions, and tends to invest in lower-grade debt issues.

At the quarterly review, Foppiano meets with Rafael Porto, the CFO of Catapult Systems, to discuss Exhibit 8-1.

EXHIBIT 8-1: Total Returns on Index and Funds

	Quarterly Return
Merrill Lynch High-Yield Index	3.87%
Tuscany Fund	3.96%
Feliciano Fund	4.75%

Porto is pleased with these results. He makes the following two statements:

1. "Tuscany hit their mark right on the money."

2. "Perhaps we should overweight Feliciano Fund in the fixed-income portion of the pension fund because of its higher return."

A month later Foppiano meets with the company's plan sponsors to review the plan's performance results and to discuss the plan's current strategy. During the meeting, senior management tells the plan sponsors that they will be offering a one-time, lump sum early retirement package to eligible employees beginning in the next 24-30 months. Senior management estimates that 10 percent of the existing company workforce will accept this retirement package.

Upon returning to his office, Foppiano reviews his notes from the plan sponsors and contemplates the impact that a potential early employee retirement could have on his existing bond portfolio. Foppiano decides to shift his focus from managing the company's bond portfolio to funding of future pension plan liabilities. Based on his due diligence, Foppiano narrows his fixed-income strategies to cashflow matching and contingent immunization. During a subsequent phone conversation with Porto, Foppiano discusses his change in bond management strategy. Foppiano also makes the following three statements to Porto:

1. "I am considering a cash-flow matching strategy given the flexibility it provides for selecting bonds for the portfolio and because it minimizes trading costs."

2. "On the other hand, the upside to contingent immunization is that it allows me to manage the bond portfolio actively without immunization unless the safety margin falls to zero."

3. "Given the expected lump sum retirement payout in the next 24-30 months, the cash-flow matching strategy is clearly better for the pension plan because of the certainty of the company's pension obligations."

A. **Determine** whether you agree or disagree with each of Porto's statements. **Justify** your determination with one reason for each statement.

   Note: You may not use the same justification for both statements.

   Answer Question 8, Part A in the template provided.

(6 minutes)

Template for Question 8, Part A

Statement	Determine whether you agree or disagree with each of Porto's statements. (circle one)	Justify your determination with one reason for each statement. Note: You may not use the same justification for both statements
1. "Tuscany hit their mark right on the money."	Agree Disagree	
2. "Perhaps we should overweight Feliciano Fund in the fixed income portion of the pension fund because of its higher return."	Agree Disagree	

B.   **Determine** whether you agree or disagree with each of Foppiano's statements. **Justify** your determination with one reason for *each* statement. Answer Question 8, Part B in the template provided.

(9 minutes)

Template for Question 8, Part B

Statement	Determine whether you agree or disagree with each of Foppiano's statements (circle one)	Justify your determination with one reason for each statement.
1. "I am considering a cashflow matching strategy given the flexibility it provides for selecting bonds for the portfolio and because it minimizes trading costs."	Agree Disagree	
2. "On the other hand, the upside to contingent immunization is that it allows me to manage the bond portfolio actively without immunization unless the safety margin falls to zero."	Agree Disagree	
3. "Given the expected lump sum retirement payout in the next 24–30 months, the cash-flow matching strategy is clearly better for the pension plan because of the certainty of the company's pension obligations."	Agree Disagree	

QUESTION 9 HAS ONE PART FOR 15 MINUTES.

Alcor Investments, a firm based in Chicago, IL, has set the goal of adopting the Global Investment Performance Standards (GIPS®) beginning on January 1, 2014. On June 1, 2014, Alcor will merge with another investment firm (The Barton Co.), which is not compliant with GIPS standards. The combined firms will be considered as a single firm for GIPS purposes. All of Barton's employees will be given comparable positions within Alcor.

As management supports the incorporation of alternative investments, Alcor has invested in both real estate (new building construction) and private equity (distressed debt holdings).

Members of Alcor's Compliance Team, tasked with ensuring Alcor's compliance with GIPS, made the following statements in a June 2013 meeting. (Unless noted, the statements apply to Alcor's nonalternative investment holdings.)

1. We will use a total return calculation methodology that will include realized and unrealized gains, income, returns from cash and cash equivalents, and deductions for estimated and actual trading expenses.

2. We will disclose the minimum asset level for the inclusion of a portfolio, but will only make available upon request any calculation methodology changes which result in material performance impacts.

3. We will disclose the dispersion measure used in our performance presentations and report performance results gross of fees.

4. We will have our real estate investments valued every three months (and by a licensed appraiser every year).

5. We will include all actual fee-paying portfolios (both discretionary and non-discretionary) and all non-fee-paying discretionary portfolios in at least one composite.

6. We will (based on our discretion) create a single asset portfolio out of a multiple asset class portfolio by allocating cash return to the carve-out portfolio in a consistent and timely manner.

7. After the acquisition, we will bring Barton's results into GIPS compliance by December 31, 2014.

Determine whether *each* of the seven statements, considered independently, meets the requirements of GIPS. **Recommend**, for *each* statement not in compliance with GIPS, the appropriate change that must be made to bring Alcor into compliance with GIPS.

Answer Question 9 in the template provided.

(15 minutes)

Template for Question 9, Part B

Statement	Determine whether each of the seven statements, considered independently, meets the requirements of GIPS. (circle one)	Recommend, for each statement not in compliance with GIPS, the appropriate change that must be made to bring Alcor into compliance with GIPS requirements.
1. We will use a total return calculation methodology that will include realized and unrealized gains, income, returns from cash and cash equivalents, and deductions for estimated and actual trading expenses.	Yes No	
2. We will disclose the minimum asset level for inclusion of a portfolio, but will only make available upon request any calculation methodology changes which result in material performance impacts.	Yes No	

3. We will disclose the dispersion measure used in our performance presentations and report performance results gross of fees.	Yes No	
4. We will have our real estate investments valued every three months (and by a licensed appraiser every year).	Yes No	
5. We will include all actual fee-paying portfolios (both discretionary and nondiscretionary) and all nonfee-paying discretionary portfolios in at least one composite.	Yes No	
6. We will (based on our discretion) create a single asset portfolio out of a multiple asset class portfolio by allocating cash return to the carve-out portfolio in a consistent and timely manner.	Yes No	
7. After the acquisition, we will bring Barton's results into GIPS compliance by December 31, 2014.	Yes No	

QUESTION 10 HAS THREE PARTS (A, B, C) FOR 14 MINUTES.

Paul Price, CFA, and Michelle Adrienne, CFA, are preparing for the monthly asset allocation committee meeting of their firm, Capital Investment Advisors, LLC (CIA). The committee reviews current and expected future economic and capital market conditions monthly to establish the firm's benchmark asset allocations. To date, the economy has experienced a modest contraction with flat or slightly declining equity prices, real GDP growth of less than one percent, and an inverted yield curve.

Price is advocating increasing the firm's equity allocation. His research is based on a Grinold-Kroner discounted cash flow model to develop a three-year aggregate forecast of the expected return for stocks included in the S&P 500 index. Price projects a dividend yield of 1.25 percent, inflation at 2.5 percent (which firms will be able to pass through to customers as price increases), real earnings growth of 3.5 percent, and 4.0 percent repricing as economic activity is expected to accelerate in the next twelve months. Moreover, he expects aggregate share repurchases of 1.5 percent of outstanding shares among those firms as they take advantage of low equity prices. All rates are annualized.

Adrienne maintains the opposite view. She advocates a sharp reduction in the firm's equity allocation and increasing the firm's short positions. She bases her view on a sophisticated autoregressive time series model that she has refined and used successfully for several years. Adrienne thinks that the broad equity market will decline an additional 5 percent in the next year.

A.   **Calculate** the expected annual return on the S&P 500 based on Price's data. **Explain** *each* component of the calculation.

(6 minutes)

B. Briefly **describe** strategic and tactical asset allocation and the input from capital market expectations.

(4 minutes)

C. **Select** the analyst whose approach is *best* suited for strategic asset allocation and the analyst whose approach is *best* suited for tactical asset allocation. **Describe** *one* shortcoming of *each* approach.

(4 minutes)

QUESTION 11 HAS TWO PARTS (A, B) FOR A TOTAL OF 10 MINUTES.

Jim Conway is a currency overlay manager working with a U.S. mutual fund specializing in multinational fixed-income securities. The fund has €1 billion of investment-grade bonds issued by major EU companies. The mutual fund's portfolio manager wants exposure to the EU bond market but wants to avoid translation risk. Conway has no opinion as to the future movement of the euro against the U.S. dollar and is considering the following three alternatives to managing this exposure:

- Hedging with futures contracts (Exhibit 11-1)
- Insuring with options (Exhibit 11-2)
- Delta hedging with options (Exhibit 11-3)

The spot exchange rate is $1.30/€. Conway has gathered the following information regarding the contracts under consideration:

Exhibit 11-1: Euro Futures Contract

Contract size: €125,000
Contract price: $1.28/€
Expiration in nine months

Exhibit 11-2: Euro Option Contract

Contract size: €125,000
Expiration in three months

Strike	Call	Put
$1.35/€	0.01	0.08
$1.30/€	0.04	0.05
$1.25/€	0.07	0.02

Option premiums are quoted in dollars per euro. The current option deltas are included in the following table:

Exhibit 11-3: Euro Option Delta

Contract size: €125,000

Strike	Call	Put
$1.35/€	0.30	−0.70
$1.30/€	0.50	−0.50
$1.25/€	0.70	−0.30

A. **Recommend** *one* of the strategies being considered and **describe** how it would be implemented. **Calculate** the number of contracts required to initiate the selected strategy. **Show** your work.

(4 minutes)

B.

i. **Justify** the strategy you recommended in Part A with *one* reason in the template provided.

ii. **Explain** *one* reason why *each* of the other two strategies was not recommended.

Answer Question 11, Part B in the templates provided.

(6 minutes)

Template for Question 11, Part B

Recommended strategy (choose only one)	Justification
Hedging with futures	
Insuring with options	
Delta hedging with options	

Strategies not recommended (choose only two)	Explanation
Hedging with futures	
Insuring with options	
Delta hedging with options	

END OF MORNING SESSION

EXAM 2 AFTERNOON SESSION TOPIC BREAKDOWN

Question	Topic	Minutes
1–6	Ethics and Standards	18
7–12	Ethics and Standards	18
13–18	Execution of Portfolio Decisions; Monitoring and Rebalancing	18
19–24	Equity Portfolio Management	18
25–30	Fixed Income Portfolio Management	18
31–36	Fixed Income Portfolio Management	18
37–42	Asset Allocation/Risk Management Applications of Derivatives	18
43–48	Risk Management Applications of Derivatives	18
49–54	Global Investment Performance Standards	18
55–60	Private Wealth Management	18
	Total	180

EXAM 2 SELECTED RESPONSE ITEM SET ANSWER SHEET

The afternoon session of the Level III exam contains 10 Selected Response Item Sets, each with six questions, and you must answer them by filling in a bubble sheet with a number 2 or HB pencil. For realism, we suggest that you use this answer sheet and darken the bubbles corresponding to your answers. This sheet will also facilitate entering your answers into our online Performance Tracker. You have 180 minutes for this session of the exam. That equates to 3 minutes per item set question, so budget your time well.

1.	Ⓐ	Ⓑ	Ⓒ
2.	Ⓐ	Ⓑ	Ⓒ
3.	Ⓐ	Ⓑ	Ⓒ
4.	Ⓐ	Ⓑ	Ⓒ
5.	Ⓐ	Ⓑ	Ⓒ
6.	Ⓐ	Ⓑ	Ⓒ
7.	Ⓐ	Ⓑ	Ⓒ
8.	Ⓐ	Ⓑ	Ⓒ
9.	Ⓐ	Ⓑ	Ⓒ
10.	Ⓐ	Ⓑ	Ⓒ
11.	Ⓐ	Ⓑ	Ⓒ
12.	Ⓐ	Ⓑ	Ⓒ
13.	Ⓐ	Ⓑ	Ⓒ
14.	Ⓐ	Ⓑ	Ⓒ
15.	Ⓐ	Ⓑ	Ⓒ
16.	Ⓐ	Ⓑ	Ⓒ
17.	Ⓐ	Ⓑ	Ⓒ
18.	Ⓐ	Ⓑ	Ⓒ
19.	Ⓐ	Ⓑ	Ⓒ
20.	Ⓐ	Ⓑ	Ⓒ
21.	Ⓐ	Ⓑ	Ⓒ
22.	Ⓐ	Ⓑ	Ⓒ
23.	Ⓐ	Ⓑ	Ⓒ
24.	Ⓐ	Ⓑ	Ⓒ
25.	Ⓐ	Ⓑ	Ⓒ
26.	Ⓐ	Ⓑ	Ⓒ
27.	Ⓐ	Ⓑ	Ⓒ
28.	Ⓐ	Ⓑ	Ⓒ
29.	Ⓐ	Ⓑ	Ⓒ
30.	Ⓐ	Ⓑ	Ⓒ

31.	Ⓐ	Ⓑ	Ⓒ
32.	Ⓐ	Ⓑ	Ⓒ
33.	Ⓐ	Ⓑ	Ⓒ
34.	Ⓐ	Ⓑ	Ⓒ
35.	Ⓐ	Ⓑ	Ⓒ
36.	Ⓐ	Ⓑ	Ⓒ
37.	Ⓐ	Ⓑ	Ⓒ
38.	Ⓐ	Ⓑ	Ⓒ
39.	Ⓐ	Ⓑ	Ⓒ
40.	Ⓐ	Ⓑ	Ⓒ
41.	Ⓐ	Ⓑ	Ⓒ
42.	Ⓐ	Ⓑ	Ⓒ
43.	Ⓐ	Ⓑ	Ⓒ
44.	Ⓐ	Ⓑ	Ⓒ
45.	Ⓐ	Ⓑ	Ⓒ
46.	Ⓐ	Ⓑ	Ⓒ
47.	Ⓐ	Ⓑ	Ⓒ
48.	Ⓐ	Ⓑ	Ⓒ
49.	Ⓐ	Ⓑ	Ⓒ
50.	Ⓐ	Ⓑ	Ⓒ
51.	Ⓐ	Ⓑ	Ⓒ
52.	Ⓐ	Ⓑ	Ⓒ
53.	Ⓐ	Ⓑ	Ⓒ
54.	Ⓐ	Ⓑ	Ⓒ
55.	Ⓐ	Ⓑ	Ⓒ
56.	Ⓐ	Ⓑ	Ⓒ
57.	Ⓐ	Ⓑ	Ⓒ
58.	Ⓐ	Ⓑ	Ⓒ
59.	Ⓐ	Ⓑ	Ⓒ
60.	Ⓐ	Ⓑ	Ⓒ

Practice Exam 2
Afternoon Session

Questions 1–6 relate to Bernard Brigand.

Bernard Brigand, CFA, works for Monumental Managers. He has recently developed a model based on the analysis of wage growth in the hospitality industry. He gathered historic information covering the last six months and has concluded that there is a correlation between monthly wage changes and earnings growth.

As part of Brigand's analysis, Brigand visited the Labor Department website and noticed an interesting article. Brigand used the information in this article as the basis for some of his recommendations to clients. On a later occasion he revisited the same website and saw that not only had the article been removed, but a notice had been posted saying that the article had been placed there in error and had contained classified information. However, by this time some of Brigand's clients had acted on the recommendation and had made a profit.

Brigand manages some discretionary client portfolios. On occasions he has used Scarpers Securities when placing trades. Scarpers has a reputation for providing market-leading research and has a higher commission structure as a result. When Brigand "pays up" on trades to obtain research, he uses the research to the benefit of all of his discretionary clients. He believes the extra cost represents good value, and full details of the commission structure are disclosed to all clients in their service contracts.

On one occasion Brigand accidentally makes an error when instructing a trade through Scarpers Securities. By the time he has noticed his mistake the price has moved against the intended position. Scarpers agrees to correct the position and cover the error in return for a higher volume of trades over the next few months.

One of Brigand's discretionary clients, Antonella Stuart, is a successful businesswoman in her late 50s. She made it clear to Brigand when they were first discussing her requirements that she was willing to take on a considerable amount of risk in return for capital growth—however she didn't want anything to do with derivatives of any sort. Stuart has had some heated exchanges over the past year relating to the returns that her investments have generated.

Stuart accepted all Monumental Managers' standard terms and conditions, which included an assumption that unless contacted by the investor, the manager would use any equity voting rights in their perceived interests of the investor.

Some recent information has come to light, which has made Stuart very angry:

- In 2012, Brigand had the chance to acquire warrants (a type of derivative) in Renmeed, Inc., a lucrative potential issuer of new shares the next year. Brigand purchases a block of these warrants and adds them to the accounts of a handful of his clients; these clients subsequently enjoyed a gain of 40% on this investment.

- Early in 2013, Brigand was briefed by the CEO of Ashma Plastics that the firm had won exclusive distribution rights in China for their product, but this wasn't going to be announced for two more weeks. Brigand did not act on this information, though an investment in that company's equity would have earned a 15% return.

- During 2012, Elliot Corporation wished to take a vote of no confidence in the current Board. Stuart's holding in the company at the time was 0.2% of voting stock. Stuart heard about this vote on the news. Stuart felt that the current Board was performing well and did not want them removed. However, Brigand did not contact Stuart on this matter, and Stuart was upset when she later found out her votes were used in favor of removing the Board.
Bernard later informed Stuart that he was aware that two pension funds holding 72% between them were going to vote in favor, so it made very little difference as only a 50% voting majority was required.

1. Has Brigand breached CFA Institute's Standards of Professional Conduct in passing his hospitality industry analysis and recommendations to clients?
    A. No, Brigand is in compliance with the Standards.
    B. Yes, Brigand is in violation of Standard V(A): Investment Analysis, Recommendations, and Actions – Diligence and Reasonable Basis as he used insufficient data.
    C. Yes, Brigand is in violation of Standard II(A): Integrity of Capital Markets – Material Nonpublic Information since he used a classified Labor Department document.

2. The practice of Brigand "paying up" for the research is in:
    A. violation of the Soft Dollar Standards.
    B. compliance with the Standards of Professional Conduct.
    C. violation of Standard VI(A): Conflicts of Interest – Disclosure of Conflicts since clients should be informed of the higher commissions specifically and not generally.

3. In respect to Brigand's error when directing a trade to Scarpers Securities, if Brigand accepts Scarpers' offer of covering the error in return for additional trades, which CFA Institute Standards have been violated?
   A. Standard I(B): Professionalism – Independence and Objectivity and Standard III(B): Duties to Clients – Fair Dealing.
   B. Standard III(A): Duties to Clients – Loyalty, Prudence, and Care and Standard III(B): Duties to Clients – Fair Dealing.
   C. Standard I(B): Professionalism – Independence and Objectivity, Standard III(A): Duties to Clients – Loyalty, Prudence, and Care and Standard III(B): Duties to Clients – Fair Dealing.

4. With regard to Renmeed, Inc., did Brigand's decision not to allocate Renmeed warrants to Stuart's portfolio violate any CFA Institute Standard?
   A. Yes, because Brigand had a duty to treat all clients fairly under Standard III(B): Duties to Clients – Fair Dealing.
   B. No, because Stuart's specific requirements meant she would not want this investment.
   C. Yes, because warrants are a high risk item, and Stuart has expressed a willingness to take on high risk.

5. With respect to Ashma Plastics, which of the following is *most accurate*?
   A. Brigand should have disclosed the CEO's comments to the appropriate legal authority.
   B. Brigand has breached his duty to his clients by not purchasing shares of Ashma Plastics for his clients.
   C. Ashma Plastics' CEO breached his responsibilities under law by disclosing the insider information.

6. Did Brigand act properly with respect to his use of Stuart's votes with the Elliot Corporation?
   A. Yes, because Stuart had not contacted him to express a desire not to vote.
   B. Yes, provided he thought the action was in Stuart's interests and Stuart had not advised otherwise.
   C. No, there is always a duty to consult clients on votes irrespective of agreement—this right cannot be waived.

Questions 7–12 relate to Harold Chang and Woodlock Management Group.

Harold Chang, CFA, has been the lead portfolio manager for the Woodlock Management Group (WMG) for the last five years. WMG runs several equity and fixed income portfolios, all of which are authorized to use derivatives as long as such positions are consistent with the portfolio's strategy. The WMG Equity Opportunities Fund takes advantage of long and short profit opportunities in equity securities. The fund's positions are often a relatively large percentage of the issuer's outstanding shares and fund trades frequently move securities prices. Chang runs the Equity Opportunities Fund and is concerned that his performance for the last three quarters has put his position as lead manager in jeopardy. Over the last three quarters, Chang has been underperforming his benchmark by an increasing margin and is determined to reduce the degree of underperformance before the end of the next quarter. Accordingly, Chang makes the following transactions for the fund:

Transaction 1: Chang discovers that the implied volatility of call options on GreenCo is too high. As a result, Chang shorts a large position in the stock options while simultaneously taking a long position in GreenCo stock, using the funds from the short position to partially pay for the long stock. The GreenCo purchase caused the share price to move up slightly. After several months, the GreenCo stock position has accumulated a large unrealized gain. Chang sells a portion of the GreenCo position to rebalance the portfolio.

Richard Stirr, CFA, who is also a portfolio manager for WMG, runs the firm's Fixed Income Fund. Stirr is known for his ability to generate excess returns above his benchmark, even in declining markets. Stirr is convinced that even though he has only been with WMG for two and a half years, he will be named lead portfolio manager if he can keep his performance figures strong through the next quarter. To achieve this positive performance, Stirr enters into the following transactions for the fund:

Transaction 2: Stirr decides to take a short forward position on the senior bonds of ONB Corporation, which Stirr currently owns in his Fixed Income Fund. Stirr made his decision after overhearing two of his firm's investment bankers discussing an unannounced bond offering for ONB that will subordinate all of its outstanding debt. As expected, the price of the ONB bonds falls when the upcoming offering is announced. Stirr delivers the bonds to settle the forward contract, preventing large losses for his investors.

Transaction 3: Stirr has noticed that in a foreign bond market, participants are slow to react to new information relevant to the value of their country's sovereign debt securities. Stirr, along with other investors, knows that an announcement from his firm regarding the sovereign bonds will be made the following day. Stirr doesn't know for sure, but expects the news to be positive, and prepares to enter a purchase order. When the positive news is released, Stirr is the first to act, making a large purchase before other investors and selling the position after other market participants react and move the sovereign bond price higher.

Because of their experience with derivatives instruments, Chang and Stirr are asked to provide investment advice for Cherry Creek, LLC, a commodities trading advisor. Cherry Creek uses managed futures strategies that incorporate long and short positions in commodity futures to generate returns uncorrelated with securities markets. The firm has asked Chang and Stirr to help extend their reach to include equity and fixed income derivatives strategies. Chang has been investing with Cherry Creek since its inception and has accepted increased shares in his Cherry Creek account as compensation for his advice. Chang has not disclosed his arrangement with Cherry Creek since he meets with the firm only during his personal time. Stirr declines any formal compensation but instead requests that Cherry Creek refer their clients requesting traditional investment services to WMG. Cherry Creek agrees to the arrangement.

Three months have passed since the transactions made by Chang and Stirr occurred. Both managers met their performance goals and are preparing to present their results to clients via an electronic newsletter published every quarter. The managers want to ensure their newsletters are in compliance with CFA Institute Standards of Professional Conduct. Chang states, "in order to comply with the Standards, we are required to disclose the process used to analyze and select portfolio holdings, the method used to construct our portfolios, and any changes that have been made to the overall investment process. In addition, we must include in the newsletter all factors used to make each portfolio decision over the last quarter and an assessment of the portfolio's risks." Stirr responds by claiming, "we must also clearly indicate that projections included in our report are not factual evidence but rather conjecture based on our own statistical analysis. However, I believe we can reduce the amount of information included in the report from what you have suggested and instead issue more of a summary report as long as we maintain a full report in our internal records."

7. Determine whether Chang has violated any CFA Institute Standards of Professional Conduct with respect to Transaction 1.
   A. This is a violation of CFA Institute Standards due to use of the funds from the short position being used to partially pay for the long position.
   B. This is a violation of CFA Institute Standards since the immediate upward movement in GreenCo stock price was a result of the transaction artificially manipulating the market.
   C. No violation of CFA Institute Standards has occurred.

8. Determine whether Stirr has violated any CFA Institute Standards of Professional Conduct with respect to Transaction 2 and Transaction 3.
   A. Both Transactions 2 and 3 violate CFA Institute Standards.
   B. Neither transaction is a violation of CFA Institute Standards.
   C. Transaction 2 is a violation of CFA Institute, while Transaction 3 is not.

9. According to CFA Institute Standards of Professional Conduct, which of the following statements regarding Chang's arrangement with Cherry Creek, LLC is *most* accurate? Chang's arrangement:
   A. does not violate any Standards.
   B. violates the Standards because he has not obtained written consent from WMG to enter into the agreement.
   C. violates the Standards because he has misrepresented his ability to provide professional advice to Cherry Creek.

10. According to CFA Institute Standards of Professional Conduct, which of the following statements regarding Stirr's arrangement with Cherry Creek, LLC is *most* accurate? Stirr's arrangement:
    A. does not violate any Standards.
    B. need only be disclosed to WMG to be acceptable.
    C. is acceptable only if disclosed to WMG and to clients and prospective clients.

11. Determine whether Chang's comments regarding the disclosure of investment processes used to manage WMG's portfolios and the disclosure of factors used to make portfolio decisions over the last quarter are correct.
    A. Both of Chang's comments are correct.
    B. Neither of Chang's comments is correct.
    C. Only Chang's comment regarding disclosure of investment processes is correct.

12. Determine whether Stirr's comments regarding the use of projections in the report and the length of the report are correct.
    A. Both of Stirr's comments regarding the projections in the report, and the length of the report, are correct.
    B. Only Stirr's comment about the projections in the report is correct.
    C. Only Stirr's comment regarding the length of the report is correct.

Questions 13–18 relate to Dan Draper.

Dan Draper, CFA, is a portfolio manager at Madison Securities. Draper is analyzing several portfolios which have just been assigned to him. In each case, there is a clear statement of portfolio objectives and constraints, as well as an initial strategic asset allocation. However, Draper has found that all of the portfolios have experienced changes in asset values. As a result, the current allocations have drifted away from the initial allocation. Draper is considering various rebalancing strategies that would keep the portfolios in line with their proposed asset allocation targets.

Draper spoke to Peter Sterling, a colleague at Madison, about calendar rebalancing. During their conversation, Sterling made the following comments:

Comment 1: "Calendar rebalancing will be most efficient when the rebalancing frequency considers the volatility of the asset classes in the portfolio."

Comment 2: "Calendar rebalancing on an annual basis will typically minimize market impact relative to more frequent rebalancing."

Draper believes that a percentage-of-portfolio rebalancing strategy will be preferable to calendar rebalancing, but he is uncertain as to how to set the corridor widths to trigger rebalancing for each asset class. As an example, Draper is evaluating the Rogers Corp. pension plan, whose portfolio is described in Exhibit 1.

Exhibit 1: Rogers Corp Pension Plan

Asset Class	Expected Return	Standard Deviation	Average Transaction Cost	Correlation With Other Assets in Portfolio
U.S. small-cap stocks	10%	15%	0.30%	0.21
Emerging market stocks	14%	22%	0.40%	0.10
Real estate limited partnership	16%	10%	3.00%	0.16
U.S. government bonds	6%	2%	0.05%	0.14

Draper has been reviewing Madison files on four high net worth individuals, each of whom has a $1 million portfolio. He hopes to gain insight as to appropriate rebalancing strategies for these clients. His research so far shows:

Client A is 60 years old, and wants to be sure of having at least $800,000 upon his retirement. His risk tolerance drops dramatically whenever his portfolio declines in value. He agrees with the Madison stock market outlook, which is for a long-term bull market with few reversals.

Client B is 35 years old and wants to hold stocks regardless of the value of her portfolio. She also agrees with the Madison stock market outlook.

Client C is 40 years old, and her absolute risk tolerance varies proportionately with the value of her portfolio. She does not agree with the Madison stock market outlook, but expects a volatile stock market, marked by numerous reversals, over the coming months.

13. Indicate whether Sterling's comments related to calendar rebalancing are correct or incorrect.
    A. Only comment 1 is correct.
    B. Only comment 2 is correct.
    C. Both comments are correct.

14. Draper believes that the risk tolerance for tracking error relative to the target asset mix and the volatility of any other asset classes in a portfolio are important factors in determining an appropriate rebalancing corridor. Assuming all other factors are equal, the optimal rebalancing corridor will be wider when:
    A. the risk tolerance for tracking error is high and the volatility of other asset classes is low.
    B. the risk tolerance for tracking error is high and the volatility of other asset classes is high.
    C. the risk tolerance for tracking error is low and the volatility of other asset classes is high.

15. Based on the information provided in Exhibit 1, which asset class of the Rogers pension plan should have the narrowest rebalancing corridor width?
    A. U.S. small cap stocks.
    B. Emerging market stocks.
    C. U.S. government bonds.

16. In selecting a rebalancing strategy for his clients, Draper would *most likely* select a constant mix strategy for:
    A. Client A.
    B. Client B.
    C. Client C.

17. A buy and hold strategy:
    A. would be appropriate for Client C.
    B. is an example of a concave strategy.
    C. is a linear strategy with a floor greater than zero and a multiplier equal to 1.

18. Which of the following statements is *most* accurate regarding rebalancing strategies? The constant:
    A. proportion strategy has a concave payoff curve and a multiplier greater than 1.
    B. proportion strategy has a convex payoff curve and a multiplier less than 1.
    C. mix strategy has a concave payoff curve and a multiplier less than 1.

Questions 19–24 relate to the Highwings Academy Endowment.

Flynn Fountain, CFA, is the investment consultant for the $120 million Highwings Academy Endowment (Highwings). At its last meeting, Highwings's Investment Committee (Committee) voted to place half of the portfolio's 40% U.S. large-capitalization equity allocation with a Russell 1000 Index manager; the remaining half is to be divided equally between two additional managers. The Committee hopes the two non-indexers will be able to generate positive active returns relative to their respective benchmark indexes. Highwings benchmarks its overall large-capitalization domestic equity allocation to the Russell 1000 Index.

Three managers are under consideration for the two additional large-capitalization assignments: Osprey Investment Management (Osprey), Eagle Capital Management (Eagle), and Hawk Associates, LLP (Hawk). One of the managers uses an enhanced indexing style. Performance data relative to each firm's stated style benchmark are detailed below:

Exhibit 1: Annualized Performance Statistics – 5 Years Ending June 30, 2015

	Osprey	Eagle	Hawk	Index
Active return	2.4%	2.2%	1.7%	0.0%
Tracking risk	5.7%	4.2%	2.0%	0.1%
R^2	0.9430	0.9469	0.9689	
Index style	S&P/Citigroup	S&P/Citigroup	S&P/Citigroup	Russell
Benchmark	500 Growth	500 Growth	500 Value	1000

In addition to assembling the performance data, Fountain has completed a returns-based style analysis of the three investment managers. His study examined five years of quarterly data as of June 30, 2015. Fountain used the following index benchmarks in the analysis:

- Large-cap growth (LCG): S&P/Citigroup 500 Growth Index
- Large-cap value (LCV): S&P/Citigroup 500 Value Index
- Mid-cap growth (MCG): S&P/Citigroup 400 Growth Index
- Mid-cap value (MCV): S&P/Citigroup 400 Value Index
- Small-cap growth (SCG): S&P/Citigroup 600 Growth Index
- Small-cap value (SCV): S&P/Citigroup 600 Value Index
- T-bill: Citigroup 3-month T-bill Index

The following exhibits show Fountain's results:

Exhibit 2: Osprey Investment Management

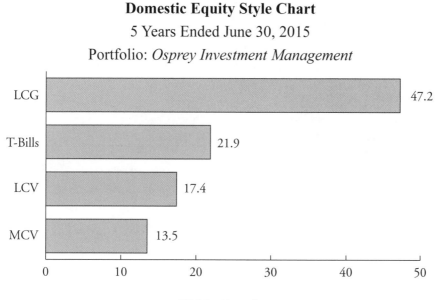

Domestic Equity Style Chart

5 Years Ended June 30, 2015

Portfolio: *Osprey Investment Management*

Weight % total = 100

Exhibit 3: Eagle Capital Management

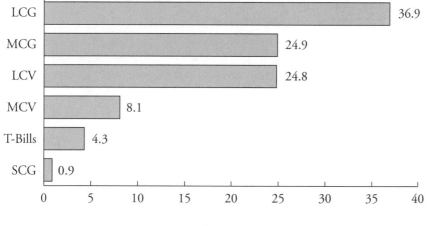

Domestic Equity Style Chart

5 Years Ended June 30, 2015

Portfolio: *Eagle Capital Management*

Weight % total = 100

Exhibit 4: Hawk Associates, LLP

Domestic Equity Style Chart

5 Years Ended June 30, 2015

Portfolio: *Hawk Associates, LLP*

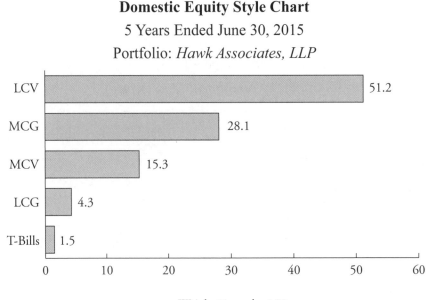

Weight % total = 100

As Highwings's Investment Committee reviews the results of Fountain's returns-based style analysis, Committee members make the following statements:

Statement 1: "We should add the Russell 1000 Index to this analysis because it is our main benchmark."

Statement 2: "None of these managers meet our selection guidelines. We want two large-capitalization equity managers, and these managers invest in mid-capitalization stocks and T-bills in addition to large-cap stocks."

19. Highwings's implementation approach for large-capitalization equity securities is *most likely* to be characterized as which of the following strategies?
    A. Core-satellite.
    B. Completeness fund.
    C. Alpha and beta separation.

20. Based solely on the data in Exhibit 1, which of the following investment firms would *most likely* be classified as the best active manager?
    A. Eagle.
    B. Hawk.
    C. Osprey.

21.   Are the Committee members' statements regarding the returns-based style analysis accurate?
       A. Only statement 1 is accurate.
       B. Only statement 2 is accurate.
       C. Neither statement is accurate.

22.   Which of the following statements about Osprey is *most accurate*?
       A. On average, over the past five years, Osprey held approximately 22% in cash equivalents.
       B. The S&P/Citigroup 500 Growth Index is not the most appropriate normal portfolio benchmark for Osprey.
       C. Osprey's returns over the past five years could not have been passively replicated because the R^2 value of the style analysis regression is less than 0.95.

23.   Which of the following statements about Hawk is *most accurate*?
       A. Hawk may be undergoing style drift.
       B. Hawk's regression style fit indicates that most of its active returns are attributable to market timing.
       C. The most appropriate normal style benchmark for Hawk is the S&P/Citigroup 500 Value Index.

24.   To meet the properties of valid benchmarks, it is *most accurate* to say the Highwing's Investment Committee must inform the new managers:
       A. of their respective style benchmarks.
       B. the Russell 1000 Index is the overall equity benchmark.
       C. of their respective style benchmarks and the Russell 1000 Index is the overall equity benchmark.

Questions 25–30 relate to Kashyap Kompella.

Kashyap Kompella, CFA, manages the defined benefit plan of Grease-Z Wheel Bearings. A high percentage of the employee participants in the plan are risk averse, middle-aged men, with 25% of the participants over 50 years old. Exhibit 1 shows the plan's current status.

Exhibit 1: Portfolio Characteristics

Fixed Income	Present Value	Effective Duration	Average Maturity
Assets	$150 million	3.0 years	5.0 years
Liabilities	$100 million	6.0 years	8.0 years

The plan trustees believe interest rates will increase over the next year while credit spreads will narrow. The trustees believe in active management of the portfolio and have decided to decrease the portfolio duration and adjust the portfolio holdings to take advantage of their expectations. Kompella agrees with these views.

The plan trustees have asked Kompella to review potential benchmarks for the plan. Exhibit 1 shows the benchmarks under consideration.

Exhibit 2: Potential Benchmarks

Benchmark	Effective Duration	Average Maturity
1. Short-term government bonds	3.0 years	5.0 years
2. Short-term corporate bonds	3.0 years	5.0 years
3. Long-term government bonds	6.0 years	8.0 years
4. Long-term corporate bonds	6.0 years	8.0 years

Kompella estimates he can earn 7% annually through active management of the corporate bond portfolio over the next five years. The plan trustees will allow Kompella to actively manage the portfolio as long as the minimum annual return does not fall below 5%.

Kompella has started his buying program to shorten duration and buy corporate bonds. A broker has offered him a 7-year, single-B rated, 9% coupon bond trading at par. Kompella expects to hold the bond for two years, assumes a reinvestment rate of 8%, and believes the bond will be priced to yield 10% at the investment horizon.

The plan actuary has projected pension payments of $6 million, $5 million, and $8 million in years 1–3, respectively. Kompella is considering buying one-year, two-year, and three-year annual pay eurobonds to match the cash flows of the payments. The eurobonds yield 6% at each maturity and are selling at par.

Kompella also manages another immunized portfolio for a different client. At the beginning of the year, that portfolio's dollar duration is $4.5 million. One year later, interest rates have declined by 100 basis points, and the dollar duration is $4.7 million.

As Kompella's time begins to free up, he decides to perform research on several immunization strategies. He begins his due diligence by comparing and contrasting risk minimization and return maximization as it pertains to immunized portfolios. He asks Franklin Stubbs, a member of his staff, to identify the differences between immunized portfolios that focus on minimizing risk versus maximizing return. Stubbs and Kompella agree to meet in the near term to discuss these immunization strategies.

25.　Which of the following risk criteria would *most likely* affect Kompella's benchmark selection?
　　A.　Credit risk.
　　B.　Income risk.
　　C.　Liability framework risk.

26.　Which combination of benchmarks from Exhibit 1 should Kompella *most appropriately* select for the plan's strategic asset allocation (SAA) and tactical asset allocation (TAA) performance evaluation?

	SAA	TAA
A.	Number 3	Number 1
B.	Number 4	Number 1
C.	Number 4	Number 2

27.　Kompella's annualized bond equivalent total return on the 7-year bond is *closest* to:
　　A.　6.7%.
　　B.　7.2%.
　　C.　8.4%.

28.　At the end of the year, which of the following portfolio change combinations must be applied to each position to restore the dollar duration of Kompella's portfolio to $4.5 million?
　　A.　Increase 4.26%.
　　B.　Decrease 4.26%.
　　C.　Decrease 4.44%.

29.　In order to fund a cash flow match of the three years projected pension payments using eurobonds, the purchase cost of the two-year eurobond is *closest* to:
　　A.　$4.3 million.
　　B.　$4.5 million.
　　C.　$5.0 million.

30. A primary difference Stubbs is *most likely* to identify between minimizing immunization risk and maximizing return subject to immunization constraints is that a return-maximized portfolio:
     A. requires duration-matching the liability stream.
     B. remains immunized regardless of a reshaping yield curve.
     C. accepts a risk trade-off between higher return and the confidence interval of possible returns.

Questions 31–36 relate to Russel Bowers and the Lake Ridge Trust Case.

Russell Bowers manages a $64 million fixed-income portfolio for the U.S.-based Lake Ridge Trust (LRT). Falling interest rates and continued contributions to the growing trust have resulted in decreasing income returns on new LRT capital at the same time that the value of the portfolio has increased. Although Bowers manages the trust to a total return requirement, he prefers to meet its income needs without liquidating assets.

One bank has offered financing for additional assets at 5.5% fixed for one year for up to 50% of portfolio value. The bank would, however, require that LRT use portfolio assets as collateral, including requiring that 5% of the portfolio be invested in short-term Treasuries. Bowers estimates LRT's fixed-income portfolio duration at 7.0 and the return on invested funds to be 5.75%. He further estimates that he could earn 5.75% on any borrowed funds. Bowers is also considering financing additional corporate debt purchases using a repurchase agreement.

Bowers is concerned that the LRT fixed-income portfolio has more credit risk (exposure) than he currently desires. He decides to explore several ways to reduce the portfolio's credit exposure while providing protection beyond the actual default of the fixed-income instruments selected. Bowers favors the use of liquid customized credit derivative instruments to meet this objective.

Looking forward one year, Bowers expects that the Federal Reserve will increase interest rates by as much as 75 basis points. He is concerned that this will affect the asset values of his portfolio and wishes to have a strategy in place to offset prevailing interest rate increases.

As the time approaches for a potential rate increase at the end of the first year, LRT's unleveraged fixed-income portfolio is now $67.5 million and has a duration of 7.0, which is much greater than its benchmark index duration of 4.0. Bowers receives information that the cheapest-to-deliver (CTD) bond is trading at a duration of 6.5 with a conversion factor of 1.09 (assume the CTD bond price is 100). Futures contracts can be purchased or sold in increments of $100,000.

Bowers observes that China bonds offer a comparable interest rate to U.S. bonds. In contrast, short-term U.S. interest rates are currently 3% higher than short-term China rates. The forward currency market is active and efficiently priced, and Bowers expects that the current China bonds spread over comparable Treasuries will remain the same, should the Federal Reserve increase interest rates as forecasted. An analytical firm has furnished a country beta of 0.36 for China with the United States, and a particular China bond issue that Bowers is interested in has a duration of 3.8.

31. The additional return to the portfolio from 50% leverage using bank financing is *closest* to:
   A. 0.125%.
   B. 0.250%.
   C. 0.375%.

32. Assuming a repurchase agreement is used for financing, Bowers could expect to pay the highest repo rate when the:
   A. lender needs those specific securities for a short sale.
   B. repo agreement does not require LRT to deliver collateral physically.
   C. Federal Reserve cuts interest rates 25 basis points prior to the transaction.

33. Which of the following credit derivative instruments would *best* meet Bowers's credit exposure reduction needs and minimize the probability he will expend any capital initially or during the credit derivative's life to acquire the position?
   A. Credit default swap.
   B. Credit default option.
   C. Credit spread forward.

34. The transaction and the number of contracts required to bring LRT's portfolio to the benchmark duration are:

	Transaction	*Number of Contracts*
A.	Buy	312
B.	Sell	312
C.	Sell	340

35. If domestic (U.S.) interest rates increase by 75 basis points (bps) and the country beta is accurate, the price change of the China bond would be *closest* to:
   A. −3 bps.
   B. −100 bps.
   C. −135 bps.

36. Assume Bowers is correct that U.S. interest rates will increase 75 basis points and the nominal spread between U.S. and China bonds will not change. Further assume that Bowers believes the U.S. dollar will depreciate 2% over the year against the Chinese (CNY) currency, Bowers's optimal strategy to maximize total return is to buy the:
   A. U.S. bond.
   B. China bond and buy the USD forward.
   C. China bond and then sell the CNY in one year.

Questions 37–42 relate to Upsala Asset Management.

Albert Wulf, CFA, is a portfolio manager with Upsala Asset Management, a regional financial services firm that handles investments for small businesses in Northern Germany. For the most part, Wulf has been handling locally concentrated investments in European securities. Due to a lack of expertise in currency management, he works closely with James Bauer, a foreign exchange expert who manages international exposure in some of Upsala's portfolios. Both individuals are committed to managing portfolio assets within the guidelines of client investment policy statements.

To achieve global diversification, Wulf's portfolio invests in securities from developed nations including the United States, Japan, and Great Britain. Due to recent currency market turmoil, translation risk has become a huge concern for Upsala's managers. The U.S. dollar has recently plummeted relative to the euro, while the Japanese yen and British pound have appreciated slightly relative to the euro. Wulf and Bauer meet to discuss hedging strategies that will hopefully mitigate some of the concerns regarding future currency fluctuations.

Wulf currently has a $1,000,000 investment in a U.S. oil and gas corporation. This position was taken with the expectation that demand for oil in the U.S. would increase sharply over the short-run. Wulf plans to exit this position 125 days from today. In order to hedge the currency exposure to the U.S. dollar, Bauer enters into a 90-day U.S. dollar futures contract, expiring in September. Bauer comments to Wulf that this futures contract guarantees that the portfolio will not take any unjustified risk in the volatile dollar.

Wulf recently started investing in securities from Japan. He has been particularly interested in the growth of technology firms in that country. Wulf decides to make an investment of ¥25,000,000 in a small technology enterprise that is in need of start-up capital. The spot exchange rate for the Japanese yen at the time of the investment is ¥135/€. The expected spot rate in 90 days is ¥132/€. Given the expected appreciation of the yen, Bauer purchases put options that provide insurance against any deprecation of the yen. While delta-hedging this position, Bauer discovers that current at-the-money yen put options sell for €1 with a delta of −0.85. He mentions to Wulf that, in general, put options will provide a cheaper alternative to hedging than with futures since put options are only exercised if the local currency depreciates.

The exposure of Wulf's portfolio to the British pound results from a 180-day pound-denominated investment of £5,000,000. The spot exchange rate for the British pound is £0.78/€. The value of the investment is expected to increase to £5,100,000 at the end of the180 day period. Bauer informs Wulf that due to the minimal expected exchange rate movement, it would be in the best interest of their clients, from a cost-benefit standpoint, to hedge only the principal of this investment.

Before entering into currency futures and options contracts, Wulf and Bauer discuss the possibility of also hedging market risk due to changes in the value of the assets. Bauer suggests that in order to hedge against a possible loss in the value of an asset Wulf should short a given foreign market index. Wulf is interested in executing index hedging strategies that are perfectly correlated with foreign investments. Bauer, however, cautions Wulf regarding the increase in trading costs that would result from these additional hedging activities.

37. Of the following cash management approaches, the one that best reflects Wulf and Bauer's currency management strategy is a:
   A. strategic hedge ratio.
   B. currency overlay.
   C. separate asset allocation.

38. Regarding the U.S. investment in the oil and gas company, which of the following approaches would be best in eliminating potential basis risk?
   A. When the 90-day futures contract expires, Bauer should enter into another 90-day contract to further hedge against any changes in the dollar relative to the euro.
   B. Instead of the 90-day contract, Bauer should enter into a 180-day contract to cover the full 125-day period, which would eliminate additional transactions costs brought on by short-term contracts.
   C. Despite the large amount of transaction costs, Bauer should continually adjust the hedge until the futures maturity equals the desired holding period.

39. Regarding the Japanese investment in the technology company, determine the appropriate transaction in put options to adjust the current delta hedge, given that the delta changes to –0.92. Assume that each yen put allows the right to sell ¥1,000,000.
   A. Sell 2 yen put options.
   B. Sell 27 euro put options.
   C. Buy 29 yen put options.

40. Is Bauer correct in stating to Wulf that put options provide a cheaper means of hedging than futures?
   A. No, since Bauer is only concerned with unfavorable currency movements, futures would be cheaper.
   B. No, despite being less liquid, futures are less expensive to use.
   C. Yes, given that Bauer can choose to exercise the options or let them expire, options are cheaper since the payoff is only to one side.

41. Calculate the total rate of return that Wulf can expect from hedging the principal amount in the British denominated asset with currency futures. Assume that Bauer hedges the principal by selling £5,000,000 in pound futures at £0.79/€ and the value of the investment is £5,100,000. When this hedge is lifted the futures rate is £0.785/€ and the spot rate is £0.75/€.
   A. 6.08%.
   B. 5.45%.
   C. 2.00%.

42. Assuming Wulf and Bauer are successful in hedging both the foreign currency exposure and market risk exposure from the appreciation and depreciation of the asset, the expected return would be *closest* to:
   A. zero, since all risks have been hedged.
   B. the domestic risk-free rate.
   C. the foreign risk-free rate.

Questions 43–48 are related to Milson Investment Advisors.

Milson Investment Advisors (MIA) specializes in managing fixed income portfolios for institutional clients. Many of MIA's clients are able to take on substantial portfolio risk and therefore the firm's funds invest in all credit qualities and in international markets. Among its investments, MIA currently holds positions in the debt of Worth Inc., Enertech Company, and SBK Company.

Worth Inc. is a heavy equipment manufacturer in Germany. To minimize overall balance sheet volatility, Worth finances its long-term fixed assets with fixed-rate debt. Worth's current debt outstanding is in the form of non-callable bonds issued two years ago at a coupon rate of 7.2% and a maturity of 15 years. Worth expects German interest rates to decline by as much as 200 basis points (bps) over the next year and would like to take advantage of the decline. The company has decided to enter into a 2-year interest rate swap with semiannual payments, a swap rate of 5.8%, and a floating rate based on 6-month EURIBOR. The duration of the fixed side of the swap is 1.2. Analysts at MIA have made the following comments regarding Worth's swap plan:

> "The duration of the swap from the perspective of Worth is 0.95."

> "By entering into the swap, the absolute duration of Worth's long-term liabilities will become smaller, causing the value of the firm's equity to become more sensitive to changes in interest rates."

Enertech Company is a U.S.-based provider of electricity and natural gas. The company uses a large proportion of floating rate notes to finance its operations. The current interest rate on Enertech's floating rate notes, based on 6-month LIBOR plus 150bp, is 5.5%. To hedge its interest rate risk, Enertech has decided to enter into a long interest rate collar. The cap and the floor of the collar have maturities of two years, with settlement dates (in arrears) every six months. The strike rate for the cap is 5.5% and for the floor is 4.5%, based on 6-month LIBOR, which is forecast to be 5.2%, 6.1%, 4.1%, and 3.8%, in 6, 12, 18, and 24 months, respectively. Each settlement period consists of 180 days. Analysts at MIA are interested in assessing the attributes of the collar.

SBK Company builds oil tankers and other large ships in Norway. The firm has several long-term, fixed-rate bond issues outstanding. Several years ago, the firm entered receive-fixed versus pay-floating swaps to convert their liabilities to floating rate debt. SBK now fears interest rates will increase. SBK mistakenly sells a payer swaption in an effort to hedge the risk of increasing rates.

MIA is considering investing in the debt of Rio Corp, a Brazilian energy company. The investment would be in Rio's floating rate notes, currently paying a coupon of 8.0%. MIA's economists are forecasting an interest rate decline in Brazil over the short term.

43. Given Worth Inc.'s expectations regarding German interest rates, which of the following is *closest* to the effective interest rate the firm will pay on its liabilities after entering into the swap?
    A. Fixed rate of 5.8%.
    B. EURIBOR plus 140bp.
    C. EURIBOR less 140bp.

44. Determine whether the MIA analysts' comments regarding the duration of the Worth Inc. swap and the effects of the swap on the company's balance sheet are correct or incorrect.
    A. Only the comment regarding the swap duration is correct.
    B. Only the comment regarding the swap balance sheet effects is correct.
    C. Both comments are correct.

45. Which of the following is *closest* to the payoff on Enertech's collar 24 months from now? Enertech will:
    A. make a payment of $0.0020 per dollar of notional principal.
    B. make a payment of $0.0035 per dollar of notional principal.
    C. will receive a payment of $0.0035 per dollar of notional principal.

46. Which of the following is *closest* to the effective interest rate that Enertech will pay 18 months from now assuming the notional principal of the collar is equal to the outstanding principal on the firm's floating rate notes?
    A. 2.8%.
    B. 3.5%.
    C. 3.8%.

47. How will the sale of a payer swaption affect the net net cash flow risk of SBK's debt?
    A. If rates decrease, cash outflows will increase.
    B. If rates increase, cash outflows will increase.
    C. If rates increase, cash outflows will decrease.

48. Which of the following strategies would *best* hedge the risk of MIA's investment in the Rio Corp. floating rate notes?
    A. Sell an interest rate call with a strike rate of 8.0%.
    B. Sell an interest rate put with a strike rate of 7.0%.
    C. Purchase an interest rate put with a strike rate of 7.0%.

Questions 49–54 relate to Arthur Campbell and Campbell Asset Management.

Arthur Campbell, CFA, is the founder of Campbell Capital Management (CCM), a money management firm focused solely on high net worth individuals. Campbell started CCM two years ago after a 25-year career with a large bank trust department. CCM provides portfolios tailored to match the unique situation of each individual client. All of CCM's clientele have balanced portfolios. CCM does not use derivatives or exotic instruments to manage any of its portfolios. CCM's equity style is defined as growth at a reasonable price (GARP). Most of CCM's portfolios are managed under one of the following three approaches:

- Aggressive (10 accounts): 70% stocks and 30% bonds.
- Moderate (4 accounts): 50% stocks and 50% bonds.
- Conservative (25 accounts): 30% stocks and 70% bonds.

CCM has recently added the following two clients:

1. Harold Moss, a long-time acquaintance of Campbell. Campbell and Moss agreed to an investment policy statement in which Moss's portfolio will be managed under CCM's Aggressive approach. However, Moss feels he is actually much more aggressive than the other accounts in this composite and will have no allocation to bonds.

2. Richard Bateman is a successful businessman with a $5 million portfolio. Bateman wants his portfolio managed using a conservative approach, and he specifically states that no options or futures are to be used.

A current client, Stan North, has decided to retire. North would like to reduce his risk exposure from aggressive to conservative. CCM moves North's account, including its historical performance, to the conservative composite.

At the end of 2013, CCM reports the moderate portfolio composite performance but does not include the associated number of accounts.

CCM reported the 2013 returns on its conservative composite as shown in Exhibit 1:

Exhibit 1: CCM Conservative Composite Returns: Year Ending December 31, 2013

	Market Value 12/31/2013	Strategic Asset Mix	Returns
Stocks	$95,875,000	30%	8.5%
Bonds	$182,000,000	70%	5.2%
Cash	$47,125,000	0%	3.4%
Total	$325,000,000		

The data shown in Exhibit 2 relates to Moss portfolio transactions from the 2nd quarter of 2013.

Exhibit 2: Moss Cash Flows for the Second Quarter of 2013

	Moss Portfolio
Market value 3/31/2013	$2,500,000
Cash inflows (outflows)	
4/30/2013	$300,000
5/31/2013	0
Market value 6/30/2013	$3,100,000

49.   Campbell wants CCM's composites to be compliant with the Global Investment Performance Standards (GIPS)®. Should the Moss and the Bateman accounts be added to CCM's aggressive and conservative composites, respectively, to remain compliant with GIPS?
   A.   Moss's and Bateman's accounts should be added to the "aggressive" and "conservative" composites, respectively.
   B.   Moss's and Bateman's accounts should NOT be added to the "aggressive" and "conservative" composites, respectively.
   C.   Moss's account should not be added to the aggressive composite, but it would be acceptable to add Bateman's account to the conservative composite.

50.   CCM established three types of composites: aggressive, moderate, and conservative. State whether CCM's composites are *correctly* defined according to GIPS.
   A.   No, CCM must define an equity and fixed-income benchmark.
   B.   No, CCM must quantify risk parameters.
   C.   Yes, if CCM establishes a tight allowable range.

51.   Was CCM's movement of North's account from the aggressive composite to the conservative composite consistent with GIPS standards?
   A.   Yes.
   B.   No, the historical performance must remain with the aggressive composite.
   C.   No, the historical performance must be excluded from both the aggressive and conservative composites.

52. Which of the following statements concerning CCM's performance presentation is *most* accurate? According to GIPS standards:
    A. external verification of CCM's performance measurement policies is not required.
    B. CCM must report the number of accounts in the moderate portfolio composite.
    C. the cash balance in the CCM conservative composite must be excluded from any return calculations.

53. Campbell is considering carving out the bond return based on Exhibit 1. Using the strategic asset allocation method, the annual return he would report is *closest* to:
    A. 4.8%.
    B. 5.2%.
    C. He may not report a bond return for GIPS.

54. Campbell would like to report the equity performance for Moss's account for the second quarter of 2013. He computes the return using the Modified Dietz method. Which of the following statements is *most correct*?
    A. He calculates a Modified Dietz return of 11.1%.
    B. He may not report a Modified Dietz calculation for Moss.
    C. He may not report an equity return because Moss has a balanced portfolio objective.

Questions 55–60 relate to portfolio manager James Hatfield and clients.

James Hatfield, CFA, manages money for several clients. The clients reside in various countries. Some of them reside in countries that do not currently have tax-advantaged accounts. Hatfield watches for changes in the tax laws of the countries to see when accounts such as tax-exempt accounts and tax-deferred accounts become available. Hatfield wants to react quickly in such cases so that his clients respond as soon as they can to changes in the availability of these accounts.

Hatfield is also doing general counseling with his clients about how they should manage their accounts for tax purposes. One of his newest clients, Chrissie Hynde, lives in a country with a flat and heavy tax regime. She already has a small portfolio of investment assets and asks for Hatfield's advice about the current allocations. Currently, her portfolio is in a taxable account and is equally allocated among interest-paying assets, dividend-paying assets and non-dividend-paying growth stocks. Hynde is young and her income is relatively low, but she is in a job that has a high degree of job security and where she expects her income to increase dramatically in about ten years and then for the rest of her career. She expects her retirement income to be equal to the wage income she will be earning when she retires. She asks Hatfield about tax-advantaged accounts. If they become available, she wants to know which tax-advantaged account, if any, would benefit her the most.

Hynde also asks Hatfield about tax drag. She has a long investment horizon, but she is considering extending it and delaying retirement. However, she plans to reduce risk over time and shift from higher return assets to lower return assets. She asks Hatfield if this strategy would increase or decrease her tax drag.

Hatfield has another client, Rick Mars, who lives in a country with a heavy capital gains tax regime. The tax regime is not expected to change. Mars asks Hatfield about harvesting losses. Mars has a position in Chromoly stock, which he accumulated over several years at successively higher prices. Mars now plans to liquidate some of his position in Chromoly. He asks Hatfield his advice concerning the best way he should go about this.

Mars wants to make sure his portfolio of investment assets is a mean-variance optimal portfolio. In a preliminary analysis, Hatfield concludes Mars's current portfolio is optimal. As of now, however, Mars's country does not have any tax-advantaged accounts. The news has just come out that tax-exempt accounts may soon become available. Categorizing Mars's investments into the three basic categories of interest-paying investments, dividend-paying investments, and non-dividend paying growth investments, Mars asks how the availability of tax-advantaged accounts would influence the determination of the optimal weights.

55. What adjustment would Hatfield *most likely* make to Hynde's portfolio?
   A. Increase the allocation to interest-paying assets.
   B. Increase the allocation to dividend-paying assets.
   C. Increase the allocation to non-dividend-paying growth stocks.

56. Given Hynde's expectations concerning her future income and post-retirement income, would the tax-exempt account or the tax-deferred account be more beneficial?
   A. The tax-exempt account.
   B. The tax-deferred account.
   C. Neither has an advantage over the other.

57. Based on what we know about Hynde's plan to increase her investment horizon and choose assets with lower returns, the net effect would be:
   A. decreased tax drag.
   B. increased tax drag.
   C. an uncertain effect on tax drag.

58. With respect to dividend and interest income, it is likely that Mars faces favorable tax treatment for:
   A. both dividend and interest income.
   B. interest income but not dividend income.
   C. dividend income but not interest income.

59. Based on how Mars accumulated the position in Chromoly, Hatfield should advise Mars to:
   A. sell the shares that were acquired first.
   B. sell the most recently acquired shares first.
   C. sell shares from each purchase and in proportions equal to the positions.

60. If tax-advantaged accounts become available to Mars, the optimization process would become:
   A. less complicated because the new tax regime would create a level playing field.
   B. ineffective because there is no way to create an optimal portfolio given the multiple tax effects.
   C. more complicated because the number of weights to compute would increase from three to six.

END OF AFTERNOON SESSION

PRACTICE EXAM 3 MORNING SESSION QUESTION BREAKDOWN

MORNING SESSION		
Question	Topic	Minutes
1	Monitoring/Rebalancing and Risk Management	13
2	GIPS	12
3	Portfolio Management – Institutional	24
4	Equity Portfolio Management	9
5	Performance Evaluation	12
6	Fixed Income Derivatives	11
7	Portfolio Management – Individual	14
8	Portfolio Management – Individual	18
9	Portfolio Management – Individual	15
10	Portfolio Management – Individual	13
11	Portfolio Management – Institutional	21
12	Alternative Investments	18
	Total	180

PRACTICE EXAM 3 SCORE SHEET

MORNING SESSION		
Question	Maximum Points	Your Approximate Score
1A	4	
1B	6	
1C	3	
2A	6	
2B	6	
3A	16	
3B	6	
3C	2	
4	9	
5	12	
6A	4	
6B	3	
6C	4	
7A	8	
7B	6	
8A	9	
8B	9	
9A	10	
9B	5	
10A	4	
10B	9	
11A	2	
11B	9	
11C	6	
11D	4	
12A	12	
12B	6	
Total	180	

AFTERNOON SESSION		
Questions	Maximum Points	Your Approximate Score
1–6	18	
7–12	18	
13–18	18	
19–24	18	
25–30	18	
31–36	18	
37–42	18	
43–48	18	
49–54	18	
55–60	18	
Total	180	

PRACTICE EXAM 3
MORNING SESSION

QUESTION 1 HAS THREE PARTS (A, B, C) FOR A TOTAL OF 13 MINUTES

Lauren Shoemaker, CFA, is the director of equity trading for a large mutual fund group. Shoemaker oversees the execution of roughly 5 million shares of daily trading volume. Over the past several years, it has become more difficult to efficiently handle the mutual fund group's large trade volume because the average trade size on the New York Stock Exchange has fallen so dramatically. Based on a recent conference attended by Shoemaker, she believes the solution to the mutual fund group's problem is algorithmic trading. Shoemaker has told a colleague that, in the future, traders will become irrelevant and the job of the trader will be eliminated. Figure 1 provides a partial trade blotter for Shoemaker's mutual fund group.

Figure 1: Trade blotter

Stock	Trade	Size (shares)	Avg. Daily Volume	Last Price	Bid Price	Ask Price	Urgency
Star	Sell	700,000	11,500,000	$39.75	$39.74	$39.76	High
Moon	Buy	500,000	2,200,000	$150.00	$149.62	$150.37	Low
Sun	Buy	500,000	6,000,000	$80.00	$79.98	$80.02	Low

A.   **Describe** two primary characteristics of algorithmic trading.

(4 minutes)

B. **State** the appropriate trading strategy for each stock listed in the trade blotter in Figure 1 and **justify** your selection.

(6 minutes)

Answer Question 1-B in the template provided.

Template for Question 1-B

Stock	Appropriate trading strategy	Justification
1. Star		
2. Moon		
3. Sun		

C. Shoemaker has expressed concern about the role of traders in the future. **State** whether Shoemaker's statement regarding the future of the trader function is correct or incorrect and **support** your decision with one reason.

(3 minutes)

Answer Question 1-C in the template provided.

Template for Question 1-C

Circle one	Defend your selection
Correct Incorrect	

QUESTION 2 HAS TWO PARTS (A, B) FOR A TOTAL OF 12 MINUTES

Dennis Richardson is the chief investment officer for Delray Portfolio Managers. Delray provides investment management services for institutions and wealthy individuals. Richardson is discussing the requirements for compliance with the Global Investment Performance Standards (GIPS®) and makes the following comments:

> "We have not reported the performance for our real estate composite because we only have eight portfolios in it, which is less than the minimum number of portfolios required to form a composite. Once we have the required ten portfolios necessary for composite creation, we will begin reporting performance for the real estate composite."

> "We have different policies for when portfolios are added to a composite. The time period for inclusion of new portfolios is longer for the private equity composite than it is for the small cap equity composite."

A.   **State** whether or not *each* of these comments is consistent with the GIPS standards. If inconsistent, **recommend** the change necessary to bring the firm into compliance with the GIPS standards.

(6 minutes)

Answer Question 2-A in the template provided.

Template for Question 2-A

Comment	Is the comment consistent with the requirements of GIPS? (circle one)	If not, recommend the change that will bring the firm into GIPS compliance
"We have not reported the performance for our real estate composite because we only have eight portfolios in it, which is less than the minimum number of portfolios required to form a composite. Once we have the required ten portfolios necessary for composite creation, we will begin reporting performance for the real estate composite."	Yes No	
"We have different policies for when portfolios are added to a composite. The time period for inclusion of new portfolios is longer for the private equity composite than it is for the small cap equity composite."	Yes No	

Delray recently acquired BJ Asset Management (BJAM). The acquisition was amiable and Delray took possession of all BJAM records and has contracted for the investment staff to remain in place. Delray is excited about the business opportunities of the acquisition. It will significantly extend Delray's management expertise into new areas, including wrap fee accounts. BJAM was GIPS compliant, though unverified, and all of its composites are materially different from those of Delray. The only disappointment is that Ben Jones, the founder of BJAM, will retire. However, Jones ceased his involvement in the investment management side of BJAM about five years ago. The rest of BJAM's investment staff will continue to be responsible for the old BJAM asset management composites.

Richardson is reviewing a staff report of BJAM's GIPS compliance procedures and has three concerns with the report:

1. BJAM offers separately managed wrap fee accounts. BJAM manages the client assets but a separate sponsor firm handles all client communication and other portfolio management activities. In these accounts, the entire bundled fee including trading expense is deducted. This is inconsistent with Delray's policy of only deducting direct trading expenses.

2. BJAM reports internal account dispersion as a simple difference between top 25th and bottom 75th account performance within a composite, but reports standard deviation for only three years of each composite's and benchmark's monthly returns.

3. The report recommends, subject to verifying that BJAM's past reports are accurate, reporting the past performance of BJAM composites in Delray's next GIPS report.

B.   **Review** each of the concerns Richardson has with the staff report. **Determine** if there is a problem or if you agree with the recommendation and **explain** your decision.

(6 minutes)

QUESTION 3 (A, B, C) HAS THREE PARTS FOR A TOTAL OF 24 MINUTES

Gordon Brown would like to update the return objective of the $500 million Shailor College perpetual endowment so that the return includes an adjustment for long-term inflation expectations and for the costs associated with managing the endowment. Brown believes that inflation will average 4% over the next several years. The endowment's investment management fees have averaged 0.35% of assets over the past five years. Brown would also like to generate a revised asset allocation reflecting more diversification across asset classes, while maintaining the endowment's 4.5% payout.

Brown has also collected the following information:

* Under relevant tax regulations, the endowment must distribute 4% of portfolio value each year. A smoothing formula can be applied to meet this distribution target. The endowment board has directed Brown to hold 6 months of the annual minimum payout as an emergency cash reserve.
* The board has also informed Brown that $2.6 million will be distributed in 6 months as a one-time capital expenditure. Brown has noted that Treasury bills have an 8% annual return (pretax).
* The board has also informed Brown that the college has recently adopted a new tuition policy to stimulate foreign student enrolment. Foreign students (not residing in the United States at time of application) can pay their tuition in foreign currency. The program has been highly successful, and the board has asked Brown to consider how this will affect the portfolio asset allocation.

A. **Prepare** the objectives and constraints for Shailor College's endowment portfolio. **Calculate** the compounded desired and minimum return requirements. **Show** your calculations.

(16 minutes)

Answer Question 3-A in the template provided.

Template for Question 3-A

Objectives	Comments
Return	
Risk	

Constraints	Comments
Liquidity	
Legal/Regulatory	
Taxes	
Time Horizon	
Unique	

Note: Your response should include appropriate content for each objective and constraint based on Shailor College's current situation.

©2016 Kaplan, Inc.

B.   Brown has developed the asset allocation for Shailor College
      endowment shown in Figure 1. He has recomputed the desired return
      to be 8.5% based on new information regarding expected college
      expense inflation. Recommend for the T-bills, corporate bonds, and
      venture capital whether each proposed allocation should most likely
      be increased or decreased. All other factors, except desired return, are
      unchanged. **Support** each recommendation with one fact relevant to
      the college's situation. Assume that any additional funds required or
      freed up to meet the changes can be met by adjusting other allocations.

(6 minutes)

Figure 1: Proposed Asset Allocation for Shailor College Endowment

Asset Class	Expected Total Return (%)	Historical Standard Deviation (%)	Proposed Weight (%)
T-bills	1.5	0.2	20.0
Corporate bonds	6.0	6.5	10.0
Large Cap stocks	9.0	9.0	5.0
REITs	9.5	9.8	5.0
Small cap stocks	11.0	15.9	30.0
International stock	13.0	18.3	10.0
Venture capital funds	14.0	22.9	20.0
Total portfolio	9.2	n.a.	100.0

Answer Question 3-B in the template provided.

Template for Question 3-B

Recommended Change	Explanation
1.	
2.	
3.	

C. **Recommend** whether the college is more or less likely to hedge the foreign currency exposure of international stocks given their tuition program and **explain** your answer.

(2 minutes)

QUESTION 4 HAS ONE PART FOR A TOTAL OF 9 MINUTES

Jeff Stone, another trustee of the Shailor College endowment, has questioned Brown's recommendation to employ an active management strategy for the entire equity portion of the endowment portfolio. Specifically, Stone made the following three statements:

Statement 1: "Large-cap stocks are the most appropriate place for active management because managers can take big enough positions to capitalize on pockets of inefficiency."

Statement 2: "Because the S&P 500 Index is price-weighted, out-performing stocks tend to have more and more influence on its value."

Statement 3: "The Shailor College endowment should employ a passive index vehicle, such as a Russell 2000 index fund, for our small-cap stock portfolio. The market for small-cap stocks tends to be more efficient than the market for large-cap stocks and would provide more opportunities for us to benefit from active management."

Identify whether or not you agree or disagree with each of Stone's statements. **Support** each decision with one reason.

(9 minutes)

Answer Question 4 in the template provided.

Template for Question 4

Comment	Circle one	Supporting statement
"Large-cap stocks are the most appropriate place for active management because managers can take big enough positions to capitalize on pockets of inefficiency."	Correct Incorrect	
"Because the S&P 500 Index is price-weighted, out-performing stocks tend to have more and more influence on its value."	Correct Incorrect	
"The Shailor College endowment should employ a passive index vehicle, such as a Russell 2000 index fund, for our small-cap stock portfolio. The market for small-cap stocks tends to be more efficient than the market for large-cap stocks and would provide more opportunities for us to benefit from active management."	Correct Incorrect	

QUESTION 5 HAS ONE PART FOR A TOTAL OF 12 MINUTES

Amy Morgan manages a $4 billion global equity fund and has discretion to invest in the stocks of firms located in both developed and emerging markets as long as she maintains guideline weights in each. Partly due to a disagreement over her most recent performance appraisal, she has suggested changes to her benchmark. She makes the following statements:

"For a benchmark to be considered valid, it must be investable. To be investable, I should be able to recreate and hold the benchmark as a portfolio."

"Although I agree with you that market value-weighted benchmarks are generally considered the most valid, the benchmark you have applied in my performance appraisal is not truly market value-weighted because you have not included the total market capitalization of all the benchmark firms."

"Perhaps as an alternative we could use a multi-factor model-based benchmark. Factor model-based benchmarks are considered valid benchmarks and, since they are based on sound statistical methods, their results are irrefutable."

"If you do not like the idea of multi-factor-based benchmarks, we can always go back to comparing my performance to the average equity manager. At least that way I know exactly who I'm up against."

Select whether you agree or disagree with each of Morgan's statements. If you disagree, **support** your decision with one reason related to the characteristics of valid benchmarks.

(12 minutes)

Answer Question 5 in the template provided.

Template for Question 5

Comment	Agree or disagree (circle one)	If you disagree, support your decision with one reason related to the characteristics of valid benchmarks
"For a benchmark to be considered valid, it must be investable. To be investable, I should be able to recreate and hold the benchmark as a portfolio."	Agree Disagree	
"Although I agree with you that market value-weighted benchmarks are generally considered the most valid, the benchmark you have applied in my performance appraisal is not truly market value-weighted because you have not included the total market capitalization of all the benchmark firms."	Agree Disagree	
"Perhaps as an alternative we could use a multi-factor model-based benchmark. Factor model-based benchmarks are considered valid benchmarks and, since they are based on sound statistical methods, their results are irrefutable."	Agree Disagree	
"If you do not like the idea of multi-factor-based benchmarks, we can always go back to comparing my performance to the average equity manager. At least that way I know exactly who I'm up against."	Agree Disagree	

**QUESTION 6 HAS THREE PARTS (A, B, C) FOR A TOTAL OF
11 MINUTES**

Sid Mulder, CFA, manages a $250 million fixed income portfolio. Currently, the weighted average duration for his portfolio is 6.8. Mulder is concerned about rising interest rates and has decided that he should adjust the duration of his portfolio to reduce the impact of rising interest rates. Mulder plans to use Treasury futures contracts to achieve his target duration of 5.0. The duration and price of the cheapest-to-deliver (CTD) bond are 6.5 and $100,000. The conversion factor for the CTD is 1.3.

Mulder is also concerned about credit risk in his portfolio. Specifically, he is worried that there is significant risk of a spread widening for his $10 million in Blum Development bonds. Currently, the Blum bonds trade at a spread of 250 basis points (bp) over comparable maturity U.S. Treasury securities. To protect against this risk, Mulder is considering purchasing a credit forward with a notional principal of $10 million, a contract spread of 250bp, and a risk factor of 3.0.

A. **Describe** the futures transaction Mulder should execute in order to achieve his target duration. Your response should include the number of contracts and whether these contracts should be bought or sold.

(4 minutes)

B. Mulder has chosen to modify his portfolio duration using futures, as opposed to buying/selling additional securities. **Identify** one advantage of using futures in this situation, and **describe** how basis risk might affect Mulder's strategy.

(3 minutes)

C. For the credit derivative Mulder is considering, **determine** the following:

i. The maximum potential loss to Mulder on the credit forward.
ii. The payoff if the spread narrows to 200bp at the maturity of the derivative.

(4 minutes)

Answer Question 6-C in the template provided. Show your calculations.

Template for Question 6-C

	Credit forward at a contract spread of 250bp
i. The maximum potential loss to Mulder on the credit forward.	
ii. The payoff if the spread narrows to 200bp at the maturity of the derivative.	

QUESTION 7 HAS TWO PARTS (A, B) FOR A TOTAL OF 14 MINUTES

James Baltus and Uri Korkov are portfolio strategists at North Range Asset Management (NRAM). NRAM offers asset management for high net worth individuals and has expertise in maximizing after-tax wealth accumulation. Baltus and Korkov are recent hires with a background in tax exempt institutional portfolio management. They have been reviewing the literature on strategies to increase after-tax return or ending wealth and have compiled the following summary conclusions.

1. Both tax deferred and tax exempt accounts provide a tax advantage in allowing tax free compounding while funds are held in the account. However, a tax deferred account is superior for after-tax wealth maximization because it provides an initial tax deduction.

2. The accrual equivalent after-tax return is the tax-free return that if compounded annually would produce the portfolio's after-tax ending value. Therefore, it considers the impact of all the various tax rates and deferrals that may apply to a portfolio.

3. Shorter-term trading strategies have an advantage when short-term gains and losses are taxed more heavily than long-term gains and losses because the shorter-term trader will realize short-term losses to shelter short-term gains that would have been heavily taxed.

4. Maximizing after tax value will include optimizing asset location. Traditional mean-variance optimization can be modified to achieve this result or Monte Carlo simulation can be used.

A.   **Determine** whether each statement is correct or incorrect and if the statement is incorrect, state why it is incorrect.

(8 minutes)

Answer Question 7-A in the template provided.

Template for Question 7-A

Comment	Correct or incorrect	If the statement is incorrect, state why it is incorrect
Both tax deferred and tax exempt accounts provide a tax advantage in allowing tax free compounding while funds are held in the account. However, a tax deferred account is superior for after-tax wealth maximization because it provides an initial tax deduction.	Correct Incorrect	
The accrual equivalent after-tax return is the tax-free return that if compounded annually would produce the portfolio's after-tax ending value. Therefore, it considers the impact of all the various tax rates and deferrals that may apply to a portfolio.	Correct Incorrect	
Shorter-term trading strategies have an advantage when short-term gains and losses are taxed more heavily than long-term gains and losses because the shorter-term trader will realize short-term losses to shelter short-term gains that would have been heavily taxed.	Correct Incorrect	
Maximizing after tax value will include optimizing asset location. Traditional mean-variance optimization can be modified to achieve this result or Monte Carlo simulation can be used.	Correct Incorrect	

B.   Baltus and Korkov find they are unable to agree on the best method to manage unrealized tax losses in a portfolio. Baltus states that if there are multiple tax lots with different acquisition prices and only a portion of the position will be sold, the lowest tax basis lots should be sold. Korkov states that in the same situation the highest tax basis lots should be sold. **Determine** who is *more likely* to be correct and **explain** the conditions under which the other method could be correct.

(6 minutes)

Questions 8, 9, and 10 relate to Jim Wilson. *Candidates should answer the questions in order.*

Jim Wilson, age 42, helped found Tides Technology about 20 years ago and took it public ten years later. Over the last ten years Wilson has had complete control of Tides. Destiny, Inc., will soon purchase Tides by paying two shares of Destiny stock, valued at $45 per share, for each share of Tides stock. In total, Wilson holds a total of 100,000 shares of Tides stock. He holds 12,500 shares in his $1.25 million defined contribution pension plan portfolio and 87,500 shares in a taxable investment portfolio. The cost basis of the Tides stock in his taxable investment portfolio is $2.00. Exhibit 1 shows the allocation of his pension portfolio prior to the buyout by Destiny.

Exhibit 1: J. Wilson Pension Portfolio Prior to Sale of Tides

Investments	Weight (%)	Cost Basis ($)	Current Share Value ($)
Tides equity	30	8.00	30.00
Equity fund	40	10.00	15.00
Balanced portfolio	10	34.00	44.00
Bond fund	15	12.50	13.75
Money market fund	5	1.00	1.00

After the sale to Destiny is completed, Wilson wants to enter law school, which should take three years and cost $45,000 the first year, increasing annually by the rate of inflation of 3%. Given his entrepreneurial background and contacts, his future income potential after law school is high. Although he has no plans of marriage, Wilson will provide care for his autistic brother, Tom. Total after-tax current annual expenses, including care for his brother, will amount to $175,000.

With the help of a financial planner, Wilson has compiled risk and return characteristics for three asset classes as well as their correlations with one another and with Wilson's human capital. The data are shown in Exhibits 2 and 3.

Exhibit 2: Risk and Returns for Asset Classes

Asset Class	Expected Yield (%)	Expected Growth (%)	Expected Standard Deviation (%)
Cash	1.5	0.0	2.4
Bonds	5.0	0.0	8.3
Stock	3.0	6.0	15.4

Exhibit 3: Asset Class Correlations

Class	Cash	Bonds	Stock	Human Capital
Cash	1.00	0.65	0.27	0.41
Bonds	—	1.00	0.36	0.60
Stock	—	—	1.00	0.15
Human capital	—	—	—	1.00

QUESTION 8 HAS TWO PARTS (A, B) FOR A TOTAL OF 18 MINUTES

A. **Explain** using the specifics of Wilson's ownership of Tides stock in his taxable portfolio how he has progressed through the stages of executive, entrepreneur, and investor, as well as how his exposure to systematic and company-specific risk and his desire for diversification have most likely changed in each stage. Assume that Wilson's taxable portfolio starts out as 100% Tides stock.

(9 minutes)

B. Post-sale of the Tides stock, **explain** how each of the following strategies could be used to provide diversification in the portfolio. Comment on any differences between the three strategies in regard to upside or downside risk exposure to Destiny, Inc., and whether a loan will be required to provide diversification. Do not discuss taxation.

Strategy Choices:
i.   Total return equity swap.
ii.   Out-of-the-money protective put.
iii. Prepaid variable forward.

(9 minutes)

Exam 3
Morning Session

QUESTION 9 HAS TWO PARTS (A, B) FOR A TOTAL OF 15 MINUTES

Wilson is meeting with his financial adviser, Drew Goebel, CFA, to review his financial situation. Wilson is particularly interested in establishing a law practice after graduation from law school. He estimates start-up costs for the practice, including reference books, furniture, and advertizing, will total $200,000. He expects his living expenses and care for his brother, which totaled $175,000 this year, to increase at the general rate of inflation of 3% per year.

A.   **Formulate** the return portion of Wilson's investment policy statement (IPS) for his taxable investment portfolio and **calculate** the total after-tax return that portfolio must earn next year, his first year in law school. Show your calculations. (You should ignore Wilson's pension assets and any tax effects associated with the sale of Tides.)

(10 minutes)

B.   **Determine** whether Wilson's ability to tolerate for risk would be considered above average, average, or below average. **Support** your decision with *two* reasons.

(5 minutes)

Answer Question 9-B in the template provided.

Template for Question 9-B

Wilson's ability to tolerate risk would be considered: (Circle one)	Support with *two* reasons
Above average Average Below average	

QUESTION 10 HAS TWO PARTS (A, B) FOR A TOTAL OF 13 MINUTES

Jim Wilson has graduated from law school and opened his law office. Because of his popularity in the business community, his law business started out very well. Now that he is fairly certain of his future, he is meeting with his financial adviser, Drew Goebel, CFA, to determine the appropriate asset allocation for his investment portfolio. He has told Goebel that regardless of his asset allocation, how well his law practice does, or how long he (Jim) lives, he wants to be sure his brother Tom receives proper care for the rest of his life. Goebel has indicated that in determining a total asset allocation, Jim's human capital should be considered and, to care for Tom, he might consider purchasing life insurance.

A.   **Explain** the purpose of life insurance as it relates to human and financial capital. **Discuss** how and why Wilson's less risky business will affect his human capital and his need for life insurance.

(4 minutes)

B.   Based solely on the data in Exhibits 2 and 3, reproduced below, **recommend** the *best* allocation of stocks, bonds, and cash in Wilson's investment portfolio. **Support** each of your decisions with *one* reason.

(9 minutes)

Answer Question 10-B in the template provided.

Exhibit 2: Risk and Returns for Asset Classes

Asset Class	Expected Yield (%)	Expected Growth (%)	Expected Standard Deviation (%)
Cash	1.5	0.0	2.4
Bonds	5.0	0.0	8.3
Stock	3.0	6.0	15.4

Exhibit 3: Asset Class Correlations

Class	Cash	Bonds	Stock	Human Capital
Cash	1.00	0.65	0.27	0.41
Bonds	—	1.00	0.36	0.60
Stock	—	—	1.00	0.15
Human capital	—	—	—	1.00

Template for Question 10-B

Asset Class	Recommended allocation (circle one)	Support with *one* reason
Cash	0% to 5% 6% to 10% 11% to 20%	
Bonds	36% to 45% 46% to 55% 56% to 70%	
Stocks	41% to 50% 51% to 60% 61% to 70%	

**QUESTION 11 HAS FOUR PARTS (A, B, C, D) FOR A TOTAL OF
21 MINUTES**

Paris Helicopter Leasing (PHL) is the largest corporate helicopter leasing
company in Europe. PH has only a few competitors and a market capitalization
of €5 billion. The PHL Defined Benefit Pension Plan (PHLP) has assets with a
current market value of €125 million. Holly Rawlings, PHL's actuary, calculates
the value of its Projected Benefit Obligation (PBO) using a 5% discount rate.
She estimates the current PBO to be approximately €125 million with a duration
of 17. Last year PHLP implemented an option for early retirement for long-
term employees over 50 years of age, but so far no one has indicated a desire
to take advantage of it. Should anyone elect to exercise the retirement option,
they can elect to receive benefits in a lump-sum payout, a lifetime annuity, or a
combination of the two.

A mostly independent investment committee manages PHLP. The committee
recently hired Milton McCormick, CFA, as a consultant. After researching
PHL, McCormick concluded that the company is financially sound and has a
stable workforce. PHL has a low debt/equity ratio and a high return on equity
compared to the rest of the corporate helicopter leasing industry. McCormick
prepared Exhibit 1 to summarize the characteristics of the workforces for PHL
and the corporate helicopter leasing industry.

**Exhibit 1: Comparison of PHL and the Corporate Helicopter Leasing
Industry**

Workforce Characteristics	PHL	Industry Average
Average age of active employees	36 years	43 years
Active long-term employees over age 50	12%	16%
Active employees to retired employees	6 to 1	8 to 1

McCormick decides to discuss the PHLP's investments with PHL's President
Brad Mauer. During the discussion, Mauer states, "Industry analysts are currently
predicting an increase in leased transportation by corporate executives. With
this increase in profitability and growth for this industry over the next decade,
the PHLP should be able to see returns of at least 10% annually. The investment
committee should increase PHLP's investment in transportation leasing industry
equities from its current level of 15% of plan assets to at least 20%."

McCormick decides to also consult the investment committee, which states,
"We have set a return objective that is 175 basis points above PHLP's minimum
required return in order to meet our investment objective of building a fund
surplus. This return objective is consistent with the current risk tolerance of
PHLP."

A.   **Determine** the required return for the Paris Helicopter Leasing Defined
        Benefit Pension Plan (PHLP). **Show** your calculations.

                        (2 minutes)

B.   **Select** whether PHLP has a below-average, average, or above-average
        ability to take risk compared with the average for the corporate
        helicopter leasing industry with respect to sponsor financial status and
        profitability, workforce age, and retired employees and **justify** *each*
        response with *one* reason.

Answer Question 11-B in the template provided.

                        (9 minutes)

Template for Question 11-B

Risk factor	Select whether PHLP has below-average, average, or above average ability to tolerate risk compared with the average for the corporate helicopter leasing industry (circle one)	Justify *each* response with *one* reason
i. Sponsor financial status and profitability	Below average Average Above average	
ii. Workforce age	Below average Average Above average	
iii. Retired employees	Below average Average Above average	

C. **Identify** whether *each* of the following factors increases, does not affect, or decreases PHLP's ability to tolerate risk and **justify** *each* response with *one* reason.

    i. Sponsor (PHL) and pension fund (PHLP) common risk exposures.
   ii. Retirement plan features.

Answer Question 11-C in the template provided.

(6 minutes)

Template for Question 11-C

Factor	Identify whether the factor increases, does not affect, or decreases PHLP's ability to tolerate risk (circle one)	Justify *each* response with *one* reason
i. Sponsor (PHL) and pension fund (PHLP) common risk exposures	Increases Does not affect Decreases	
ii. Retirement plan features	Increases Does not affect Decreases	

D.   **Formulate** *each* of the following constraints in PHLP's investment policy statement, and **justify** *each* response with *one* reason.

     i.   Liquidity requirement.
    ii.   Time horizon.

Answer Question 11-D in the template provided.

(4 minutes)

Template for Question 11-D

Constraint	Formulate *each* of the constraints in PHLP's investment policy statement and justify *each* response with *one* reason.
i. Liquidity requirement	
ii. Time horizon	

QUESTION 12 HAS TWO PARTS (A, B) FOR A TOTAL OF 18 MINUTES

Harold Spare, CFA, is the chief financial officer (CFO) of Neptune Company. Neptune manufactures auto parts. In addition to his responsibilities as CFO, Spare oversees the company's defined benefit pension plan. The pension plan has assets of $3.5 billion. However, the plan is currently underfunded by $700 million. Spare is unhappy with the investment performance of the plan and believes the current asset allocation needs to be altered. To assist him in making a decision, Spare has hired an outside consultant.

The consultant recommends changing the asset mix from the current 60% stocks and 40% bonds (60/40) allocation to a 60% stocks, 30% bonds, and 10% hedge fund (60/30/10) allocation. The consultant justifies the recommendation by highlighting the fact that hedge funds would generate equity-like returns while reducing the portfolio's overall risk level. Thus, the 60/30/10 asset mix would produce higher returns with a risk level comparable to or less than the old asset mix. The consultant provides Figures 1 and 2 containing return, risk and correlation measures of four hedge fund strategies.

Figure 1: Performance of Hedge Fund Strategies

Strategy or Index	Annual Return	Annual Standard Deviation	Sharpe Ratio
Convertible arbitrage	13.46%	5.59%	1.64
Equity market neutral	15.90%	9.34%	1.24
Hedged equity	15.28%	6.07%	1.81
Global macro	16.98%	8.38%	1.51

Figure 2: Correlations Between Hedge Fund Strategies and Stocks and Bonds

	Stocks	Bonds	Event-Driven	Equity Hedge	Distressed Securities	Global Macro
Stocks	1.00					
Bonds	0.13	1.00				
Convertible arbitrage	0.59	0.07	1.00			
Equity market neutral	0.64	0.09	0.70	1.00		
Hedged equity	0.42	0.04	0.87	0.56	1.00	
Global macro	0.26	0.34	0.33	0.46	0.29	1.00

A. **Describe** the primary strategy of each of the hedge fund styles proposed by the consultant. Include the structure of the strategy and how the strategy is expected to generate profits.

(12 minutes)

Answer Question 12-A in the template provided.

Template for Question 12-A

Hedge Fund Style	Description
Convertible arbitrage	
Equity market neutral	
Hedged equity	
Global macro	

B.   **Identify** and **describe** three special issues a manager should consider when recommending alternative investments to private wealth clients.

(6 minutes)

Answer Question 12-B in the template provided.

Template for Question 12-B

	Alternative investments special issues
1	
2	
3	

END OF MORNING SESSION

EXAM 3 AFTERNOON SESSION
TOPIC BREAKDOWN

Questions	Topic	Minutes
1–6	Ethics and Standards	18
7–12	Ethics and Standards	18
13–18	Economic Concepts	18
19–24	Equity Portfolio Management	18
25–30	Behavioral Finance	18
31–36	Fixed Income Portfolio Management	18
37–42	Risk Management Applications of Derivatives	18
43–48	Risk Management Applications of Derivatives	18
49–54	Asset Allocation; Alternative Investments	18
55–60	Capital Market Expectations	18
	Total	180

EXAM 3 SELECTED RESPONSE ITEM SET ANSWER SHEET

The afternoon session of the Level III exam contains 10 Selected Response Item Sets, each with six questions, and you must answer them by filling in a bubble sheet with a number 2 or HB pencil. For realism, we suggest that you use this answer sheet and darken the bubbles corresponding to your answers. This sheet will also facilitate entering your answers into our online Performance Tracker. You have 180 minutes for this session of the exam. That equates to 3 minutes per item set question, so budget your time well.

1.	Ⓐ	Ⓑ	Ⓒ	31.	Ⓐ	Ⓑ	Ⓒ
2.	Ⓐ	Ⓑ	Ⓒ	32.	Ⓐ	Ⓑ	Ⓒ
3.	Ⓐ	Ⓑ	Ⓒ	33.	Ⓐ	Ⓑ	Ⓒ
4.	Ⓐ	Ⓑ	Ⓒ	34.	Ⓐ	Ⓑ	Ⓒ
5.	Ⓐ	Ⓑ	Ⓒ	35.	Ⓐ	Ⓑ	Ⓒ
6.	Ⓐ	Ⓑ	Ⓒ	36.	Ⓐ	Ⓑ	Ⓒ
7.	Ⓐ	Ⓑ	Ⓒ	37.	Ⓐ	Ⓑ	Ⓒ
8.	Ⓐ	Ⓑ	Ⓒ	38.	Ⓐ	Ⓑ	Ⓒ
9.	Ⓐ	Ⓑ	Ⓒ	39.	Ⓐ	Ⓑ	Ⓒ
10.	Ⓐ	Ⓑ	Ⓒ	40.	Ⓐ	Ⓑ	Ⓒ
11.	Ⓐ	Ⓑ	Ⓒ	41.	Ⓐ	Ⓑ	Ⓒ
12.	Ⓐ	Ⓑ	Ⓒ	42.	Ⓐ	Ⓑ	Ⓒ
13.	Ⓐ	Ⓑ	Ⓒ	43.	Ⓐ	Ⓑ	Ⓒ
14.	Ⓐ	Ⓑ	Ⓒ	44.	Ⓐ	Ⓑ	Ⓒ
15.	Ⓐ	Ⓑ	Ⓒ	45.	Ⓐ	Ⓑ	Ⓒ
16.	Ⓐ	Ⓑ	Ⓒ	46.	Ⓐ	Ⓑ	Ⓒ
17.	Ⓐ	Ⓑ	Ⓒ	47.	Ⓐ	Ⓑ	Ⓒ
18.	Ⓐ	Ⓑ	Ⓒ	48.	Ⓐ	Ⓑ	Ⓒ
19.	Ⓐ	Ⓑ	Ⓒ	49.	Ⓐ	Ⓑ	Ⓒ
20.	Ⓐ	Ⓑ	Ⓒ	50.	Ⓐ	Ⓑ	Ⓒ
21.	Ⓐ	Ⓑ	Ⓒ	51.	Ⓐ	Ⓑ	Ⓒ
22.	Ⓐ	Ⓑ	Ⓒ	52.	Ⓐ	Ⓑ	Ⓒ
23.	Ⓐ	Ⓑ	Ⓒ	53.	Ⓐ	Ⓑ	Ⓒ
24.	Ⓐ	Ⓑ	Ⓒ	54.	Ⓐ	Ⓑ	Ⓒ
25.	Ⓐ	Ⓑ	Ⓒ	55.	Ⓐ	Ⓑ	Ⓒ
26.	Ⓐ	Ⓑ	Ⓒ	56.	Ⓐ	Ⓑ	Ⓒ
27.	Ⓐ	Ⓑ	Ⓒ	57.	Ⓐ	Ⓑ	Ⓒ
28.	Ⓐ	Ⓑ	Ⓒ	58.	Ⓐ	Ⓑ	Ⓒ
29.	Ⓐ	Ⓑ	Ⓒ	59.	Ⓐ	Ⓑ	Ⓒ
30.	Ⓐ	Ⓑ	Ⓒ	60.	Ⓐ	Ⓑ	Ⓒ

Practice Exam 3
Afternoon Session

Questions 1–6 relate to Jose Verde.

Jose Verde is an international equity analyst for New World Capital Management (NWCM). Verde has been studying the potential impact of proposed joint ventures involving U.S. firms and firms partially owned by the government in a recently democratized country. There is much excitement in the investment community about the potential of these joint ventures, which concerns Verde somewhat as he has had great difficulty finding and acquiring reliable information about the quality and accessibility of inputs and labor in local markets. Furthermore, there is still considerable uncertainty about which U.S. firms will be offered partnerships, what the conditions of those partnerships will be, and the accounting rules that will govern the new ventures. However, Verde is confident that there will be demand for the output in local and international markets.

Verde contacts a friend domiciled in the foreign country in an effort to gather more information on the joint ventures. His friend claims to have reliable contacts in the government. He informs Verde that it appears that only one U.S. firm, GlobalCo, will be offered a partnership. The remaining partnerships will go to firms based in other countries.

Seeking to verify this information, Verde speaks with the CFO of one of the other U.S. firms positioning itself for a joint venture partnership, International Merchants, Inc. (IMI). In the conversation Verde learns that IMI has decided to withdraw its bid to be a joint venture partner, but that the formal announcement of the withdrawal will not occur for another week. The CFO says IMI has decided that the risk of expropriation is too high given their expectations of a change in the balance of power in the upcoming elections in the new democracy and a likely reversion to a more socialistic government.

Not wanting to miss an opportunity, Verde completes his industry analysis and concludes with a buy recommendation for GlobalCo and a sell recommendation for IMI. While Verde bases his written recommendations on the information received in the phone calls, the information is not disclosed in his analysis. Before releasing the recommendations to his clients, Verde asks some of his colleagues in the research department to review his analysis and conclusions. Normal policy is to discuss the report with his boss but she is out of the office and Verde feels speed is important and goes to his coworkers instead. Two days later Verde releases his revised recommendations to his clients.

1. Verde based his conclusions on discussions with a foreign national and the CFO of a firm involved in bidding for the joint ventures. Augmenting his own research in this way means that Verde:
   A. conformed to the standard of diligence and thoroughness by seeking additional facts and information from new sources.
   B. did not conform to the standard of diligence and thoroughness because he obtained material nonpublic information during his due diligence.
   C. did not conform to the standard of diligence and thoroughness because he lacked enough information and facts about the input markets, accounting processes, and new government to make a reasonably informed recommendation and acted on material nonpublic information.

2. Information sourced from Verde's friend is:
   A. material nonpublic information because of the personal relationship between Verde and his friend and may not be used in Verde's report.
   B. not material nonpublic information because it originated from a source that is not known to be privy to nonpublic information and may be used in Verde's report.
   C. material nonpublic information because the foreign source claimed to have access to unpublished government information and may not be used in Verde's report.

3. Information sourced from the CFO at IMI:
   A. is not material nonpublic information thus Verde can use it in his report.
   B. is similar enough to other information Verde gathered and falls under the mosaic theory thus Verde can use it in his report.
   C. may not be used in Verde's report unless he was able to gather the same information from public and nonmaterial nonpublic sources.

4. Verde shared his research with his colleagues at New World prior to releasing the report to New World clients. Concerning this action Verde:
   A. is being thorough by seeking the opinion of others before releasing his report and is thereby complying with standards rather than violating them.
   B. breached the standards by partially disseminating his findings and recommendations inside the firm prior to releasing the information to clients outside of the firm.
   C. is fulfilling his duty to his firm by giving his colleagues time to incorporate the information into clients' accounts (money under management) before the report is released.

5. Verde attempted to maintain the confidence of his sources by not revealing them in his report. By doing so, Verde:
   A. is exercising discretion in order to maintain a competitive edge.
   B. is neither helping nor harming the consumers of his report, as long as he reaches logical conclusions from the information the sources provide.
   C. may have violated the standards related to known limitations of his analysis and material misrepresentation by omitting the source of his information and other facts that led to his conclusions.

6. Verde's superior is concerned with potential problems related to his recent analysis on the firms seeking joint ventures. The best recommendation the superior can give to Verde is to:
   A. omit the recommendation for IMI and disseminate the rest of the report.
   B. omit the recommendation for GlobalCo and disseminate the rest of the report.
   C. delay disseminating the report until the conflict of nonpublic information related to IMI's decision can be resolved and the other issues related to thoroughness, accuracy, limitations, and misrepresentations can be properly overcome.

Questions 7–12 relate to Shirley Smith.

Shirley Smith, CFA, has just been promoted to the position of Chief Investment Officer (CIO) at Kirk Investment Co (KIC), a large investment management firm that offers mutual funds as well as managed accounts for individuals and employment benefit plans. As a CFA charterholder, Smith's first task is to ensure that KIC is in compliance with the Asset Manager Code of Professional Conduct. For the past few weeks, Smith has encountered the following issues:

Employee Incentive Scheme

KIC has recently changed its portfolio managers' compensation scheme and has tied manager bonuses to portfolio performance. The change was outlined in a letter that was sent to clients and prospects before the new bonus structure took effect. David Lee, CFA, is one of the best portfolio managers at KIC and manages both individual investors and institutional investor employee benefit plans. His clients have done extremely well, but lately they have underperformed due to limited exposure to the biotech sector, one of the strongest performing sectors over the recent few months. Lee placed an order for all employee benefit plans to receive an allocation of Star, Inc.'s initial public offering (IPO). Star is expected to be over-subscribed and Lee knew that this IPO would make money for his employee benefit plans. Lee did not consider allocating any shares to his individual clients.

KIC is considering allowing its portfolio managers and other staff to buy IPO shares as a form of incentive compensation. For the scheme to work in an orderly manner, KIC is thinking of centralizing all the purchase of IPO shares through a designated department. For portfolio managers, they are allowed to buy up to 5% of the IPO shares that they purchased on behalf of their client accounts. For other staff, they are allowed to purchase IPO shares by placing an order with the designated department. KIC will allocate IPO shares to the portfolio managers' clients first, then, if sufficient shares are available, to the portfolio managers and finally, any excess IPO shares are then allocated to the other staff.

Pricing methodology

KIC has a fund that invests in small capitalization issues. Due to the risk related to these small cap issues, the fund is only available to very high net worth clients. Some of these small cap stocks are thinly traded, and hence prices of these securities for monthly statements that are sent to clients are often difficult to obtain. Ryan Haywood, the portfolio manager that is managing this fund uses various methods—third party services and in-house valuation models—to price these small cap stocks. Sometimes, Haywood will enter an order during the last trading hour of the month to purchase a small number of these illiquid shares to establish a market price. Typically, Haywood has to offer a premium to the last traded price to ensure that a trade will be executed. The executed price will then be used as the market price in the monthly statements. These trades do not materially affect the overall shareholding in any specific company due to the small number of shares purchased. Shirley Smith has met with Haywood and is concerned about the multiple pricing methods used by Haywood. Smith suggests that Haywood adopt one pricing method and apply it consistently. Haywood disagrees with Smith and mentioned that as long as pricing sources are fully disclosed to clients, it is acceptable to use various methods.

Trade allocation

Peter Armstrong, a portfolio manager for individual clients, is interested in the IPO of Telstar, Inc. Telstar is a firm in the telecom industry and is expected to have excellent growth prospects. However, due to recent political events, Armstrong believes that the stock volatility could be quite high in the first year. He places an order for the Telstar IPO and begins to allocate the IPO shares among his clients. He divides his clients into two groups—an income-based group and a capital gains-based group. The income-based group of clients is more risk-averse than the capital gains-based group, so he decides to allocate Telstar IPO only to his capital gains-based group of clients. Within the capital gains-based group of clients, he allocates the shares pro rata to the size of assets in each account.

7. Has David Lee violated the Asset Manager Code of Professional Conduct by investing in Star, Inc. IPO for the employee benefit plans?
   A. Yes. Lee did not allocate the trades fairly to all his clients.
   B. No. Lee has used reasonable care and prudent judgment when managing client assets since he knew that Star, Inc. would be a profitable trade.
   C. Yes. Lee did not manage the employee benefit plans according to the plans' mandates.

8. Is KIC's new compensation scheme of linking bonuses to portfolio performance a potential violation of the Asset Manager Code of Professional Conduct?
   A. Yes. Portfolio managers may take investment actions that conflict with client interests.
   B. No. The Asset Manager Code of Professional Conduct does not deal with compensation issues.
   C. No. KIC's compensation scheme would ensure that portfolio managers provide the best service to clients in order to retain clients' accounts.

9. Is Shirley Smith's recommendation to Haywood or his response correct?

	Shirley Smith	Ryan Haywood
A.	Correct	Correct
B.	Correct	Incorrect
C.	Incorrect	Correct

10. Is Peter Armstrong's trade allocation method in violation of the Asset Manager Code of Professional Conduct?

	Divide clients into two groups	Allocate according to size of account
A.	No	No
B.	Yes	No
C.	Yes	Yes

11. Would the proposal of how IPO shares are allocated and purchased among portfolio managers and staff be a potential violation of the Asset Manager Code of Professional Conduct?

	Portfolio Manager	Other staff
A.	Yes	Yes
B.	Yes	No
C.	No	Yes

12. Does trading stocks during the last trading hour of a month to establish a fair market price violate the Asset Manager Code of Professional Conduct?
    A. Yes. Haywood has no reasonable basis to execute the trades.
    B. No. Haywood is simply acting in the client's best interests to obtain fair market price to value the fund assets.
    C. Yes. This is a form of market manipulation to depress the price for the securities.

Questions 13–18 relate to Monica Garza.

Monica Garza is a portfolio manager for Southwood Group, a large investment management firm, where she is in charge of economic and capital market forecasting. Brett Crosby, director of research at Southwood, has asked Garza to assist him in identifying the forecasting approach that would best suit an equity long-short hedge fund the company would like to open. The fund will purchase securities from its investment universe that are considered to have the highest forecasted alphas and sell short securities with negative forecasted alphas. The overall long-short exposure will vary based on the number of securities with positive and negative forecasted alphas.

After reviewing the forecasting method to be used by the new hedge fund, Crosby asks Garza to forecast GDP growth. To do this, Garza obtains predictions for changes in several underlying macroeconomic factors, including those listed Exhibit 1 with their predicted changes.

Exhibit 1: Predicted Changes in Economic Factors

Factor	Predicted Change
Savings rate	Decrease
Pollution controls	Increase
Retirement age	Increase

Garza then gathers the data in Exhibit 2 for the periods 1991–2000 and 2001–2010.

Exhibit 2: Historical Economic Data

	Growth in Total Factor Productivity	Growth in Capital Stock	Growth in Labor Input	Output Elasticity of Capital (α)
1991–2000	1.25%	–0.50%	2.50%	0.6
2001–2010	2.35%	1.25%	0.42%	0.6

Using the data she gathered, Garza will calculate the implied price of the market index. She notes that the major equity market index value is currently 1600 and the last dividend was $75. She believes the required rate of return for the market is 8.0%.

Crosby then asks Garza to review the major relative valuation models and provide short descriptions of each. Garza reviews the Fed model, the Yardeni model, and the 10-year moving average price/earnings ratio model, P/10-year MA(E), and makes the following comments:

Comment 1: The Fed model compares the earnings yield for the S&P 500 index to the yield on U.S. Treasury securities. When the earnings yield for the S&P 500 is greater than the yield on Treasury securities, equities are said to be over-valued and should fall.

Comment 2: The Yardeni model is used to estimate earnings yield for a market index and is computed as the yield on A-rated corporate bonds less the long-term growth rate forecast multiplied by a weighting factor. Although the Yardeni model incorporates a risk premium above that of Treasuries, the premium is not a true measure of equity risk.

Comment 3: The 10-year moving average price/earnings ratio model is computed as the value of the S&P 500 index divided by the average of the previous 10-years' reported earnings. One of the major drawbacks of this model is that it does not consider the effects of inflation.

After completing a review of the relative valuation models, Garza turns back to evaluating the value of the market index. She now decides to employ the equity q ratio and gathers the information in Exhibit 3:

Exhibit 3: Valuation Data ($Billions)

Market value (replacement cost) of assets	50
Book value of assets	35
Market value of liabilities	26
Market value of equity	20

13. In response to Crosby's question regarding the forecasting approach that would be *best* suited for the hedge fund, Garza should suggest using a:
A. top-down approach.
B. bottom-up approach.
C. combination of top-down and bottom-up approaches.

14. Which of the following is *most likely* correct regarding the predicted changes in the underlying factors? All else equal, the predicted change in:
A. the savings rate will lead to an increase in GDP growth.
B. the retirement age will lead to an increase in GDP growth.
C. pollution controls will lead to an increase in GDP growth.

15. The component of economic growth that contributed the *most* to real GDP growth during 1991–2000 is:
A. labor input.
B. capital stock.
C. total factor productivity.

16. If Garza assumes that the sustainable economic growth rate will be the same as the growth rate realized over the period 2001–2010, the intrinsic value of the market index would be *closest* to:
A. 1578.
B. 1586.
C. 1637.

17. Which of Garza's comments regarding relative equity market valuation models is correct?
A. Comment 1.
B. Comment 2.
C. Comment 3.

18. Based on the equity *q* ratio, Garza would *most likely* conclude that the equity index is:
A. overvalued.
B. undervalued.
C. fairly valued.

Questions 19–24 relate to Geneva Management.

Geneva Management (GenM) selects long-only and long-short portfolio managers to develop asset allocation recommendations for their institutional clients.

GenM Advisor Marcus Reinhart recently examined the holdings of one of GenM's long-only portfolios actively managed by Jamison Kiley. Reinhart compiled the holdings for two consecutive non-overlapping 5-year periods. The Morningstar Style Boxes for the two periods for Kiley's portfolio are provided in Exhibits 1 and 2.

Exhibit 1: Morningstar Style Box: Long-Only Manager for 5-Year Period 1

	Value	*Blend*	*Growth*
Large-cap	20	30	40
Mid-cap	2	3	5
Small-cap	0	0	0

Exhibit 2: Morningstar Style Box: Long-Only Manager for 5-Year Period 2

	Value	*Blend*	*Growth*
Large-cap	45	30	20
Mid-cap	1	2	2
Small-cap	0	0	0

Reinhart contends that the holdings-based analysis might be flawed because Kiley's portfolio holdings are known only at the end of each quarter. Portfolio holdings at the end of the reporting period might misrepresent the portfolio's average composition. To compliment his holdings-based analysis, Reinhart also conducts a returns-based style analysis on Kiley's portfolio. Reinhart selects four benchmarks:

1. SCV: a small-cap value index.

2. SCG: a small-cap growth index.

3. LCV: a large-cap value index.

4. LCG: a large-cap growth index.

Using the benchmarks, Reinhart obtains the following regression results:

Period 1: $R_P = 0.02 + 0.01(SCV) + 0.02(SCG) + 0.36(LCV) + 0.61(LCG)$

Period 2: $R_P = 0.02 + 0.01(SCV) + 0.02(SCG) + 0.60(LCV) + 0.38(LCG)$

Kiley's long-only portfolio is benchmarked against the S&P 500 Index. The Index's current sector allocations are shown in Exhibit 3.

Exhibit 3: S&P 500 Index Sector Allocations

Sector	Percent Allocation
Energy	12
Materials	3
Industrials	11
Consumer Discretionary	9
Consumer Staples	10
Health Care	12
Financials	19
Information Technology	17
Telecommunications	4
Utilities	3

GenM strives to select managers whose correlation between forecast alphas and realized alphas has been fairly high, and to allocate funds across managers in order to achieve alpha and beta separation. GenM gives Reinhart a mandate to pursue a core-satellite strategy with a small number of satellites each focusing on a relatively few number of securities.

In response to the core-satellite mandate, Reinhart explains that a Completeness Fund approach offers two advantages:

Advantage 1: The Completeness Fund approach is designed to capture the stock selecting ability of the active manager, while matching the overall portfolio's risk to its benchmark.

Advantage 2: The Completeness Fund approach allows the Fund to fully capture the value added from active managers by eliminating misfit risk.

19.   Which one of the following statements about Kiley's long-only portfolio is *most correct*? Kiley's portfolio:
       A. is only exposed to systematic risk.
       B. is only exposed to unsystematic risk.
       C. attempts to earn a positive alpha through security selection.

20.   Reinhart is concerned that the portfolio managed by Kiley has style drift. Is Reinhart's concern supported by either holdings-based style analysis or returns-based style analysis?
       A. Only the holdings-based style analysis supports style drift.
       B. Only the returns-based style analysis supports style drift.
       C. Both approaches support style drift.

21.   Assuming Kiley feels that the Utilities Sector is overvalued now, the largest active weight that Kiley can apply to the Utilities sector is:
       A. –3%.
       B. 0%.
       C. 3%.

22.   Reinhart is *more likely* to satisfy the GenM alpha and beta separation objective by:
       A. allocating funds to his long-only active managers and to his passive market index fund manager.
       B. allocating funds to his market-neutral long-short managers and to his passive market index fund manager.
       C. allocating funds solely to his market-neutral long-short managers.

23.   Assuming no material change in the forecasting ability of GenM's managers and considering the core-satellite mandate faced by Reinhart, which of the following statements is *correct*?
       A. The GenM information coefficient will be relatively low.
       B. The GenM investor breadth will be relatively low.
       C. The GenM information ratio will be relatively low.

24.   State whether the two advantages to the Completeness Fund approach explained by Reinhart are *correct*.
       A. Only advantage 1 is correct.
       B. Only advantage 2 is correct.
       C. Both advantages 1 and 2 are correct.

Questions 25–30 relate to Robert McGriff.

Robert McGriff and Marshall Hemp are eating lunch at their favorite downtown spot. The restaurant is within a few blocks of their law office and across the street from a large FDIC-insured bank that they pass by almost every day. McGriff mentions that his wife recently inherited $250,000 and they want to "park" it somewhere until they decide what to do with it. They want to protect the cash and be able to access it quickly once they make their decision.

Pointing across the street, Hemp suggests to McGriff that they simply deposit the money in a checking account in the bank. "A checking account there would fill all your short term needs for the cash. The deposit would be totally insured, you'd make a bit of interest on it, and you could simply write a check when you need it." When they finish eating, McGriff contacts his wife who opens the checking account that afternoon.

About a year later, well after McGriff and his wife have closed the checking account and invested the money in stocks and bonds, McGriff meets with his advisor, Jean Little. Little complains about McGriff's tendency to want to sell stocks that have experienced a bit of a run up but hold onto stocks that have experienced declines. McGriff's reply is that he wants to grab the profits on those stocks before they disappear, but he has confidence that the others will recover. In addition to these tendencies Little has noticed that the McGriffs, especially Robert, tend to be difficult to deal with when new market or company information is released. Little has difficulty even getting Robert to consider the implications of the information. "It's probably not worth going to all that trouble to interpret the information, Jean!"

Another year has passed, and Robert McGriff has assumed almost total control of the McGriffs portfolio. Little has almost given up on advising him, although she still meets with him regularly and tries to explain fundamental portfolio theory to him. In spite of Little's efforts, McGriff makes his own investment decisions, which in most cases turn out sub-optimal at best. In spite of the results, McGriff seems to always be able to find evidence that his decisions are correct, sometimes seeming to deliberately ignore evidence to the contrary. Partly due to his ever-increasing confidence, he is now quick to interpret new information and adjust his portfolio in response, even when the amount of information he has is limited. In addition he is usually reluctant to change his decisions based on Little's suggestions, and has frequently even blamed poor performance on Little.

In addition to the investment portfolio that he and his wife own, Robert McGriff participates in a 401(k) defined contribution plan administered by his employer. When he started his 401(k), the plan offered 15 equity and 10 fixed income mutual funds as well as several money market funds. For various reasons, McGriff almost immediately eliminated 5 of the equity funds, 3 of the bond funds, and all of the money market funds. He then allocated almost evenly across the remaining mutual funds, over-allocating only to the fund that contains his employer's stock. As he devotes so much attention to his investment portfolio, McGriff effectively ignores his 401(k) portfolio.

25. By following Hemp's advice and depositing his wife's inheritance into the insured, interest-bearing checking account, McGriff is *most likely* exhibiting which of the following?
   A. Irrational behavior.
   B. Rational behavioral.
   C. Bounded rationality.

26. McGriff's tendency to sell stocks that have appreciated in value but hold others that have fallen is *least likely* to indicate:
   A. loss aversion.
   B. bounded rationality.
   C. the disposition effect.

27. Which of the following is *least likely* to explain McGriff's statement, "It's probably not worth going to all that trouble to interpret the information, Jean!" McGriff:
   A. is subject to confirmation bias.
   B. feels the cognitive cost is too great.
   C. fails to properly utilize a Bayesian framework to evaluate information.

28. After Robert McGriff has assumed almost total control of the McGriff's portfolio, his management techniques would *most likely* be classified as which of the following behavioral investor types?
   A. Friendly follower.
   B. Active accumulator.
   C. Independent individualist.

29. In consideration of McGriff's behavioral investor type, Little would *probably* be hesitant to:
   A. present educational material to McGriff on a regular basis.
   B. present McGriff's bad investments as evidence of a need to consult with Little.
   C. use statistics and a periodic table of investments to help influence McGriff's decisions.

30. There are several behavioral biases routinely exhibited by participants in defined contribution plans. Which of the following statements is *least likely* to be true about McGriff's behavior with respect to his 401(k) portfolio?

A. His employer's stock is held by one of the alternative funds offered in the plan and he intentionally over-weighted that fund. This could indicate over-confidence and familiarity bias.

B. McGriff originally set up the portfolio and contribution allocations and has since ignored them. He is subject to status quo bias because he has done nothing to evaluate the way funds are deposited into the fund or the portfolio allocation.

C. 1/n diversification is when investors allocate evenly across all the alternative funds offered by a defined contribution plan. McGriff is technically not subject to 1/n diversification bias because he only allocated evenly across remaining funds after eliminating several of them.

Questions 31–36 relate to Integrated Analytics.

Jack Higgins, CFA, and Tim Tyler, CFA, are analysts for Integrated Analytics (IA), a U.S.-based investment analysis firm. IA provides bond analysis for both individual and institutional portfolio managers throughout the world. The firm specializes in the valuation of international bonds, with consideration of currency risk. IA typically uses forward contracts to hedge currency risk.

Higgins and Tyler are considering the purchase of a bond issued by a Norwegian petroleum products firm, Bergen Petroleum. They have concerns, however, regarding the strength of the Norwegian krone currency (NKr) in the near term, and they want to investigate the potential return from hedged strategies. Higgins suggests that they consider forward contracts with the same maturity as the investment holding period, which is estimated at one year. He states that if IA expects the Norwegian NKr to depreciate and that the Swedish krona (Sk) to appreciate, then IA should enter into a hedge where they sell Norwegian NKr and buy Swedish Sk via a 1-year forward contract. The Swedish Sk could then be converted to dollars at the spot rate in one year.

Tyler states that if an investor cannot obtain a forward contract denominated in Norwegian NKr and if the Norwegian NKr and euro are positively correlated, then a forward contract should be entered into where euros will be exchanged for dollars in one year. Tyler then provides Higgins the following data on risk-free rates and spot rates in Norway and the U.S., as well as the expected return on the Bergen Petroleum bond.

Return on Bergen Petroleum bond in Norwegian NKr	7.00%
Risk-free rate in Norway	4.80%
Expected change in the NKr relative to the U.S. dollar	–0.40%
Risk-free rate in United States	2.50%

Higgins and Tyler discuss the relationship between spot rates and forward rates and comment as follows.

- Higgins: "The relationship between spot rates and forward rates is referred to as interest rate parity, where higher forward rates imply that a country's spot rate will increase in the future."
- Tyler: "If one-year U.K. and Japanese interest rates are 5.5% and 2.3%, respectively, I should expect the unhedged return on currency, if I invest in Japan, to be –3.2%."

The following day, Higgins and Tyler discuss various emerging market bond strategies and make the following statements.

- Higgins: "Over time, the quality in emerging market sovereign bonds has declined, due in part to contagion and the competitive devaluations that often accompany crises in emerging markets. When one country devalues their currency, others often quickly follow and as a result the countries default on their external debt, which is usually denominated in a hard currency."
- Tyler: "Investing outside the index can provide excess returns. Because the most common emerging market bond index is concentrated in Latin America, the portfolio manager can earn an alpha by investing in emerging country bonds outside of this region."

Turning their attention to specific issues of bonds, Higgins and Tyler examine the characteristics of two bonds: a 6-year maturity bond issued by the Midlothian Corporation and a 12-year maturity bond issued by the Horgen Corporation. The Midlothian bond is a U.S. issue and the Horgen bond was issued by a firm based in Switzerland. The characteristics of each bond are shown in the table below. Higgins and Tyler discuss the relative attractiveness of each bond and, using a total return approach, which bond should be invested in, assuming a 1-year time horizon.

	Currency of Denomination	Annualized Bond Yield	Bond Modified Duration
Midlothian Bond	U.S. dollars	8.00%	4.69
Horgen Bond	Swiss franc	9.00%	7.25

31. What are the currency hedge strategies for the Bergen Petroleum bond that Higgins and Tyler are referring to? Higgins is referring to:
    A. a cross-hedge, and Tyler is referring to a proxy-hedge.
    B. an indirect-hedge, and Tyler is referring to a proxy-hedge.
    C. an indirect-hedge, and Tyler is referring to a correlation-hedge.

32. On the basis of expected return, should the Bergen Petroleum bond be hedged against currency risk and what is the hedged return?
    A. No, the hedged return is 4.70%.
    B. No, the hedged return is 6.60%.
    C. Yes, the hedged return is 6.60%.

33. Regarding their comments concerning the relationship between spot rates and forward rates, determine whether Higgins and Tyler are *correct*.
    A. Both Higgins's and Tyler's comments are correct.
    B. Both Higgins's and Tyler's comments are incorrect.
    C. Only Higgins's comment is correct.

34. Regarding their statements concerning the emerging market bond investments, determine whether Higgins and Tyler are *correct*.
    A. Both Higgins and Tyler are correct.
    B. Both Higgins and Tyler are incorrect.
    C. Only Tyler is correct.

35. Assume that both the Midlothian and Horgen bonds are being considered for purchase. Determine which of the following statements provides the *best* description of the appropriate strategy using breakeven spread analysis. If the yield for the Horgen bond:
    A. is expected to increase more than 14 basis points, invest in the Midlothian bond.
    B. is expected to increase more than 7 basis points, invest in the Midlothian bond.
    C. is expected to fall more than 21 basis points, invest in the Midlothian bond.

36. Which of the following statements provides the *best* description of the advantage of using breakeven spread analysis? Breakeven spread analysis:
    A. provides an estimate of exchange rate risk.
    B. quantifies the change in spread needed to offset a foreign yield advantage.
    C. assesses the risk of a foreign bond investment independent of the bond's duration.

Questions 37–42 relate to United Global Group.

United Global Group (UGG) is a major property and casualty insurance company. UGG has a total investment portfolio of $25 billion. The portfolio is divided into $22 billion in bonds and $3 billion in equities. UGG's equity strategy employs enhanced indexing with the S&P 500 Index as the benchmark. UGG adjusts its equity portfolio by employing a simple 200-day moving average technical indicator. When stocks increase in value above their 200-day moving average, this is a bullish indicator. In contrast, when they fall below their 200-day moving average, this is a bearish indicator. UGG management uses this indicator to move in and out of equities. Rather than actually selling their equities, UGG uses futures to create a synthetic cash position to execute any bearish trigger. Relevant data is shown in Figure 1.

Figure 1: Selected Data

S&P 500 Index futures contract	1058
S&P 500 Index dividend yield	1.60%
Time to expiration	5 months
Risk free rate (annual)	3.00%
UGG equity portfolio beta	1.00
S&P 500 Index futures contract beta	1.00
UGG bond portfolio modified duration	5.90
Treasury bond futures contract price	$150,000
Treasury bond futures modified duration	5.10
Cash equivalents modified duration	0.20
S&P 500 Index futures contract multiplier	$250

UGG's management applied its technical indicator to the Japanese market and discovered that prices have crossed above their 200-day moving average. Based on this bullish signal, management allocated half of UGG's equity portfolio, 162,225,000,000 yen, to the Japanese market. Relevant data are shown in Figure 2.

Figure 2: Selected Data

Nikkei 225 index futures contract (USD)	10,337
Nikkei 225 index dividend yield	1.00%
Time to expiration	6 months
Japanese risk-free rate (annual)	2.00%
Multiplier	$5.00
Nikkei 225 index futures contract beta	1.00
UGG's Japanese portfolio beta	0.90
Exchange rate	108.15 yen to $1

37.   Assuming the initial $3 billion position in U.S. equities and the
      information in Figure 1, if UGG wishes to convert the entire position
      to synthetic cash, the *most appropriate* strategy would be to sell
      approximately:
      A. 11,108 S&P futures contracts.
      B. 11,342 S&P futures contracts.
      C. 11,483 S&P futures contracts.

38.   Assume the S&P 500 Index is at 1,125 when these futures contracts
      expire. The payoff on the futures position would be a loss:
      A. of less than $1 million.
      B. between $1 million and $100 million.
      C. greater than $100 million.

39.   UGG management intends to adjust its $22 billion in bonds and $3 billion
      in equities to 75% bonds and 25% stocks. Using the information provided
      in Figure 1, the strategy to adjust to the new bond and stock allocation is
      to sell bond futures contracts and buy approximately:
      A. 12,290 equity futures contracts.
      B. 13,387 equity futures contracts.
      C. 15,199 equity futures contracts.

40.   UGG has now purchased the Japanese equities and would like to fully
      hedge against a possible decline in the Japanese market. Using the data
      in Figure 2, the number of (short) contracts needed to hedge the yen-
      denominated portion of the equity portfolio is *closest* to:
      A. 24,000 and 25,000 contracts.
      B. 25,000 and 26,000 contracts.
      C. 26,000 and 27,000 contracts.

41.   Which of the following statements is *most correct*?
      A. UGG can use country beta to adjust their exposure to equities.
      B. UGG can hedge their foreign currency equity risk by buying the
          foreign currency forward.
      C. UGG can replicate a long foreign stock position by buying equity
          futures and a risk-free bond.

42.   UGG is exposed to the U.S. bond market and both the U.S. and Japanese
      equity markets. Given these exposures, which of the following statements
      is *most correct*?
      A. UGG is likely to use a mixture of corporate and Treasury bond futures
          to hedge their U.S. bond portfolio.
      B. UGG is likely to manage exchange rate risk using forward contracts on
          the yen/USD exchange rate for liquidity reasons.
      C. UGG can lock in the Japanese risk-free rate by using futures to hedge
          the equity portfolio and using a forward to hedge yen/USD currency
          risk.

Questions 43–48 relate to Director Securities.

Walter Skinner, CFA, manages a bond portfolio for Director Securities. The bond portfolio is part of a pension plan trust set up to benefit retirees of Thomas Steel Inc. As part of the investment policy governing the plan and the bond portfolio, no foreign securities are to be held in the portfolio at any time and no bonds with a credit rating below investment grade are allowable for the bond portfolio. In addition, the bond portfolio must remain unleveraged. The bond portfolio is currently valued at $800 million and has a duration of 6.50. Skinner believes that interest rates are going to increase, so he wants to lower his portfolio's duration to 4.50. He has decided to achieve the reduction in duration by using swap contracts. He has two possible swaps to choose from:

1. Swap A: 4-year swap with quarterly payments.

2. Swap B: 5-year swap with semiannual payments.

Skinner plans to be the fixed-rate payer in the swap, receiving a floating-rate payment in exchange. For analysis, Skinner assumes the duration of a fixed rate bond is 75% of its term to maturity.

Several years ago, Skinner decided to circumvent the policy restrictions on foreign securities by purchasing a dual currency bond issued by an American holding company with significant operations in Japan. The bond makes semiannual fixed interest payments in Japanese yen but will make the final principal payment in U.S. dollars five years from now. Skinner originally purchased the bond to take advantage of the strengthening relative position of the yen. The result was an above average return for the bond portfolio for several years. Now, however, he is concerned that the yen is going to begin a weakening trend, as he expects inflation in the Japanese economy to accelerate over the next few years. Knowing Skinner's situation, one of his colleagues, Bill Michaels, suggests "You need to offset your exposure to the Japanese yen."

Skinner has also spoken to Orval Mann, the senior economist with Director Securities, about his expectations for the bond portfolio. Mann has also provided some advice to Skinner in the following comment:

> "I know you expect a general increase in interest rates, but I disagree with your assessment of the interest rate shift. I believe interest rates are going to decrease. Therefore, you will want to synthetically remove the call features of any callable bonds in your portfolio by purchasing a payer interest rate swaption."

43.   From Skinner's perspective, the duration of Swap A would be *closest* to:
         A. –2.50.
         B. –2.88.
         C. –3.00.

44.   Determine the approximate notional principal required for Skinner to achieve a portfolio duration of 4.5 using Swap B.
         A. $320 million.
         B. $457 million.
         C. $492 million.

45.   To implement Michaels's suggested strategy to offset the dual currency bond's yen exposure Skinner should enter a:
         A. pay JPY versus receive USD currency swap.
         B. special receive USD versus pay JPY currency swap with no notional principal exchange.
         C. special pay USD versus receive JPY currency swap with no notional principal exchange.

46.   After considering Mann's comments, Skinner reverses his views and believes interest rates will decline. To hedge the risk of the callable bonds he owns in his portfolio with swaptions, Skinner should:
         A. sell payer swaptions.
         B. sell receiver swaptions.
         C. buy receiver swaptions.

47.   After his long conversation with Director Securities' senior economist, Orval Mann, Skinner has completely changed his outlook on interest rates and has decided to extend the duration of his portfolio. The *most* appropriate strategy to accomplish this objective using swaps would be to enter into a swap to pay:
         A. fixed and receive floating.
         B. floating and receive fixed.
         C. floating and receive floating.

48.   Skinner has been consulting with Dwayne Barter, a client of Director Securities and CFO of a large corporation. Barter is interested in using interest rate swaps to convert his firm's floating rate debt to fixed rate debt. Barter is planning to enter into a swap to pay a fixed rate and receive a floating rate in exchange. How would the swap impact the firm's debt?
         A. Increase the market value risk.
         B. Reduce both the cash flow risk and market value risk.
         C. Increase the cash flow risk.

Questions 49–54 relate to Alternate Investments.

Dan McDonald manages the Singer Family (Singer) family offices, including the $500 million family portfolio. Singer's Investment Policy Statement (IPS) maintains fairly specific risk and return objectives, but gives McDonald a great deal of latitude in selecting asset classes that can be used to meet these objectives. McDonald has no IPS constraints other than balancing Singer's return with tax effect and not taking an active management role in any Singer investment.

Each current family member receives an equal income allocation from the fund when they reach 21 years of age, so McDonald must grow the fund more rapidly than inflation to prepare for the next generation. Therefore, McDonald is willing to invest up to 10 percent of the Singer portfolio in return-enhancing alternative investments.

McDonald contacted several consultants to assist him with alternative investment asset classes that he doesn't feel comfortable managing alone. He first turns his attention to a real estate consultant who says:

Statement 1:   "Direct real estate investments have good diversification benefits with stocks, but they have poor diversification benefits with bonds because of the income aspect inherent in a real estate investment."

McDonald then consults with a private equity consultant who states the following:

Statement 2:   "Venture capital funds typically finance only expansion-stage companies."

Statement 3:   "Buyout funds purchase established companies and participate in taking public companies private."

After further discussion with the private equity consultant, McDonald believes that private equity is potentially a viable investment alternative for the Singer portfolio. He decides to further investigate the key investment differences between venture capital funds and buyout funds before making any IPS and asset allocation changes.

McDonald is also concerned about unexpected inflation and is considering adding commodities to the Singer portfolio as a means to hedge this risk. He next consults a commodities advisor who discusses the sources of return from a commodity investment. The commodities advisor states:

Statement 4:   "There are three types of return available from a commodities investment."

Statement 5: "Contango and backwardation are conditions that can result in additional returns on commodities investments; contango produces positive returns while backwardation produces negative returns."

McDonald is intrigued by the risk reduction benefits offered by adding commodity investments. Upon further analysis, McDonald concludes that the commodity market under review is currently exhibiting a downward-sloping term structure.

49. Was McDonald's real estate consultant correct in Statement 1 about the correlation of real estate direct investment with stocks and bonds?
   A. Only his opinion regarding bonds is correct.
   B. Only his opinion regarding stocks is correct.
   C. Both his opinion regarding stocks and his opinion regarding bonds are correct.

50. Assuming that McDonald completes his due diligence on private equity investing, what is the *most accurate* investment difference between venture capital and buyout funds?
   A. Buyout funds are usually less leveraged than venture capital funds.
   B. Venture capital investors generally receive cash flows later than buyout fund investors.
   C. Venture capital investments have more risk of loss than buyout funds, but their return estimates are less subject to error.

51. Is McDonald's private equity consultant correct with regard to:

	Statement 2?	Statement 3?
A.	No	No
B.	No	Yes
C.	Yes	Yes

52. Are the statements made by the commodity advisor correct?
   A. Only statement 4 is correct.
   B. Only statement 5 is correct.
   C. Both statements are correct.

53. If McDonald's conclusion regarding the commodity markets is correct, the corresponding commodity investment will *most likely* result in:
   A. A negative roll return because the markets are in contango.
   B. A positive roll return caused primarily by increased volatility.
   C. A positive roll return because the markets are in backwardation.

54. To hedge against unexpected inflation, McDonald should consider adding commodities to a portfolio consisting primarily of bonds if:
   A. markets are in contango.
   B. the commodity is related to agriculture or non-energy.
   C. the commodity is related to energy or precious metals.

Questions 55–60 relate to Otterbein forecasting.

Jimena Mora, CFA, and Jack Wieters, CFA, are economists for Otterbein Forecasting. Otterbein provides economic consulting and forecasting services for institutional investors, medium-sized investment banks, and corporations. In order to forecast the performance of asset classes and formulate strategic asset allocations, Mora and Wieters are currently examining the capital market expectations for four developed countries: Alzano, Lombardo, Bergamo, and Linden. Wieters was hired in 2009 and Mora is his supervisor.

Mora and Wieters use the Grinold and Kroner model to forecast equity market performance. Macroeconomic forecasts and capital market expectations for three countries are given below:

	Alzano	Bergamo	Lombardo
Change in Correlation with World Index	7.30%	12.20%	0.30%
Change in P/E ratio	0.70%	1.10%	–0.20%
Change in Shares Outstanding	–0.20%	1.20%	–0.80%
Dividend Yield	2.70%	0.60%	3.60%
Growth in Real Earnings	4.80%	5.70%	2.20%
Growth in Exports	3.70%	2.30%	1.70%
Growth in Imports	4.60%	7.20%	2.60%
Liquidity Risk Premium	2.00%	3.60%	0.70%
Long-Term Inflation Rate	2.80%	5.30%	1.90%

Mora is also examining the return on federal government bills and bonds of various maturities for the country of Linden. The data are provided below:

Maturity in Years	Yield
0.25	4.54
0.50	4.48
1.00	4.47
2.00	4.39
3.00	4.36
4.00	4.33
5.00	4.31
10.00	4.08
15.00	3.92
20.00	3.57

One of Otterbein Forecasting's largest clients is an institutional investor in Linden, the Balduvi Endowment. The current and potential asset allocations for the endowment are shown below:

Asset Class	Current and Potential Portfolios Asset Allocation Percentages (%)			
	Current	A	B	C
Cash Equivalents	3	3	3	3
Government Bonds	21	22	11	34
Investment Grade Bonds	21	22	11	33
High-Yield Bonds	10	17	26	5
Non-Cyclical Stocks	25	22	31	20
Cyclical Stocks	20	14	18	5

Mora asks Wieters for his opinion on the future of the economy in Linden and the appropriate investment for the Balduvi Endowment.

Mora has been asked by the Otterbein CEO to develop a model for explaining stock returns. In her master's degree training, Mora was instructed that the default risk premium has predictive power for stock returns; however, the CEO has asked her to include other macroeconomic variables. Mora examines the following data for the capital market history of Bergamo:

1. Default risk premiums, which she measures as the difference in yields between high-yield bonds and government bonds.

2. Maturity risk premiums, which she measures as the difference in yields between 10-year and 1-year government bonds.

3. Lagged changes in the stock market.

Mora uses these variables to explain stock returns in the following year. Using 40 years of data, she finds the following results for the significance of the variables in explaining stock returns:

	Variable		
Analysis	Default Risk Premium	Maturity Risk Premium	Lagged Changes in the Stock Market
Correlation	Significant	Insignificant	Significant
Regression	Significant	Insignificant	Significant

Mora concludes from the correlation analysis that, of the three variables studied, the default risk premium has the most predictive power for stock returns.

As the most recent hire at Otterbein Forecasting, Wieters is well versed on the latest evidence on asset pricing and financial engineering. However, Mora suspects that his limited experience results in erroneous forecasts.

For instance, during the credit crisis of 2007–2008, annual stock returns in Lombardo averaged –12.6%. However, using the 80-year history of its capital market, annual stock returns in Lombardo have averaged 13.6%. For his clients' strategic asset allocations in 2010 and onward, Wieters projects Lombardo stock returns of 6.5%. As his supervisor, Mora questions him about this, and she suggests that Wieters revise his projections upward.

Mora and Wieters are discussing the valuation and risk analysis of emerging market securities and economies. In their discussion, Mora makes the following comments:

Statement 1: "Emerging countries are dependent on foreign financing of growth, but it is important that a country not take on too much debt. A financial crisis can lead to currency devaluations and capital flight. Foreign debt levels greater than 50% of GDP or debt greater than 200% of current account receipts may indicate that a country is over-levered."

Statement 2: "In financial crises, emerging market debt is particularly susceptible, as currency devaluations will quickly reduce the principal and coupon value. Because most emerging debt is denominated in a domestic currency, the emerging government must have foreign currency reserves to defend its currency in the foreign exchange markets."

55. Using the Grinold and Kroner model, which of the three countries has the highest expected return for its equity market?
    A. Alzano.
    B. Bergamo.
    C. Lombardo.

56. What does the bond data predict for the future of the economy in Linden?
    A. The economy is likely to expand in the future.
    B. The economy is likely to contract in the future.
    C. The economy is likely to experience no growth in the future.

57. Using only the forecast for the Linden economy, which of the following portfolios should Wieters recommend for the Balduvi Endowment?
    A. Portfolio A.
    B. Portfolio B.
    C. Portfolio C.

58. Which of the following psychological traps is Mora *likely* susceptible to in her analysis of Bergamo stock returns?
    A. Status Quo trap.
    B. Recallability trap.
    C. Confirming Evidence trap.

59. Which of the following psychological traps is Wieters likely susceptible to in his forecast of Lombardo stock returns?
    A. Anchoring trap.
    B. Status Quo trap.
    C. Recallability trap.

60. Regarding the statements made by Mora on the analysis of emerging market securities and economies, are both statements *correct*?
    A. Yes.
    B. No, both statements are incorrect.
    C. No, only Statement 1 is correct.

END OF AFTERNOON SESSION

PRACTICE EXAM 1
MORNING SESSION ANSWERS

QUESTION 1

Source: Study Session 3, LOS 7.c

A.   1/n diversification: Joe divides his assets equally among all available alternatives.

Status quo bias: Joe has made no changes to his portfolio.

Candidate discussion:
Joe may show loss aversion, but that is not the same thing as myopic loss aversion. Myopic loss aversion is a macro issue when large numbers of investors under-allocate to stocks, keeping their prices low and biasing upward their return premium. Joe is not showing conservatism because that is a cognitive error when an initially rational view is formed but then retained without further consideration as new information comes in. Joe made an initial, uninformed, and not well-thought-out decision that he does not change. It is conceivable he has some of these other biases, but we know he exhibited the two selected, so other selections will receive no credit. 1 point each for a correct identification and 1 point for supporting it.

Source: Study Session 3, LOS 7.a

B.

Personality Type (circle one)	Comments
Guardian	• Joe's primary concern is avoiding losses, suggesting he has low risk tolerance. or • Joe is cautious and wants to protect his assets.

Candidate discussion: 2 points for guardian and 1 point for one reason supporting the classification.

C. Structure the plan in three layers, one for each priority level of goals. The highest priority goals would be funded with lower risk assets, the lowest priority with higher risk assets, and the middle priority with medium risk assets.

The advantage to the client is to see how high priority goals are less likely to be endangered by market declines and, thus, help the client stick with the investment plan during stressful market periods.

Candidate discussion: 1 point for covering the 3 layers and 1 point for the risk characteristics in each layer. 2 points for conveying that the client is more likely to stay with such a plan and, thus, come out ahead in the long run.

D.

- Deviate because their biases are mainly emotional and that will make convincing them to change difficult.
- Do not deviate because there is high standard of living risk. Their assets are small enough that meeting primary goals will be difficult. Therefore, they cannot afford to deviate from traditional finance efficiency.

Candidate discussion: 1 point each for identifying the two relevant pieces of information and 1 point each for why one supports less and one more deviation from traditional efficiency.

QUESTION 2

Source: Study Session 4, LOS 8.f, g, h

A.

Retirement starts in one year: first year cash flow needs:

Lachlan's After-Tax Company Pension	AUD 51,000
Living expenses (263,000 × 1.03 inflation)	−270,890
Year 1 net required after-tax cash flow	AUD −219,890
Net Investable Assets	
Inheritance, after-tax	AUD 9,000,000
Mortgage debt repayment	−3,700,000
Other debt repayment	−160,000
Investable asset base (beginning Year 1)	AUD 5,140,000
Return Objective	
Year 1 after-tax required cash flow	AUD −219,890
Divided by investable asset base	AUD 5,140,000
Equals after-tax real return	4.28%
Plus expected inflation	3.00%
Equals after-tax nominal rate of return	7.28%
Before tax nominal return:	7.28 / (1 − 0.2) = 9.10%
Or	
Geometrically (1.0428)(1.03) − 1	7.41%
Before tax nominal return:	7.41 / (1 − 0.2) = 9.26%

Candidate discussion:

1 point each for 1) components of need, 2) 219,890, 3) components of asset base, 4) 5,140,000, 5) setting up the after-tax real calculation, 6) 4.28%, 7) including inflation, and 8) dividing by 1 − marginal tax rate.
- Retirement starts in one year and all the figures given are in one year except the 263,000; remember to increase it for inflation.
- An effective annual tax rate considers the effects of deferring some taxes and is the pertinent annual tax rate to apply.
- Exam answers for individuals have been accepted using either addition or geometric compounding, only show one method. Addition is preferred for individuals.

B. Factors that decrease the Martins' risk tolerance:
- Retired with no additional income from working to replace any investment shortfalls.
- Small pension relative to living expenses and must depend primarily on their investment portfolio.
- Large amount of living expenses relative to investable assets making them less able to tolerate volatility and negative short-term returns.
- They want their portfolio invested conservatively—an indication of low willingness to bear risk.
- Inherited wealth (passive source of wealth), may indicate a reduced willingness to take risk.

Factors that increase risk tolerance:

- They plan to leave their estate to charity; if this is a lower priority goal, they could spend the principal on living expenses if needed.
- They consider their investment base to be large, which increases willingness to bear risk.
- They have a long time horizon, which gives the portfolio time to recover from market losses.

Candidate discussion: Only discuss the requested two items that decrease and one that increases risk tolerance. 2 points each for two factors that decrease risk tolerance, and 2 points for one factor that increases risk tolerance.

C.

    i.   Liquidity needs:

- AUD 3,860,000 total debt repayments in one year comprised of the mortgage and other debts.
- AUD 219,890 ongoing living expenses.
- Expect an AUD 9 million after-tax inheritance in one year.

    ii.   Time horizon is long-term (they are age 50):

- One year until retirement.
- Retired when both spouses are alive.
- After one spouse dies and expenses drop 25%.

Candidate discussion:

- Listing the debt payoff items is essential for full credit. Listing the inheritance is recommended.
- Past exam answers are inconsistent in discussing a need for ongoing distributions under liquidity. It needs to be discussed and analyzed under return, and to be safe you can list it under liquidity as well.
- It is not necessary to call the next year a stage as the portfolio investment does not start until retirement in one year, two stages and only listing the second two is also full credit.
- The discussion of pre- and post-death of one spouse is unusual. This case provided specific information, so ignoring the information will reduce the score.

QUESTION 3

Source: Study Session 8, LOS 17.j

A.   The portfolio Sharpe ratio is $(6.5 - 2.5) / 7.8 = 0.51$
- Int'l Eq: $0.51(0.4) = 0.20$, the addition's Sharpe (0.50) is higher and is beneficial to add
- Real estate: $0.51(0.1) = 0.05$, the addition's Sharpe (0.72) is higher and is beneficial to add
- Mgd. Fut: $0.51(-0.2) = -0.1$, the addition's Sharpe (0.48) is higher and is beneficial to add

Candidate discussion: 1 point for computing the portfolio Sharpe ratio and 1 point each for the 3 asset addition calculations (and correct conclusions).

Source: Study Session 13, LOS 24.d, f, g

B.   Real estate is an illiquid security and the price data is subject to infrequent pricing and smoothing. This lowers the reported standard deviation and increases the reported Sharpe ratio. Real estate Sharpe is the most likely to be overstated.

Candidate discussion: 1 point for real estate. For a 2-point explanation, it must be clear the candidate refers to infrequent pricing/smoothing of prices and this lowers the reported standard deviation. If only one issue is included, only 1 point. The other asset classes are based primarily on liquid traded securities and are unacceptable answers.

Source: Study Session 13, LOS 24.d, t

C.   Managed futures are not really an asset class, but they reflect the skill of the manager. They are the least likely to exhibit persistent return characteristics so their Sharpe ratio is the least likely to persist.

Candidate discussion: 1 point for managed futures. For a 2-point explanation, it must be clear the candidate refers to manager skill issues and/or the lack of persistence in return parameters. Referring to the generally shorter history of data for managed futures is not as good an explanation and receives only 1 point.

Source: Study Session 9, LOS 18.b

D.   Hedge the international bond currency exposure.

Bonds are less volatile than equity, making the currency volatility relatively a greater source of risk of bonds (i.e., foreign currency would be a smaller contributor to return volatility for the Martins in foreign equity than in foreign bonds).

Alterative reason: The correlation of foreign bond return to foreign currency is more positive than the correlation between foreign equity and foreign currency. The + correlation contributes to volatility for the investor in the foreign market and makes currency hedging more important in foreign bonds.

Candidate discussion: 1 point for foreign bonds and 2 points for either explanation.

Source: Study Session 9, LOS 18.i

E.   Contagion refers to the observation that in crisis periods of market decline, correlations between markets move upward towards +1 and the benefits of diversification are not present.

The tool used is conditional correlation matrices. One set of correlations is for normal conditions and another higher set is for crisis conditions.

Candidate discussion: 1 point for explaining that correlations increase in declines, 1 for the effect on portfolios, and 1 for using conditional correlation matrices. If the candidate says the conditional matrices solve the problem, the last point is not awarded. They can be used to quantify the issue or jointly optimize, but do not solve the underlying problem of convergence and loss of diversification.

Source: Study Session 9, LOS 18.f

F.   Unhedged return: 12 + 2 = 14%

Hedged return: 12 + 5 − 2 = 15%

Hedged currency standard deviation: 29%

Unhedged currency standard deviation:

Variance is: $1^2(0.29^2) + 1^2(0.14^2) + 2(1)(1)(0.3)(0.29)(0.14) = 0.1281$

Making standard deviation: 0.3579 = 35.79%

Candidate discussion: 1 point each for the first three calculations and 2 points for the last. Return is approximately $R_{FC} + R_{FX}$. R_{FC} is given as 12%. The projected unhedged R_{FX} is given as a 2% change in value of the EUR. This is 12 + 2 = 14%. With hedging, R_{FX} is determined by IRP; lose the r_f of the currency sold forward (the EUR, so -2%) and gain the r_f of the currency purchased forward (the AUD, so +5%). This is 12 − 2 + 5 = 15%. With hedging, the standard deviation of R_{FX} is 0, and the unhedged standard deviation of the investment is the standard deviation of R_{FC}, which is given as 29%. With currency unhedged, the standard deviation of R_{FX} (given as 14%) is used in the standard variance formula, recognizing that the weights for both R_{FC} and R_{FX} are 1.0 when investing in a foreign asset.

QUESTION 4

Source: Study Session 6, LOS 13. b, c, i

Disagree—Statement 1. DB plan time horizons are primarily determined by the duration of the liabilities and are not perpetual. (They may be legally perpetual, but that is irrelevant to the IPS.)

Disagree—Statement 2. For DB plans, future inflation may only apply to some liabilities, not all. Or, inflation is already incorporated in the actuary's determination of future and PV of liabilities of DB plans. Inflation is not a component of return for the DB manager to consider in the way it is done for foundations.

Agree—Statement 3. The correlations are relevant to both. If the receiving foundation is highly dependent on portfolio distributions, it reduces risk tolerance. So, if low returns correlated with increased needs, portfolio risk tolerance would need to be lower. For DB plans, the high correlation described reduces risk tolerance to avoid contribution requirements increasing when business results are poor.

Disagree—Statement 4. The need to hold cash equivalents and fund payouts varies for both.

Candidate discussion: 1 point for each correct determination and 1 point for the explanation if the decision is correct.

QUESTION 5

Source: Study Session 13, LOS 24.b, d, g, i, k, l, m, n, o

A. These investments use a limited partnership (or similar) structure. Each partnership can differ, so it is essential to review the document for legal or tax implications. One common stock is legally like another common stock, but one partnership may not be the same as another in legal or tax details.

Candidate discussion: 2 points for discussing the unique structure details of each partnership contract.

B. Direct RE will be more expensive:
- For the firm: each property is unique and information is generally not publically available, so the property must be thoroughly researched prior to any recommendation. (Or property must be physically managed and maintained, which will involve time and expense).
- For the client: investment management fees are generally higher (or commission and other transaction costs are generally higher).

Candidate discussion: 1 point for direct, 2 points each for the two reasons. One must relate to the firm and one the client.

C. Direct RE: It should provide lower correlation to other portfolio assets and more diversification benefit. (Or REITs provide less diversification benefit because they behave partially like stock. They are in fact stock in publically traded shares of companies that invest in real estate.)

Candidate discussion: 1 point for direct RE and 2 points for one reason.

D. Decision risk refers to investors investing in securities they do not really understand and then exiting the strategy at an inopportune time and at high cost. It is higher for PE.

Or PE is generally illiquid and has a multiyear time horizon. The investor may be unable to exit and then assert they never understood the risks. In contrast, commodity futures are both liquid, have low transaction costs, and have short expiration dates. Being able to exit lowers the decision risk.

Candidate discussion: 1 point each for explaining what decision risk is and that it is a bigger issue for PE. 1 point for an explanation of why it will be lower for futures contracts or higher for PE.

E.
- BO funds often use leverage and VC do not.
- Underlying VC investments are more risky.
- BO fund returns are typically more consistent.
- BO funds generally begin to return cash to investors sooner and complete their liquidation in a shorter period.

Candidate discussion: 1 point each, for the four issues.

F. Vintage year is the year in which initial investments are made. The initial economic conditions generally have a significant effect on subsequent returns and, therefore, the benchmark should have the same vintage year as the investment.

   Candidate discussion: 1 point for explaining vintage year and 2 points for the discussion. For a 2-point discussion, it must be clear the benchmark must have the same vintage year.

G. Periodic roll is: change in f − change in S:

   Roll for May: $(1{,}215 − 1{,}132) − (1{,}195 − 1{,}101) = 83 − 94 = −11$

   Roll for the contract life if held to expiration is: $S_0 − f_0$

   Roll from end of April to contract expiration will be: $1{,}101 − 1{,}132 = −31$

   Therefore, June roll must be −20

   Candidate discussion: 2 points for May and 1 point for the June computation. There are several equivalent methods to calculate June. June is an expiration month, so it can also be calculated as $1{,}195 − 1{,}215 = −20$. (You could also calculate end of March to end of June total roll as $1{,}244 − 1{,}289 = −45$. Then calculate roll for April and May as −14 and −11, which again makes June −20. This later method is excessively long and not a wise choice of approach as it can make math mistakes more likely.)

H. Gold: Energy and precious metals that are storable and tied to the business cycle have had positive correlation to changes in inflation.

   Candidate discussion: 1 point for gold and 1 point for the explanation.

QUESTION 6

Source: Study Session 12, LOS 23.s

Answer for Question 6-A

Active return is the weighted average for the managers:

$$1.0(0.9\%) + (-1.0)(0.0\%) + 1.0(1.5\%) = 2.4\%$$

Active risk uses the standard portfolio variance formula, assuming 0 correlations unless indicated otherwise:

$$1.0^2(1.3^2) + (-1.0^2)(0.1^2) + 1.0^2(2.7^2) = 8.99 = \text{variance}$$

$$8.99^{0.5} = 3.0\% = \text{standard deviation}$$

$$\text{True IR} = 2.4/3.0 = 0.80$$

Candidate discussion: 2 points each for active risk and return. A correct setup but incorrect calculation is 1 point. 1 point for correct IR setup.

Source: Study Session 12, LOS 23.g, i, h, m, n, r, t

Answer for Question 6-B

- This is a long/short portfolio that is net 100% long using active management.
- A and C are each funded with 100% of portfolio capital, and the leverage is funded by shorting 100% in B for net 100% long. A and C are active managers based on their active return and risk numbers.

Candidate discussion: The Q is vague on what detail to give so give a direct short answer. The directions are a 3 minute question. It is not a hard question based on what is covered in the readings. Full credit for answers reflecting the strategy is long/short, net 100% long, and using active managers.

Answer for Question 6-C

1 is false. If the portfolio was equally long and short, the underlying capital could be invested in other asset classes. But this portfolio is net 100% long, so there is no capital to invest elsewhere.

2 is true. The benefit of portable alpha is misvaluations in equity can be captured while the capital is invested in another and better performing asset class. That is desirable if equity is under-performing.

Candidate discussion: 1 point for each correct true and false decision and if that is correct, 1 point each for an explanation.

Answer for Question 6-D

Manager A

A has the higher information ratio at 0.9/1.3 versus 1.5/2.7 for C, but both have the same number of insights, investor breadth (IB). Therefore, A must have a better information coefficient (IC).

In an inefficient market, it is more likely that A can find significant misvaluation, which would be a form of IC.

Candidate discussion: 1 point for A and 2 points for each reason. An alternative way to explain the second reason is that value stocks are often out-of-favor securities, which may be the reason significant misvaluation and high IC could exist. Remember that IR = active return / active risk and that it is a function of IC × square root of IB. It is these two interpretations that are behind the question and answer.

QUESTION 7

Source: Study Session 4, LOS 10.c

A.   Year 2:
Combined probability: $(0.7644) + (0.8244) - (0.7644)(0.8244) = 0.9586$
Projected real spending: $\$128,750(1.03) = \$132,612.50$
Expected real spending: $132,612.50(0.9586) = \$127,122.34$
PV is Core Capital Year 2: $\$127,122.34 / (1.04^2) = \$117,531.75$

Candidate discussion: 1 point each for the 4 necessary steps, if correct and the work is shown. Remember that the solution can be done with all real or all nominal numbers. The spending was given as real, so a real discount rate was used. The spending for year 1 was given and 3% growth in real spending was specified, so real spending was increased for 1 year.

B.   MCS focuses the client and manager on the most important risk, outliving the assets, instead of short term volatility.
MCS can visually display for the client the prospects of outliving the assets.
MCS can incorporate path dependency issues such as how changes in inflation affect both distributions and market value.
MCS can incorporate taxes and other factors in addition to return.

Candidate discussion: 2 points each for three reasons favoring MCS. Because the question specified favoring MCS, a discussion of drawbacks to mortality tables was not accepted.

C.   Excess capital is PVA – PVL = 1.2M – 0.45M = $750,000
Distribution needs can be higher than projected.
Return can be less than projected.
Once funds are distributed they cannot be recovered.
The clients can live longer than expected and need more capital.
MCS is complex and any of the assumptions and interactions can be wrong.

Candidate discussion: 1 point for the correct calculation and 2 points each for two reasons. The 0.45M PVL is the core capital given in part B.

Source: Study Session 4, LOS 10.i

D.

Country	Tax Jurisdiction: For the exam
United States	Residence Jurisdiction
Country X	Source Jurisdiction

Candidate discussion: 1 point each for the two correct classifications.

Source: Study Session 4, LOS 10.k

E.   Credit: 60,000(0.25) = $15,000 to X
                      (60,000)(0.3) = $18,000 to U.S. less 15,000 credit = $3,000 to the U.S.
                      = $18,000 total

      Exemption: 60,000(0.25) = $15,000 to X
                      exempt in U.S.
                      = $15,000 total

      Deduction: 60,000(0.25) = $15,000 to X
                      (60,000 − 15,000)(0.3) = $13,500 to U.S.
                      = $28,500 total

Candidate discussion: 2 points each for the three correct results.

QUESTION 8

Source: Study Session 13, LOS 24.u, v

A.   i.   Buy the bonds and short the stock.

          ii.   The premise is that because the bonds have first claim on company assets, they should appreciate more than the stock. In Baker's case, she also assumes the bonds are excessively depressed.

               In bankruptcy, no dividend or coupon payments are normally made. Even if they were, Baker should have positive cash flow because bond yields normally exceed dividend yields. Shorting the stock would obligate her to pay the dividends, but long the bonds would generate coupon inflows.

               Candidate discussion: 2 points for part i. 4 points for part ii, explaining that bond investors have first claim on company assets, the bond's relative performance to stocks, and the potential positive cash flow.

Source: Study Session 13, LOS 24.u, v

B.   i.   Event risk is company or situation specific and would be important if it causes the bonds to decline relative to the stock of the company.

          ii.   Market liquidity risk is very significant for distressed debt investors. These are illiquid securities that most investors avoid. A forced, quick exit could be costly.

          iii.   Market risk is likely the least important risk here. Being long the company's bonds and short the stock is designed to remove market (systematic) risk.

               Candidate discussion: 6 points total; for each of the three items, there is 1 point for ranking its importance and 1 point for explaining what it is relative to distressed debt investing. Make your answer specific to the question that stated Baker is long the bonds and short the stock.

Source: Study Session 13, LOS 24.v

C.   J factor risk refers to the effect of the judge on the results of any bankruptcy proceeding, which can be important in distressed debt strategies. The judge may rule more in favor of debt or equity security holders, and thus have a dramatic impact on their respective returns.

          Candidate discussion: 1 point for referring to the judge, and 1 point for describing the uncertainty of the judge's ruling.

QUESTION 9

Source: Study Session 8, LOS 17.i, r

A.   CPs 3 and 4 will bracket the required return of 8.5%.
Solve for the weighting: $8.5 = 9.7(w_3) + 8.2(1 - w_3)$: $w_3 = 20\%$ and $w_4 = 80\%$
U.S. eq $= 0.2(41.3\%) + 0.8(38.4\%) = 8.26\% + 30.72\% = 38.98\%$

Candidate discussion: 1 point for using CPs 3 and 4, 1 point for their weights, and 2 points for the correct U.S. equity allocation.

B.   Standard deviation $= 0.2(12.1\%) + 0.8(9.0\%) = 9.62\%$. The actual sigma will be lower because the diversification benefit of less than +1 correlation was ignored.

Candidate discussion: 1 point for using the correct weights (the same ones as in the previous part). 1 point each for the correct sigma calculation and stating lower. No explanation for why lower was required for the last point.

C.   Use CP 4.

CP 4 has the highest Sharpe ratio; therefore, any combination of CP 4 and the risk-free asset will also have a higher Sharpe ratio than combinations of risk-free and any other CP. It will also have a higher Sharpe ratio than any combination of CPs.

Candidate discussion: 1 point each for CP 4 and the explanation. Given the low number of minutes assigned, a simple statement that it has the highest Sharpe ratio is sufficient.

D.   A foundation is ongoing. It has no one discrete time period to consider and no true risk-free asset (0 standard deviation) exists to borrow or lend at. Use two CPs.

Candidate discussion: 1 point each for stating use two CPs and for the explanation. Any clear indication the candidate is aware of the foundation's multi-period nature or lack of a true risk-free asset was acceptable for the 1 point explanation.

E.   The instability of the efficient frontier is the most serious problem. Asset class returns are difficult to estimate accurately, and small changes in estimates may produce large shifts in the appropriate asset allocation.

Resampling addresses this by forecasting a range of possible returns around the initial single point estimate. Each set of estimates produces a different frontier and asset allocation for a given return. An average asset allocation is then used from the multiple sets of assumptions. This allocation is less sensitive to additional changes in asset class return estimates.

Candidate discussion: 2 points for addressing the most serious problem. Some explanation of why it is an issue is needed for 2 points. The problem can also be discussed in terms of MVO typically selecting a small number of asset classes. 2 points for explaining how resampling works to address the problem.

QUESTION 10

Source: Study Session 17, LOS 31.p

$$S_P = \frac{\bar{R}_P - \bar{R}_F}{\sigma_P}; \ T_P = \frac{\bar{R}_P - \bar{R}_F}{\beta_P}$$

$$\text{Jensen's alpha} = R_P - \left[R_F + \beta_P \left(R_M - R_F \right) \right]$$

$$M_P^2 = \bar{R}_F + \left[\frac{\bar{R}_P - \bar{R}_F}{\sigma_P} \right] \sigma_m = \bar{R}_F + \left(\bar{R}_P - \bar{R}_F \right) \frac{\sigma_m}{\sigma_P}$$

Measure	Portfolio	Calculation	Value
Sharpe, S	1	(0.42 − 0.06) / 1.2	0.300
	2	(0.25 − 0.06) / 0.4	0.475
	3	(0.16 − 0.06) / 0.2	0.500
Treynor, T	1	(0.42 − 0.06) / 1.8	0.200
	2	(0.25 − 0.06) / 1.2	0.158
	3	(0.16 − 0.06) / 0.5	0.200
M^2	1	0.06 + (0.42 − 0.06)(0.50 / 1.2)	0.210
	2	0.06 + (0.25 − 0.06)(0.50 / 0.4)	0.298
	3	0.06 + (0.16 − 0.06)(0.50 / 0.2)	0.310
Jensen	1	0.42 − [0.06 + 1.8(0.20 − 0.06)]	0.108
	2	0.25 − [0.06 + 1.2(0.20 − 0.06)]	0.022
	3	0.16 − [0.06 + 0.5(0.20 − 0.06)]	0.030

Candidate Discussion: 1 point for each correct calculation for 12 points.

QUESTION 11

Source: Study Session 8, LOS 17.g, h, r

A.   Portfolio E
   • Sufficient cash for early retirement payments.
   • Meets shortfall risk: $[9.04 - (-8.0)] / 8.19 = 2.08$.
   • No exposure to lumber stocks.
   • Each of the other portfolios is unacceptable:

   Portfolio A is not most appropriate because it:
      • has insufficient cash.
      • does not meet the shortfall risk: $[8.65 - (-8.0)] / 8.53 = 1.95$

   Portfolio B is not most appropriate because it has:
      • insufficient cash.
      • exposure to lumber industry equities.

   Portfolio C is not most appropriate because it:
      • does not meet the shortfall risk: $[9.06 - (-8.0)] / 8.83 = 1.93$
      • has exposure to lumber industry equities.

   Portfolio D is not most appropriate because it:
      • has insufficient cash.
      • does not meet the shortfall risk: $[8.29 - (-8.0)] / 8.35 = 1.95$

Candidate discussion:
Three points for portfolio E and 2 points each for three reasons. Early retirement payments are 10% of portfolio assets, so the selected allocation must have at least 10% in cash equivalents. In addition, the portfolio should avoid stocks that are highly correlated with the sponsor, such as lumber industry equities. Per the question, no credit is given for discussing the return.

Source: Study Session 8, LOS 17.h

B.   Global fixed income

   Asset classes should be mutually exclusive, and assets within a class should have similar return and risk characteristics. Blending domestic and international fails to meet these characteristics. It is better to treat them as separate asset classes. Note that this does not mean global is never used as an asset class and it does not mean you should have raised it in the earlier question. There were much more specific portfolio issues to address in the earlier question. Also note you can argue mixing equity of Europe and Asia is not optimal, but any divergence of characteristics in mixing two different international categories should be less than mixing domestic and international categories.

Candidate discussion:
1 point for global fixed income and 2 points for the reason. The reason must make it clear the candidate understands that the underlying issue is for assets within a class to be homogeneous, similar, highly correlated with each other, or similar reasoning. Note that lumber industry equity is not usually an asset class, but in a DB plan of a company in the same industry, it becomes a relevant category of assets to consider and avoid.

PRACTICE EXAM 1
AFTERNOON SESSION ANSWERS

To get detailed answer explanations with references to specific LOS and SchweserNotes™ content, and to get valuable feedback on how your score compares to those of other Level III candidates, use your Username and Password to gain Online Access at schweser.com and choose the left-hand menu item "Practice Exams Vol. 1."

1.	A	21.	A	41.	C
2.	C	22.	C	42.	A
3.	B	23.	B	43.	A
4.	A	24.	C	44.	C
5.	B	25.	B	45.	B
6.	C	26.	B	46.	A
7.	A	27.	A	47.	A
8.	C	28.	B	48.	A
9.	C	29.	B	49.	C
10.	C	30.	B	50.	B
11.	C	31.	C	51.	C
12.	C	32.	B	52.	A
13.	B	33.	B	53.	C
14.	C	34.	B	54.	A
15.	B	35.	B	55.	B
16.	B	36.	A	56.	A
17.	B	37.	C	57.	B
18.	A	38.	A	58.	C
19.	A	39.	B	59.	C
20.	C	40.	A	60.	C

PRACTICE EXAM 1
AFTERNOON SESSION ANSWERS

QUESTIONS 1–6

Source: Study Session 1

1. **A**   Since Blackmore is Lange's supervisor and well experienced (including holding the CFA designation), and Lange has no knowledge of wrongdoing, Lange's professional responsibility is to follow his supervisor's directions and execute the trade. (Study Session 1, LOS 2.a)

2. **C**   This question is related to Disclosure of Conflicts. Blackmore's relationship with the 7MOD7 Corporation must be disclosed in the research report because it could impair Blackmore's ability to make an unbiased judgment. Under the same standard, the position of 7MOD7 in the children's trust fund must be mentioned because it is beneficial ownership that could reasonably impair Lange's judgment. Even though Lange is the one writing the report, both potential conflicts need to be disclosed since Blackmore is supervising Lange. (Study Session 1, LOS 2.a)

3. **B**   This question relates to Loyalty, Prudence, and Care. Blackmore's primary duty is to the participants and beneficiaries of the DB pension plan. This does not preclude some secondary responsibility to the plan sponsor. Blackmore can certainly consider the sponsor's views and implement them if they are not a violation of responsibility to the beneficiaries. But it is not an equal allocation of duty. (Study Session 1, LOS 2.a)

4. **A**   Blackmore's use of derivatives without knowing whether they are allowed according to the Plan's IPS is a violation of Loyalty, Prudence, and Care. When questionable activities occur, the best course of action for a member is to disassociate (and potentially seek legal counsel). (Study Session 1, LOS 2.a)

5. **B**   Lange violated loyalty to employer by contacting his cousin and advising him. This is because his cousin could potentially be a client for Lange's current firm. Since Lange's friend had said he would not do business with Blackmore and Lange gave him no instructions, there was no violation. Preparing to compete, by setting up an office and other related activities, is not a violation of the Standards. (Study Session 1, LOS 2.a)

6. **C**   Lange may not put "CFA (expected 2016)" following his name because it is a violation of the Standards. However, he may state that he is a Level III candidate in the CFA program if he wishes. The printing of the business cards is not a violation, as long as they are not distributed prior to receiving the designation. (Study Session 1, LOS 2.a)

QUESTIONS 7–12

Source: Study Session 1

7. **A** All the direct information supports that Smithers was diligent and acted appropriately. He researched PCD, including talking to Carson, who is in a related business. Carson shared information regarding an LP his firm is marketing. Smithers talked to a knowledgeable client who shared information from a newspaper. Smithers applied the mosaic theory to link information together and tried to confirm his research with a source, Carson. He then put together a detailed report. Note that there is no evidence anyone shared material nonpublic information. (Study Session 1, LOS 2.a)

8. **C** Sharing information on an upcoming recommendation with outsiders is disloyal to his firm. Acting on his new views before the firm approves the report (by using it to take other actions) without discussing what he is doing is also disloyal. Plus, he is not disclosing the real reason for the other actions. Sharing information with others in the firm who may have a reason to know could be acceptable, making C the least questionable action. (Study Session 1, LOS 2.a)

9. **C** Engaging in significant outside activities with clients is not prohibited per se, though it could be questionable and would require full disclosure to those involved and could not be harmful to clients. This kind of activity is specifically discussed in the Asset Manager Code, Loyalty to Clients, and therefore cannot be in violation of the Code and Standards, if properly handled. (Study Session 1, LOS 2.a)

10. **C** Both situations have significant conflicts of interest, but between the Code and Standards plus the Asset Manager Code it is clear they could, under certain conditions, be allowed. Complex interrelated activities between client and manger are not prohibited.

    The O'Toole issue is even more complicated than the one with Carson. The condo use could be a gift or seen as required to make Smithers a participant in the deal. Smithers is O'Toole's manager, and Smithers may become a client of O'Toole if he invests in the deal.

    Both actions are questionable and a safe course would be to avoid both. But there are provisions in the AMC (and therefore Code) that might allow them. (Study Session 1, LOS 2.a and Study Session 2, LOS 4.c)

11. **C** These are both recommendations and are intended to manage the issue of potentially sharing material nonpublic information or confidential client information. (Study Session 1, LOS 2.a)

12. **C** The AMC applies to organizations, not individuals. It does not conflict with the AMC but requires actions only the firm can take. That produces some additional requirements. Both logically and when you look at the lists, there are multiple additional requirements in regard to Risk Management, Compliance, and Support. (Study Session 1, LOS 2.a and Study Session 2, LOS 4.c)

QUESTIONS 13–18

Source: Study Session 7

13. **B** Cobb-Douglas assumes constant returns to scale (e.g., a 1% change in labor or capital from 2% to 3% has the same incremental effect on real output as a change from 4% to 5%). This is a simple linear relationship. It assumes TFP is a constant. (Study Session 7, LOS 16.a)

14. **C** The percentage change in capital and labor can be obtained from the national accounts. The Solow residual is equal to the percentage change in total factor productivity and is estimated as follows:

$$\text{Solow residual} = \%\Delta A = \%\Delta Y - \alpha(\%\Delta K) - (1-\alpha)\%\Delta L$$

(Study Session 7, LOS 16.a)

15. **B** To determine the country with the highest expected real GDP growth rate, use the following formula to solve for the expected real GDP growth rate for each country.

$$\%\Delta Y \cong \%\Delta A + \alpha(\%\Delta K) + (1-\alpha)(\%\Delta L)$$

Country 1: $\%\Delta Y \cong 2.0\% + 0.7(4.0\%) + (1-0.7)(9.0\%) = 7.5\%$
Country 2: $\%\Delta Y \cong 4.0\% + 0.4(4.5\%) + (1-0.4)(7.5\%) = 10.3\%$
Country 3: $\%\Delta Y \cong 3.0\% + 0.3(8.5\%) + (1-0.3)(5.5\%) = 9.4\%$

(Study Session 7, LOS 16.b)

16. **B** The H-model should be employed to evaluate the intrinsic value of the equity market for Country 4, because the H-model assumes that the current "super-normal" growth rate will decline linearly to a long-term sustainable growth rate:

$$\text{H-Model: } P_0 = \frac{D_0}{r-g_L}\left[(1+g_L) + \frac{N}{2}(g_S - g_L)\right]$$

The (current) rate of supernormal growth is estimated using the data for year 1. This growth rate will decline linearly over the next 20 years to the long-term, sustainable growth rate, which is estimated using the data for year 21:

$$g_S \cong 5.2\% + 0.4(6.9\%) + (1-0.4)(8.9\%)$$
$$\cong 5.2\% + 2.76\% + 5.34\% = 13.30\%$$
$$g_L \cong 0.5\% + 0.7(1.7\%) + (1-0.7)(2.0\%)$$
$$\cong 0.5\% + 1.19\% + 0.6\% = 2.29\%$$

The estimated intrinsic value of the equity market for Country 4 is:

$$P_0 = \frac{15}{0.12-0.0229}\left[(1+0.0229) + \frac{20}{2}(0.133-0.0229)\right]$$

$$= 154.48[1.0229 + 1.101] = 328.10$$

(Study Session 7, LOS 16.c)

17. **B** The Yardeni model calculates the fair earnings ratio (i.e., the ratio of earnings to price) as the yield on long term bonds less a growth factor.

$$\frac{E_1}{P_0} = Y_B - d(LTEG) = 0.075 - 0.15 \times 0.05 = 0.0675$$

The intrinsic forward P/E ratio is the inverse of the ratio of earnings to price computed using the Yardeni model.

$$\frac{E_1}{P_0} = 0.0675 \Rightarrow \frac{P_0}{E_1} = \frac{1}{0.0675} = 14.81$$

The forward P/E ratio can be calculated from the current trailing P/E ratio by using the long-term earnings growth rate:

$$\frac{P_0}{E_1} = \frac{P_0}{E_0 \times (1 + LTGR)} = 15 \times \frac{1}{1.05} = 14.28$$

The forward P/E is less than the intrinsic forward P/E indicating that Country 5's equity market is slightly undervalued. (Study Session 7, LOS 16.g)

18. **A** In this case, the top-down approach is most appropriate as the fund is only concerned with the direction of currencies and markets and not the relative returns between securities. (Study Session 7, LOS 16.e)

QUESTIONS 19–24

Source: Study Sessions 9 and 15

19. **A** To hedge the interest payments on the U.K. bonds, Point University needs to enter into a currency swap in which it pays GBP (at a rate of 5.3% per GBP of notional principal) and receives USD (at a rate of 4.9% per USD of notional principal). Such an arrangement will effectively lock in an exchange rate for the term of the swap. First, we must determine the face value of the U.K. bonds. Since the U.K. bonds are trading at face value, the USD allocation in the portfolio can be converted at the current exchange rate to determine the GBP face value:

U.K. Bond face value = Portfolio value × U.K. Bond allocation × GBP/USD exchange rate

U.K. Bond face value = USD 800,000,000 × 0.05 × 0.45 GBP/USD = GBP 18,000,000

Next calculate the interest due every six months from the bonds:

GBP 18,000,000 × (0.047 / 2) = GBP 423,000

In order to pay GBP 423,000 in the swap (so that a USD amount can be received), the notional principal of the swap based on a U.K. swap rate of 5.3% is calculated as follows:

$$\text{Notional Principal}\left(\frac{\text{Annual Swap Rate}}{\text{Number of Periods per year}}\right) = \text{Swap Payment}$$

Rearranging the equation to isolate the Notional Principal yields the following:

$$\text{Notional Principal} = \text{Swap Payment}\left(\frac{\text{Number of Periods per year}}{\text{Annual Swap Rate}}\right)$$

$$\text{Notional Principal} = \text{GBP}423,000\left(\frac{2}{0.053}\right) = \text{GBP}15,962,264 \approx 16,000,000$$

We could also convert the notional principal into a USD amount:

$$\text{GBP } 15,962,264\left(\frac{1}{0.45 \text{ GBP/USD}}\right) = \text{GBP } 15,962,264\left(2.22 \text{ USD/GBP}\right) = \text{USD}35,436,226$$

(Study Session 15, LOS 28.f)

20. **C** In order to adjust the allocation of an existing equity portfolio, two futures contracts are needed. The first contract should have an underlying equal (or highly similar) to the existing equity exposure to be reduced. This contract is sold to reduce a portion of the existing portfolio to a zero beta, effectively canceling the exposure to that equity sector. The second futures contract should have an underlying equal to the desired equity exposure. This contract is purchased to provide the desired equity exposure. The number of contracts to use is calculated using the following formula:

$$\text{number of contracts} = \left(\frac{\beta_{target} - \beta_{position}}{\beta_{futures\ contract}}\right)\left(\frac{\text{Value of position}}{\text{Futures price} \times \text{multiplier}}\right)$$

For Point University, should sell 417 mid-cap contracts:

$$\text{number of contracts} = \left(\frac{0-1.3}{1.1}\right)\left(\frac{80,000,000}{908 \times 250}\right) = -416.5 \approx -417 \text{ contracts}$$

Note that the negative sign indicates that the contracts should be sold.

(Study Session 15, LOS 26.e)

21. **A** The number of European index contracts to purchase is 778:

$$\text{number of contracts} = \left(\frac{1.2-0}{1.05}\right)\left(\frac{80,000,000}{2,351 \times 50}\right) = 777.78 \approx 778 \text{ contracts}$$

(Study Session 15, LOS 26.e)

22. **C** Regressing the foreign market return measured in the investor's domestic currency versus the foreign currency value produces a minimum variance hedge ratio, and the intent is to minimize the volatility of the return to the domestic investor. It jointly minimizes the volatility of the foreign market and currency. It would be a form of a cross hedge because the hedged item (R_{DC}) is not the same thing as the hedging vehicle (the foreign currency), but that is a vague answer and much less specific than correctly describing it as a MVH. (All MVHs are cross hedges, but most cross hedges are not MVHs.) A transaction exposure generally refers to hedging a known in or out flow of a foreign currency. There are elements of that here, but it is a much less specific answer and so is not acceptable. (Study Session 15, LOS 26.f)

23. **B** The slope coefficient for a regression of the foreign asset returns measured in the investor's domestic currency (USD) is the MVHR. JPY 200,000,000 x 0.8 = JPY 160,000,000

(Study Session 9, LOS 18.h)

24. **C** The MVHR is based on regressing historical returns and its future performance is therefore less predictable and riskier. The relationship (correlation) can change. Buying calls on the USD is equivalent to buying puts on the yen and the statement correctly describes the consequences of a protective put on the yen: downside protection, full upside participation, but an initial option premium expense.

(Study Session 9, LOS 18.g, h)

QUESTIONS 25–30

Source: Study Session 10

25. **B** The fund compares emerging market bond issues to U.S. bond issues of similar credit risk, interest rate risk, and liquidity risk. The analyst is starting at the bottom (i.e., at the individual issue level), not at the economy-wide level as in the top-down approach. (Study Session 10, LOS 21.a)

26. **B** Statement 1: In the primary bond market in the United States, there are a declining number of callable and putable bonds being sold. The option adjusted spread accounts for options imbedded in bonds and is therefore becoming less useful for analyzing the attractiveness of bond investments. Thus, Watson is incorrect.

    Statement 2: Watson is correct. Swap spread analysis allows a fixed rate bond to be transformed into a floating rate bond, and vice versa. It is therefore useful in comparing the relative attractiveness of fixed-rate and floating-rate bond markets. (Study Session 10, LOS 21.b, e)

27. **A** She makes her trade based on which issues she believes could be downgraded, in light of her forecasts for a U.S. economic slowdown. She reallocates away from credit risky bonds towards investment grade bonds. This describes a credit-defense trade. (Study Session 10, LOS 21.d)

28. **B** Smith is swapping bonds in order to obtain a higher yield. The Quincy Corporation bond has a yield that is 50 basis points higher. This describes a yield/spread pickup trade.

    However, notice also that the Quincy Corporation bond has a lower credit rating, which probably accounts for its higher yield. Given its higher credit risk, its yield is more likely to rise in the future than the yield on the Mahan Corporation bond. If the yield on the Quincy bond does rise, its price will fall.

    Smith has failed to evaluate the Quincy bond on a total return basis (i.e., he has not examined the return from both the yield and the potential change in price). If the yield on the Quincy bond rises high enough, its price could fall such that its total return is lower.

    Note that it is probably true that the liquidity of the Mahan bond is lower because the Quincy bond is newly issued and newly issued bonds typically have higher liquidity. However, he has already sold the Mahan bond, so this is not a consideration. (Study Session 10, LOS 21.d)

29. **B** A slowing economy coupled with an increase in interest rate volatility typically produces increased risk premiums (increased yield spreads over Treasuries) and the increase in risk premiums will vary directly with the risk of the bonds; low quality bonds experience a greater increase in the risk premium than high rated bonds, so the switch to investment grade bonds is justified. MBS, on the other hand, include embedded call options which increase in value with increased interest rate volatility. Because of the embedded option that produces the negative convexity in MBS, MBS do not increase in value as much as bullets when rates fall. The increase in volatility will only serve to increase the negative convexity, so a switch to MBS is not warranted. Swapping out of corporate bullets into MBS is considered a structural trade, because it is based on the assumption that different bond structures react differently to changing circumstances. (Study Session 10, LOS 21.d, e)

30. **B** Bond B is likely to have the greatest liquidity. Its characteristics are common to those bonds with the greatest liquidity. It is large (greater than a billion dollars in issue), sold publicly, and is a medium term note (maturity of five to twelve years). Privately placed bonds are less liquid than publicly sold bonds.

    Note that bond liquidity is cyclical with the economy and declines as defaults increase. The longer term trend however is for increasing liquidity in the global bond market. (Study Session 10, LOS 21.c)

QUESTIONS 31–36

Source: Study Sessions 10 and 11

31. **C** Historical variance measures for individual bonds are not good predictors of future risk because the bonds are constantly moving towards maturity. Therefore, the variance in the past was for a bond with higher interest rate sensitivity than the bond will have in the future. The historical standard deviation would include price changes due to interest rates. Duration does directly address volatility due to changes in interest rates, and a portfolio duration measure is much simpler to calculate than the historical variance and covariance numbers needed to measure bond portfolio standard deviation.
(Study Session 11, LOS 22.c)

32. **B** Portfolio duration is simply a weighted average, taken as follows:

Sector	% of portfolio	Duration	Duration Contribution
U.S. Treasury	14.6%	7.54	1.101
U.S. agencies	23.7%	9.02	2.138
U.S. corporates	31.8%	4.52	1.437
U.S. mortgages (MBS)	11.4%	1.33	0.152
Non-U.S. governments	18.5%	3.22	0.596
	100.0%		5.424

Since 5.42 > 5.25, the portfolio has slightly more interest rate risk than the benchmark.
(Study Session 10, LOS 20.e)

33. **B** The spread for Treasury securities is zero, so adding Treasuries reduces the weighted average portfolio spread duration. The spread duration of 6.25 is greater than the effective duration of 5.42, indicating more sensitivity to spreads than to interest rate levels. A 50 basis point change in the zero volatility spread (another name for static spread) should lead to a 6.25 / 2 = 3.125% change in portfolio value. (Study Session 10, LOS 20.i)

34. **B** The market view is for interest rates to rise, Hickock should reduce portfolio duration and can do so by selling bond forwards. The market view is for spreads to narrow. A credit forward is designed to provide protection to the buyer if spreads widen. The buyer would receive if spreads widen but pay if spreads narrow. As the seller, Hickock will receive if spreads narrow. (Study Session 11, LOS 22.g)

35. **B** The portfolio is following a contingent immunization strategy. It has a target amount and payoff date. It was initially overfunded with a surplus. A successful contingent immunization strategy would increase the surplus. The current surplus is the difference between the current market value of the portfolio [$20,100,0000 and the PV of the future payout based on the current immunization rate (4%/2 is the periodic rate)]. That value is: $24,000,000 / (1.02^{10}) = 19,688,359. The surplus is now $411,641. The surplus of $1,250,000 has declined indicating the strategies used in the portfolio have not been successful up to now. (Study Session 10, LOS 20.j)

36. **A** The previous question calculated the portfolio has a positive surplus. With a positive surplus, the portfolio can be actively managed. Expecting a rise in interest rates, the portfolio duration can be lowered by selling bond futures. (More precisely the portfolio duration should be set as less than the remaining time horizon of five years, but with what is given reducing duration is the best answer choice available.) If the surplus were zero, the portfolio would have to be immunized with a duration of 5.0. Immunization and contingent immunization are focused on interest rate risk and duration. Spread duration is not relevant to this question. (Study Session 11, LOS 22.d)

QUESTIONS 37–42

Source: Study Session 16

37. **C** effective spread (buy order) = 2 × (actual execution price – midpoint of the market at the time an order is entered)

effective spread for the order of 700 shares = 2 × (79.25 – [(79.25 + 79.00) / 2)]) = 0.25

effective spread for the order of 1,300 shares = 2 × (80.00 – [(80.10 + 79.75) / 2)]) = 0.15

Average effective spread (arithmetic) equals the mean effective spread over all transactions for Technology Company. In this case: average effective spread = (0.25 + 0.15) / 2 = 0.20. The weighted-average effective spread is:

$$\frac{700}{2,000}(0.25) + \frac{1,300}{2,000}(0.15) = 0.0875 + 0.0975$$
$$= 0.185$$

For the exam:
You will note that the letter answer to this question does not change if you use the arithmetic or weighted-average method. If asked as part of an essay question on the exam, be sure to use the method requested.

(Study Session 16, LOS 29.b)

38. **A** The Technology Company trade was based on information-motivated trading. Simpson's analyst must have obtained some piece of information that motivated her to have Simpson acquire more shares of Technology Company. Simpson quickly executed the order through a market order.

Since the trade was completed in a single day using market orders, it is not likely motivated by value considerations. Value-motivated investors are usually patient and utilize limit orders to ensure getting the desired prices. Also, a liquidity-motivated trade is used to either (1) reinvest temporary cash or (2) generate cash for necessary liquidity concerns, such as meeting client withdrawals. Since the Technology Company trade was a leveraged purchase, it was not performed to generate or to reinvest cash. (Study Session 16, LOS 29.j)

39. **B** The factors listed by Simpson that make a market liquid are not all correct. The major factors that contribute to making a market liquid are the presence of many buyers and sellers, diversity of opinion and information, convenience and market integrity. A liquid market will have narrow bid-ask spreads, not wide bid-ask spreads. Simpson's discussion of the factors evaluated when assessing market quality is correct. To evaluate market quality, the following factors must be assessed: market liquidity, market transparency, and the certainty with which investor orders will be completed. (Study Session 16, LOS 29.e)

40. **A**   Implementation shortfall can be decomposed into explicit costs, realized profit/loss, delay costs, and missed trade opportunity cost (MTOC).

Paper portfolio investment $= (35 \times 100,000) = 3,500,000$

$$\text{Explicit costs} = \frac{\text{commission}}{\text{paper portfolio investment}} = \frac{(2,500 + 2,500)}{3,500,000} = 0.00143 = 0.143\%$$

The additional components of total implementation shortfall can be calculated as follows:

$$\text{Nano's execution price} = \left[\left(36.75 \times \left(\frac{50,000}{100,000}\right)\right) + \left(40.00 \times \left(\frac{50,000}{100,000}\right)\right)\right] = 38.375$$

$$\text{realized loss} = \left(\frac{\text{Nano's execution price} - \text{day one closing price}}{\text{original benchmark price}}\right) \times \left(\frac{\text{shares purchased}}{\text{shares ordered}}\right)$$

$$\text{realized loss} = \left(\frac{38.375 - 36.50}{35.00}\right) \times \left(\frac{100,000}{100,000}\right) = 0.05357$$

$$\text{delay costs} = \left(\frac{\text{day one closing} - \text{benchmark price}}{\text{original benchmark price}}\right) \times \left(\frac{\text{shares purchased}}{\text{shares ordered}}\right)$$

$$\text{delay costs} = \left(\frac{36.50 - 35.00}{35.00}\right) \times \left(\frac{100,000}{100,000}\right) = 0.04286$$

$$\text{MTOC} = \left(\frac{\text{cancellation price} - \text{benchmark price}}{\text{original benchmark price}}\right) \times \left(\frac{\text{shares not purchased}}{\text{shares ordered}}\right)$$

$$\text{MTOC} = \left[\left(\frac{0 - 35.00}{35.00}\right) \times \left(\frac{0}{100,000}\right)\right] = 0$$

Total implementation shortfall = 0.00143 + 0.05357 + 0.04286 + 0 = 0.09786 (sum of components method)

(Study Session 16, LOS 29.f)

Candidate discussion: Note that the limit order price of 34.75 is not explicitly used in IS analysis. It may have subsequent effects. DP is market price at the time the trade decision is made. Because the market was closed, the previous close is DP.

41. **C**   total implementation shortfall $= \dfrac{\text{paper portfolio gain} - \text{real portfolio gain}}{\text{paper portfolio investment}}$ (direct method)

paper portfolio gain $= (40 - 35) \times 100{,}000 = 500{,}000$

real portfolio gain $=$ terminal value $-$ investment

terminal value $= (40 \times 100{,}000) = 4{,}000{,}000$

investment $= \left[(36.75 \times 50{,}000) + 2{,}500 \right] + \left[(40 \times 50{,}000) + 2{,}500 \right] = 3{,}842{,}500$

real portfolio gain $= 4{,}000{,}000 - 3{,}842{,}500 = 157{,}500$

total implementation shortfall $= \dfrac{500{,}000 - 157{,}500}{3{,}500{,}000} = 0.09786$

This reconciles with the individual components sum shown in the previous answer.

(Study Session 16, LOS 29.g)

42. **A** The Institute report specifies four characteristics of best execution:

1. Best execution cannot be judged independently of the investment decision. Some strategies might have high trading costs, but that alone does not mean the strategy should not be pursued as long as it generates the intended value.

2. Best execution cannot be known with certainty ex ante; it depends on the particular circumstances of the trade. Each party to a trade determines what best execution is.

3. Although best execution can be measured ex post over time, it cannot be measured for a single trade, because a particular trade may have been subject to extreme market conditions. Over time, however, a trader's effectiveness can be ascertained.

4. Relationships and practices are integral to best execution. Best execution is ongoing and requires diligence and dedication to the process.

Business relationships are indeed integral to the concept of best execution. Also, high portfolio turnover, in and of itself, does not necessarily imply the manager is not pursuing a best execution strategy. Best execution, concerned with the implementation of portfolio decisions, implies that trades should generate the intended value, and this says nothing about the frequency of trading. In the vignette, we are not told whether the considerable portfolio turnover (once per year) is excessive or whether it is an intentional strategy designed to achieve the intended increase in wealth. If over many trades the strategy produces the intended wealth gain, we could potentially classify it as best execution. In this case, with no information other than "as long as the portfolio value is greater after trading costs," we would most likely conclude this does not meet CFA Institute guidelines for best execution.

(Study Session 16, LOS 29.n)

QUESTIONS 43–48

Source: Study Session 15

43. **A** Both calls and puts increase in value if volatility increases. A straddle is composed of a long call and put with the same strike price, so it will have the greatest increase in value if volatility increases. Another way to look at it is the intrinsic value of the straddle increases 1 for 1 if the underlying increases or decreases from the strike price. The reverse butterfly can be built using the same straddle, but a call with higher strike and put with lower strike are sold, which reduces the potential upside from increasing volatility. A bull spread using either puts or calls is a directional play on the underlying increasing in value but with limited upside and downside, not a direct play on volatility. (Study Session 15, LOS 27.b)

44. **C** In a long butterfly call strategy, the investor purchases a call with a low strike price (X_1), sells two calls with a strike price between the high and low strike prices (X_2), and purchases a call with a high strike price (X_3).

    The maximum profit of the strategy is calculated as follows:

    1. Determine the initial investment:

        Buy the X = 1475 call for 35.40.

        Buy the X = 1515 call for 7.90.

        Sell two X = 1500 calls for 2 × 18.10 = 36.20.

        = net paid 7.10.

    2. Examine the payoff graph. Max gain is if the underlying closes at 1500.

    3. Determine intrinsic value of the positions at 1500:

        The X = 1475 call is worth 25.

        The X = 1515 and X = 1500 calls are worthless.

        = net ending value 25.

    4. Versus initial investment, this is a gain of 17.90 per share of the underlying.

    Or it can be solved by the formula:

    $X_2 - X_1 - c_1 + 2c_2 - c_3$

    where:
    X_2 = Strike price of the option with the middle strike price
    X_1 = Strike price of the option with the low strike price
    c_1 = Premium of option with the low strike price
    c_2 = Premium of the option with the middle strike price
    c_3 = Premium of the option with the high strike price

Using the data in Figure 2, the maximum profit on the butterfly spread strategy is equal to:

1,500 – 1,475 – 35.40 + 2(18.10) – 7.90 = 17.90

(Study Session 15, LOS 27.b)

45. **B** First, calculate the payoff of the option at expiration:

notional principal × max(0, underlying rate at expiration – exercise rate)(days in underlying rate / 360)

50,000,000 × max(0, 0.073 – 0.06)(180 / 360) = 325,000

Next, calculate the compounded value of the option premium:

option premium[1 + (current LIBOR + spread)(days until option expiration / 360)]

120,000[1 + (0.065 + 0.015)(110 / 360)] = 122,933

Next, calculate the effective loan proceeds:

loan proceeds – compounded value of option premium

50,000,000 – 122,933 = 49,877,067

Next, calculate the interest on the loan taken in 110 days:

loan proceeds(underlying rate at option expiration + spread)(days in underlying rate / 360)

50,000,000(0.073 + 0.015)(180 / 360) = 2,200,000

Finally, calculate the effective annual interest rate on the loan:

$$\left(\frac{\text{Loan proceeds} + \text{Interest on loan} - \text{Option payoff}}{\text{Effective loan proceeds}} \right)^{(365/\text{days in underlying rate})}$$

$$\left(\frac{50,000,000 + 2,200,000 - 325,000}{49,877,067} \right)^{(365/180)} - 1 = 8.29\%$$

If the manager had not utilized the interest rate option, the rate on the loan would have been 8.8% = 7.3% + 1.5%. (Study Session 15, LOS 27.c)

46. **A** A box spread is a combination of bull and bear spread but using only two strike prices. It will have a known ending value. If the difference in the initial investment and that known ending value does not reflect the periodic risk free rate, arbitrage is possible. (Study Session 15, LOS 27.b)

©2016 Kaplan, Inc.

47. **A**   The manager of Fund C is correct regarding the method of determining the delta hedge position (Comment 1), but is not correct regarding adjustments to the delta hedge position (Comment 2). In a delta hedge, a short position in call options is offset with a long position in the underlying security (or vice versa). Delta is the ratio of change in value of the option for change in value of the underlying. A dealer who is short call options can buy shares equal to delta × the number of calls sold. This case is the reciprocal situation; shares are owned, so 1/delta × shares is the number of calls to sell. In all cases, delta hedging requires delta to determine the hedge ratio.

    The delta of a call option will change in response to a change in any of the variables affecting the option value (i.e., volatility, time, price of the underlying, and risk-free rate). Any time the delta of the option changes, the delta hedge must be adjusted. (Study Session 15, LOS 27.e)

48. **A**   Gamma is a measure of the change in delta resulting from a change in the price of the underlying security. Gamma is largest for options that are at-the-money and/or near expiration. This implies that at-the-money options nearing expiration have unstable deltas which will move rapidly with any change in the price of the underlying security. Delta hedging in such an environment is difficult. (Study Session 15, LOS 27.f)

QUESTIONS 49–54

Source: Study Session 14

49. **C** The first part of Nicholson's comment is correct. Thomasville's contract with Boston Advisors is asymmetric because managers are paid for profits but not penalized for losses. As a result, Thomasville will pay for Amato's positive performance, even though Boston Advisors only earned a *net* of $5 million ($20 – $15) for Thomasville. The loss incurred by Garvin is not penalized in the contract. Thomasville would have been better off investing in two managers with, say profits of $2.5 million each. The small positive profits would result in lower performance fees and higher net profits for Thomasville.

The second part of Nicholson's comment is incorrect. Thomasville's compensation contract with Boston Advisors more closely resembles a call option (from Boston Advisors' perspective) as it pays off as returns increase but expires worthless if they decrease. That is, managers at Boston are paid if there are profits but do not suffer if there are losses. This increases the manager's incentive to take risk, which is apparently what Garvin did in the last quarter. Entering the fourth quarter, he may have had no profits and realized that he had to earn a return quickly in order to earn the 20% compensation fee. This may have been why he sustained his largest losses in the fourth quarter. (Study Session 14, LOS 25.d)

50. **B** To calculate the monthly VAR, we must first calculate a monthly expected return and monthly standard deviation. Note that to obtain a monthly standard deviation from an annual standard deviation, we must divide the annual standard deviation by the square root of 12. We then calculate a monthly percent VAR by subtracting 1.65 times the monthly standard deviation from the monthly expected return. The monthly dollar VAR is calculated last using the fund's asset base:

Monthly expected return = 14.4% / 12 = 1.20%

Monthly standard deviation = $\left(\frac{21.5\%}{\sqrt{12}} \right) = 6.2065\%$

Monthly percent VAR = 1.20% – (1.65 × 6.2065%) = –9.0407%

Monthly dollar VAR = $80 × 9.0407% = $7.2 million. (Study Session 14, LOS 25.e)

51. **C** Fluellen is incorrect regarding the Moffett option. There is no *current* credit risk of this option because it is a European option and cannot be exercised until maturity. It only has potential credit risk (i.e., the risk of non-payment at maturity, at which time the value of the option will likely be different than its current value). However, it would be correct to say that the *value of the potential credit risk* is its current market value, which is the $2.86.

Fluellen is incorrect regarding the McNeill option. There is no credit risk in an option to the seller (Thomasville). Once the option is sold, it is the buyer of the option who faces the risk that the seller will not honor the contract. That is, the only possible inflow to the writer (seller) of the option is the premium received. (Study Session 14, LOS 25.i)

©2016 Kaplan, Inc.

52. **A** The VAR measure calculated for the Special Strategies Portfolio is accurate. At a 5% VAR, losses exceeding the threshold of $13.9 million should occur about 5% of the time. With 250 trading days and a 5% VAR, losses exceeding the threshold should occur in 12.5 (5% × 250) days out of a year. This is very close to the 13 observed.

    However, the fact that the losses usually exceed $13.9 million by a significant amount suggests that the fund has the potential to suffer very large losses. Because of this, scenario analysis should be performed as a supplement to VAR so management can be aware of the potential for large losses and better protect the firm against such a scenario.

    Note also that although the calculated VAR has been accurate, the presence of options and their non-normal return distributions indicates that the variance-covariance VAR should probably not be used as a final risk measurement. The variance-covariance or analytical VAR assumes a normal distribution of returns. Delta normal VAR is a version of the variance-covariance VAR in which the deltas for options are used as part of the VAR methodology in determining potential losses. Note: since the delta normal method is not explained in the Level III curriculum, you will not have to explain it on the exam. (Study Session 14, LOS 25.f)

53. **C** The swap with the highest credit risk is swap C. At the beginning of a swap's life, the parties would not enter into the contract if credit risk was too high and any existing credit risk would be priced into the contract. So swaps A and B probably have low credit risk because they have been recently initiated.

    Credit risk is highest for interest rate swaps near the middle of their life because as the swap ages, the counterparties' credit worthiness may have changed. As the swap nears its maturity and the number of remaining settlement payments decreases, credit risk decreases.

    In a currency swap, the credit risk is highest between the middle of its life and its maturity due to the exchange of principal on the maturity date. Thus, swap C, which is three-quarters into its life, likely has the highest credit risk. (Study Session 14, LOS 25.i)

54. **A** Both comments are wrong. Cross-default is designed to protect creditors by triggering default on all contracts if there is a default on any one contract. It prevents the defaulter from selectively defaulting on some, but not other, contracts (where the defaulter might be receiving rather than paying). It is not easy to aggregate credit VaR, which is high when returns are high and value is up, with general VaR, which is typically high when returns are negative. (Study Session 14, LOS 25.i)

QUESTIONS 55–60

Source: Study Sessions 9 and 18

55. **B** Under GIPS, all fee-paying, discretionary portfolios must be included in at least one composite. There is no minimum number of portfolios or minimum asset level for composite formation, so the Contrarian composite can be formed. However, the number of portfolios and dispersion does not have to be reported because there are less than six portfolios in the composite. (Study Session 18, LOS 32.a, k)

56. **A** The Cypress University portfolio is still a discretionary portfolio (i.e., the ethical investing restriction does not limit the ability of the manager to implement the investment strategy because Nigel does not hold any stocks in the countries of concern). Therefore, the historical and future record of performance for the Cypress University portfolio should be kept in the Global Equity Growth composite.

    If, at some point, the ethical investing concern *does* limit the ability of the manager to implement the investment strategy, it would be deemed nondiscretionary and its *future* record of performance would not be included in the Global Equity Growth composite. Its historical record of performance would not be removed. (Study Session 18, LOS 32.f)

57. **B** Statement 1 is consistent with GIPS. GIPS requires at least monthly valuation and on the date of large external cash flows. In addition, GIPS requires valuation in accordance with fair value principles. Fair value is market value when that is available, as it will generally be for marketable securities. Fair value would not allow book or cost basis accounting.

    Statement 2 is not consistent with GIPS. The discussion of composites and discretion is correct, but not the discussion of exclusion. If, for any reason, such as a large external cash flow, the manager cannot manage the portfolio in a way reflecting the manager's style, the account is temporarily non-discretionary and must be excluded from the composite. (Alternatively, the large external cash flow can be segregated from the account and managed separately.) However, for any full month the account is managed with discretion, it must be included in the composite. (Study Session 18, LOS 32.c, e)

58. **C** Matching the benchmark is passive, and choosing to vary from the benchmark is active.

    The Global Equity Growth benchmark is fully hedged against currency risk but the manager is not, thus the manager is using active currency management.

    The manager of the Emerging Markets Equity composite weights country exposure the same as in the index, which also makes her currency weights the same. In addition, she does not hedge foreign currency exposures and neither does her benchmark. She is matching the benchmark currency exposures, which is a passive approach. (Study Session 9, LOS 18.b)

59. **C** From their description, it is apparent that frontier markets have fundamentally different investment characteristics than emerging markets. Thus, the investment strategy has fundamentally changed. Under GIPS, composites are defined by their investment strategy. Therefore, a new composite should be created to reflect the change in the investment strategy. The benchmark for the new composite should reflect the new investment strategy. (Study Session 18, LOS 32.g)

60. **C**   Statement 3 is incorrect in applying the special real estate provisions to private debt. Both private and public debt instruments are excluded and are instead covered by the general provisions of GIPS. Statement 4 is incorrect because external valuation is required every 12 months unless the client agrees to less frequent external valuations, in which case 36 months is the minimum. (Study Session 18, LOS 32.n, o)

QUESTION 1

Source: Study Session 4, LOS 8.g, h

A.   Jackson has stated several investment goals:

Primary goals, which must be met:
- Purchase a home
- Pay her debts
- Provide adequate income
- Provide for her children's education
- Retire in 35 years

Secondary goal:
- Quit her job and return to school herself within the year.

The analysis includes both her primary and secondary goals.

Inflows:	
After-tax proceeds from lottery lump-sum payment	$3,700,000
	3,700,000

Outflows:	
Payoff of debt to lawyers	($158,000)
Payoff of credit card debt	(57,000)
Purchase of home	(385,000)
	(600,000)

Net investable assets	$3,100,000
Annual living expenses	$125,000
College expenses for Helen	15,500
Annual family health insurance premium	15,000
Total **after-tax** income needs	$155,500

To determine the after-tax return objective for the Jackson portfolio, take her annual after-tax income needs as a percent of the investable assets:

$155,500/$3,100,000 = 5.02 percent

5.02%	
3.50	adust for inflation
8.52%	= nominal after-tax

To calculate the required before-tax nominal return:

8.52% / (1 − 25%) = 11.36%

(15 points)

Candidate discussion: 2 points for listing the primary goals, 1 point for the secondary goal, and 1 point for determining the secondary goal will be addressed in year one of the return. **Ignoring her college aspirations when it will increase her total wealth and she has the capital to attend college is incorrect in this case.** It is essentially a capital investment she is making.

1 point for listing the $3.7 million, 1 for the deductions, and 1 for calculating $3.1 million.

1 point for stating annual living expenses, 1 for deducting her first year college tuition, and 1 for deducting insurance premiums of 12 months times $1,250 monthly premium. 1 point for correct after-tax need of $155,500.

1 point for the process of calculating need divided by investable base. 1 point for converting to nominal after-tax by including 3.5% inflation. 1 point to gross up by dividing by 1 minus tax rate and 1 point if 11.36 is correctly calculated.

Compounding for inflation is also acceptable: $(1.0502 \times 1.035) - 1 = 8.70\%$ making pre-tax real: $8.70 / (1 - 0.25) = 11.60\%$.

B.   Her ability is high as Jackson has a substantial portfolio even after paying off her debts and purchasing a home and, at age 29, a very long investment time horizon.

But her ability is low as the portfolio is essentially her sole source of support. Her current salary is minimal in relation to her objectives. Jackson is almost completely dependent on the portfolio for her family's income.

Her overall ability to tolerate portfolio risk is average.

Jackson and her mother, because of their life experiences and current situation, are both highly reluctant to take risk in the portfolio. They have even stated that they do not want to risk losing any amounts from the portfolio. Their willingness to take portfolio risk is clearly below average.

Taking the lower of the two, risk tolerance is below average.

(5 points)

Candidate discussion: 1 point for listing a factor that increases ability and 1 point for a factor that lowers ability. 2 points for explaining her level of willingness and concluding willingness is low. 1 point for concluding her overall risk tolerance is low or below average.

Over time, the manager may attempt to educate and work with Jackson to resolve the inconsistency between her willingness and ability to take risk. Jackson's statement that she never wants to risk losing anything should be addressed directly because it is unrealistic from an investment management perspective.

C.   Time horizon, multistage:
  *   Now until the first child enters college in about five years.
  *   Then while children are in college, about nine more years.
  *   Then until Jackson retires, 35 years from now.
  *   Then retirement.

Taxes are 25% on income and short-term gains with 15% on long-term gains. 25% is to be used for analysis.

Liquidity:
- In the first year, Jackson needs $385,000 to buy a house, plus $158,000 and $57,000 to retire debts.
- Also meet ongoing distribution needs.

Legal: None specific. Be sure the annual lottery form is filed.

Unique: Sudden wealth from a lottery with limited financial experience. Jackson has a strong aversion to debt and any risk. Ongoing financial education will likely be needed.

(10 points)

Candidate discussion: 2 points for each constraint. For time horizon, two stages are also acceptable: (1) now until Helen and the children finish college and (2) then until retirement. Discussing after retirement is not wrong but earns no credit as it is not part of what has been discussed with the advisor. The 25% and 15% tax rates must both be disclosed for full credit. The use of 25% for planning must be done in the return calculation as it was given in the case. Under unique circumstances, the sudden wealth issue could be discussed or it could be discussed under risk. It must be included in the IPS because the extreme aversion to loss will be a problem in managing the portfolio; essentially it would mean keeping all the assets in money market type securities, which is not a realistic answer.

QUESTION 2

Source: Study Session 8, LOS 17.r

Answer for Question 2 (15 points total)

Asset Class	Recommend the most appropriate asset allocation range for each of the asset classes in Exhibit 2-1. (Circle one for each asset class.)	Justify your recommendations with one reason from the objectives and constraints developed in the previous question.
Cash Equivalents	(circled) **0.0% to 5.0%** (1 point) 5.0% to 10.0% 10.0% to 20.0%	Jackson has only limited liquidity needs now that she has met her one time distributions. Excess liquidity would impose a cash drag on her portfolio's return. (2 points)
Investment-grade U.S. Bonds	10.0% to 20.0% 20.0% to 30.0% (circled) **30.0% to 40.0%** (1 point)	Given Jackson's below-average risk tolerance and modest return objective, investment-grade U.S. bonds should have a larger allocation in her portfolio. (2 points)
U.S. Stocks	20.0% to 40.0% (circled) **40.0% to 60.0%** (1 point) 60.0% to 80.0%	Given Jackson's return objective, which is long term and higher than would be achievable with bonds alone, U.S. stocks should make up most of the rest of her portfolio. (2 points)
REITs	(circled) **0.0% to 10.0%** (1 point) 10.0% to 15.0% 15.0% to 20.0%	Jackson's home ownership and belowaverage risk tolerance does not allow a larger allocation to this relatively riskier asset class. (2 points)
Diversified International (non-U.S.) Stocks	(circled) **0.0% to 10.0%** (1 point) 10.0% to 20.0% 20.0% to 30.0%	A small allocation provides diversification benefits when combined with a portfolio of domestic equity and fixed-income securities. (2 points) Jackson's below-average risk tolerance does not allow a larger allocation to this relatively riskier asset class.

Candidate discussion: Following the process of elimination leaves little discretion in answering this question. The one-time distributions have been made so more than 0 to 5% cash equivalents creates unwarranted cash drag. The conservative risk objective could support even more than 40% fixed income. Selecting less than 30% to 40% is inappropriate. REITs are inappropriate as Jackson already has RE exposure in her home and these are high risk REITs. Jackson's conservative nature also limits the suitability of the higher risk international stocks offered.

QUESTION 3

Source: Study Session 16, LOS 29.g, h, LOS 30.g, h

A. i. The implementation shortfall can be calculated directly for the CMS transactions:

Hypothetical Portfolio Beginning Value: 8,000 shares × $75/share = $600,000

Hypothetical Portfolio Ending Value: 8,000 shares × $79/share = $632,000

Actual Portfolio Beginning Value:
 4,000 shares × $77/share + $1,500 (commissions) = $309,500

Actual Portfolio Ending Value:
 ($600,000 − $309,500) + (4,000 shares × $79/share) = $606,500

Implementation Shortfall:
 Hypothetical Portfolio Ending Value − Actual Portfolio Ending Value
 $632,000 − $606,500 = $25,500

(4 points)

Candidate discussion: Other approaches to calculating the implementation shortfall are also consistent with the CFA Program curriculum. As long as you show and label your work and correctly calculate $25,500, they will be acceptable. You may also show the implementation shortfall in basis points, 425 basis points = $25,500 / $600,000.

Individual components of IS can also be calculated and will sum to the same $25,500:
- Commissions = $1,500.
- Delay = (75.75 − 75.00) × 4,000 = $3,000
- Realized profit/loss = (77.00 − 75.75) × 4,000 = $5,000
- Missed trade = (79.00 − 75.00) × 4,000 = $16,000
- Total IS = $25,500

Be prepared to make the direct calculation as shown in the answer (the short method) or calculate the four individual components (the long method) if directed to do so.

ii. Implementation shortfall (IS) measures the total impact of portfolio performance attributable to implementation costs. This measure compares actual portfolio performance to a hypothetical portfolio based on the value of positions when decisions are reached.

Volume-weighted average price (VWAP) is the average price (weighted for corresponding volume) at which a security trades during any given day. It is used as a benchmark measure for evaluating trading costs.

(2 points)

Two advantages of IS are (only one required for 1 point):

1. It can be used to evaluate the total portfolio effect of transaction implementation.

2. This measure can be used to analyze the different components of implementation costs (perform trading cost attribution analysis).

Two disadvantages of IS are (only one required for 1 point):

1. This measure requires more extensive transaction data to evaluate the trading transactions.

2. It uses a potentially unfamiliar framework to evaluate traders.

Two advantages of VWAP are (only one required for 1 point):

1. This measure is simple to compute and easy to understand.

2. It is useful for evaluating small trades.

Two disadvantages of VWAP are (only one required for 1 point):

1. It can result in gaming by delaying trade placement when market prices do not compare favorably to VWAP.

2. This measure ignores opportunity costs if orders are not filled.

Answer for Question 3-B (9 points total)

Strategy	Briefly describe each of the three asset class rebalancing strategies; Buy-and-Hold, Constant Mix, and Constant-Proportion Portfolio Insurance (CPPI).	Determine under which market conditions (Rising trend, Falling trend, Flat) each strategy would outperform relative to the Buy-and-Hold strategy. (Circle all that apply.)	Identify (circle) the shape of the payoff diagram (Concave, Convex, Linear) for each of the rebalancing strategies.
Buy-and-Hold	A passive strategy that combines risk free assets with risky assets ("do nothing" strategy). (1 point)		Concave Convex (Linear) (1 point)
Constant Mix	Rebalance asset mix to initial weightings when changes in asset values cause drift from initial position (dynamic strategy). (1 point)	Rising Falling (Flat) (1 point)	(Concave) (1 point) Convex Linear
CPPI	A buy high/sell low dynamic trend following strategy. This strategy is conducive to investors with zero risk tolerance if the portfolio falls to a floor and high risk tolerance when cushion is positive. (1 point)	(Rising) (1 point) (Falling) (1 point) Flat	Concave (Convex) (1 point) Linear

QUESTION 4

Source: Study Session 6, LOS 13.c, d

Answer for Question 4-A (9 points total)

IPS Item	Formulate each of the following investment policy statement (IPS) items for HEMI-PP. Justify each response with one reason. Note: Your answer should specifically address HEMI's circumstances.
i. Return requirement	HEMI's return objective is to be fully funded within five years without additional contributions from the plan sponsor. If the plan were fully funded, earning the discount rate would maintain the zero surplus. Because the plan is underfunded, the required return will have to be greater than 5.6 percent. (1 point) FV of PBO in 5 years @ 5.6% = $10,697(1.056)^5 = 14,047$ FV of plan assets in 5 years must match the FV of the PBO: $9,441(1 + r)^5 = 14,047$ Solve for r: $(1 + r)^5 = 14{,}047 / 9{,}441 = 1.488$ $r = (1.488)^{1/5} - 1 = 8.27\%$ (2 points for the correct calculation)
ii. Liquidity requirement	• HEMI-PP's liquidity requirement is low. (1 point) • Adding 8,000 (10 percent) younger employees will reduce the percentage of plan participants currently drawing payouts and reduce current liquidity needs. • The plan will probably not need to make sizable payouts in the near-term given the 17-year average duration of HEMI-PP's liabilities. • Liquidity needs are not expected to increase substantially because early retirement buyouts are not planned. (2 points for any one of the above justifications)
iii. Time Horizon	• HEMI's time horizon should be long. (1 point) • HEMI-PP's liabilities have a 17-year duration. (2 points) First Bullet point: HEMI is a going concern, a profitable company, and an industry leader; thus, the time horizon should be long. Second Bullet point: HEMI has an average active employee age less than the industry average.

Answer for Question 4-B (8 points total)

Risk factor	Determine whether each of the following factors increases or decreases HEMI-PP's ability to take risk. (circle one)	Justify each response with one reason.
i. Risk exposures that are common to both the plan sponsor and stocks in the industrials sector.	Increases ⟨Decreases⟩ (1 point)	HEMI-PP invests 10 percent of the plan's equity assets in industrials. These investments will be highly correlated with HEMI's business. This presents the possibility that HEMI's investments in the industrials sector may decrease dramatically at the same time that its own ability to make contributions has diminished because of the business cycle. (3 points)
ii. Increasing the workforce with younger workers.	⟨Increases⟩ (1 point) Decreases	• Increasing the percentage of younger workers in the active labor force means that the plan's investment time horizon has extended. • This means that there will be a greater lead time before the younger workers can claim their benefits, and more of an overall cushion if plan returns fail to materialize as planned. (3 points for one correct justification)

Answer for Question 4-C (9 points total)

Risk factor	Determine whether HEMI-PP has a below-average, average, or above-average ability to assume risk relative to the average firm in the industry for each of the following factors. (circle one)	Justify each response with one reason.
i. HEMI's financial condition	Below-average Average ~~Above-average~~ (1 point)	HEMI has above average ROE and below average D/E and will be in a position to contribute additional amounts to HEMI-PP, should the plan fail to meet its expected return requirements. This gives HEMI-PP an increased ability to assume risk relative to other plans in the industry. (2 points)
ii. Workforce age	Below-average Average ~~Above-average~~ (1 point)	HEMI's workforce is younger than average for the industry. This increases the plan's ability to assume risk relative to other plans in the industry because its required cash flows will come later, giving the plan a longer-than-average time horizon. (2 points)
iii. Retired employees	Below-average Average ~~Above-average~~ (1 point)	HEMI has a higher percentage of active employees and a lower percentage of retired employees than average for the construction industry. This was probably aided by the recent hiring of 8,000 younger workers. This increases the plan's ability to assume risk relative to other plans in the industry because of the longer time horizon and lower liquidity constraints. (2 points)

QUESTION 5

Source: Study Session 8, LOS 17.r

Answer for Question 5-A (6 points total)

A.   Select E
- Shortfall risk is $8.6 - 2(8.4) = -8.2\%$ and better than the required -8.3%.
- It meets the requirement to underweight U.S. equity industrials with a 5% weight versus 10% in the S&P 500.
- It has a sufficient cash allocation to meet the proposed lump sum payouts of $2,500 \times \$300,000 = \$750,000,000$. This is 750M / 14.2B = 5.3%.

Candidate discussion: Following the process of elimination, only portfolio E is acceptable. Selecting any other portfolio scores 0 of 6 points. 2 points for selecting E and 2 points each for two reasons. Giving a reason to exclude each of the other portfolios could usually also count as one reason to select E. That will not work in this question because it is required for the next question.

Answer for Question 5-B (4 points total)

B.

A: Insufficient cash for the 750 million payout, or 20% allocation to industrials exceeds <10% maximum constraint.

B: 15% allocation to industrials is too high, or shortfall risk of $9.2 - 2(8.8) = -8.4$ exceeds the max of -8.3% specified.

C: 10% allocation to industrials is not less than 10%.

D: Cash is below the 750 million, or shortfall of $8 - 2(8.2) = -8.4\%$ is too high.

Candidate discussion: 1 point each for a reason to exclude each of the other 4 portfolios. Again, follow directions and do not refer to return. If you say E is unacceptable, that is wrong, but you could still get 3 points if you correctly explain why the other three are excluded.

QUESTION 6

Source: Study Session 4, LOS 9.a, b, c

A.

Income Bracket	×Tax Rate	= Tax Owed
First $30,000	0.00	$0
Next $30,000	0.15	$4,500
Next $40,000	0.25	$10,000
Last $75,000	0.35	$26,250
Total $175,000		$40,750

Average tax rate is:

$$t_{ave} = \frac{\text{Tax Liability}}{\text{Wage Income}} = \frac{\$40,750}{\$175,000} = 0.23 = 23\%$$

Candidate discussion: 2 points to set up the calculation and 1 point for a correct result.

B.   First, compute annualized return after realized taxes (r^*):

$$r^* = 8.0[1 - 0.3(0.25) - 0.0833(0.15) - 0.2(0.25)] = 0.069 = 6.9\%$$

Second, compute the effective long-term capital gains tax rate (T^*):

$$T^* = t_{LTG}\left(\frac{\text{Proportionate Long-term Gain}}{1 - p_i t_i - p_d t_d - p_g t_g}\right)$$

$$= 0.20\left(\frac{0.4167}{1 - 0.3(0.25) - 0.0833(0.15) - 0.2(0.25)}\right)$$

$$= 0.20\left(\frac{0.4167}{0.8625}\right) = 0.0966 = 9.66\%$$

Third, compute the future value of the portfolio, where B is the cost basis as a percent of current market value:

$$V_n = V_0\left[(1 + r^*)^n(1 - T^*) + T^* - (1 - B)t_{LTG}\right]$$

$$= 750,000[(1 + 0.069)^5(1 - 0.0966) + 0.0966 - (1 - 1.0)0.20]$$

$$= 750,000(1.35776) = 1,018,316.57$$

Candidate discussion: 1 point each for 1) setting up to calculate r^*, 2) 6.9%, 3) setting up to calculate T^*, 4) 9.66%, and 5) 1,018,317. 2 points for setting up to calculate V_n.

C.   When there are limits on contributions to tax deferred accounts, the most heavily taxed items should go to the tax deferred accounts and more lightly taxed to taxable accounts. Stock should go to the taxable account because dividend tax rates at 15% are lower than interest tax rates at 25%, and by extending the holding periods the effective tax rates on stock can be further reduced.

     Candidate discussion: 2 points for using the taxable account and 2 points for the explanation. The explanation must reference the specific and relevant case facts to get full credit.

D.   Because tax rates are expected to be higher in the future, the contributions should be made with after-tax dollars to the TEA now in order to avoid higher tax rates on withdrawals in the future.

     Candidate discussion: 1 point for TEA and 2 points for discussing the implications of the tax rate change.

QUESTION 7

Source: Study Session 4, LOS 9.d, g

A. i.

Ruby can gift GBP15,000 to each child now without paying any gift tax and also removing the funds from the future taxable estate. Each child can invest and earn 5.5% pre-tax which must be adjusted down for 25% taxes each year. For both children the FV of the gifts are:

$$2 \times \{GBP15,000 \ [1 + 0.055(1 - .25)]^{25}\} = GBP82,413.17$$

A. ii.

$$\text{relative value of taxfree gift} = \frac{FV_{gift}}{FV_{bequest}} = \frac{[1 + r_g(1 - t_{ig})]^n}{[1 + r_e(1 - t_{ie})]^n(1 - T_e)}$$

$$= \frac{[1 + 0.055(1 - 0.25)]^{25}}{[1 + 0.055(1 - 0.45)]^{25}(1 - 0.60)}$$

$$= \frac{2.747106}{2.106520(0.40)} = \frac{2.747106}{0.842608} = 3.26$$

The 3.26 implies that the relative value of gifting to Ruby's children is much higher than waiting 25 years to transfer the assets in a bequest. In addition to the benefits listed above, the gifted assets compound over the 25 year time horizon.

Candidate discussion:
*   The results are on an inflation-adjusted basis, as only real rates of return were given in the vignette.
*   Both parts of the question specify gifting that will qualify for the tax-free exclusion. That means the amount per child in A.i is $15,000, and no gift tax rate is used in A.ii.
*   A.i: 2 points for showing the calculation, 1 point for correct final number.
*   A.ii: 1 point each for correct numerator, denominator, and final answer.

B.   Use the discretionary trust.

Albert is irresponsible with money; the discretionary trust allows the trustee to decide when, how much, and for what purpose to give Albert money.

or

A discretionary trust may provide better protection from Albert's creditors as the trustee decides what to distribute to Albert.

Candidate discussion: 1 point for discretionary and 2 points for one reason.

QUESTION 8

Source: Study Session 10, LOS 20.b, l

Answer for Question 8-A (6 points total)

Statement	Determine whether you agree or disagree with each of Porto's statements. (circle one)	Justify your determination with one reason for each statement. Note: You may not use the same justification for both statements
1. "Tuscany hit their mark right on the money."	Agree (Disagree) (1 point)	A bond-indexing strategy will closely reflect the index performance less fees. Tuscany's return being higher than the index indicates they are not indexed. (2 points)
2. "Perhaps we should overweight Feliciano Fund in the fixed income portion of the pension fund because of its higher return."	Agree (Disagree) (1 point)	• One quarter of performance is an insufficient amount of time to draw performance conclusions. • Overweighting the Feliciano Fund in this strategy may improve overall performance, but could subject the pension fund to significantly more risk than expected. • Because the fund is not tied exclusively to high- yield bonds, overweighting the Feliciano Fund in the fixed-income portion of the pension fund may cause overlap with other fixed-income bond funds used by the plan. (2 points for any one justification)

Answer for Question 8-B (9 points total)

Statement	Determine whether you agree or disagree with each of Foppiano's statements (circle one)	Justify your determination with one reason for each statement.
1. "I am considering a cashflow matching strategy given the flexibility it provides for selecting bonds for the portfolio and because it minimizes trading costs."	Agree **(Disagree)** (1 point)	Cash-flow matching limits asset selection to only those with cash flows matching liability dates. It is the least flexible in bond selection. (2 points)
2. "On the other hand, the upside to contingent immunization is that it allows me to manage the bond portfolio actively without immunization unless the safety margin falls to zero."	**(Agree)** (1 point) Disagree	Contingent immunization requires an initial overfunding of the portolio to create a positive dollar safety margin (DSM). As long as this DSM is positive, active management is allowed. (2 points)
3. "Given the expected lump sum retirement payout in the next 24–30 months, the cash-flow matching strategy is clearly better for the pension plan because of the certainty of the company's pension obligations."	Agree **(Disagree)** (1 point)	Cash-flow matching generally locks in the lowest return. The majority of the pension plan funding requirements are unknown. These other payouts are less certain and cannot be addressed by cash flow matching. (2 points)

QUESTION 9

Source: Study Session 18, LOS 32.d, e, o

Answer for Question 9 (15 points total)

Statement	Determine whether each of the seven statements, considered independently, meets the requirements of GIPS. (circle one)	Recommend, for each statement not in compliance with GIPS, the appropriate change that must be made to bring Alcor into compliance with GIPS requirements.
1. We will use a total return calculation methodology that will include realized and unrealized gains, income, returns from cash and cash equivalents, and deductions for estimated and actual trading expenses.	Yes ⟨No⟩ (1 point)	Total return calculation must be based on actual incurred trading expenses, not estimated. (2 points)
2. We will disclose the minimum asset level for inclusion of a portfolio, but will only make available upon request any calculation methodology changes which result in material performance impacts.	Yes ⟨No⟩ (1 point)	The material changes in calculation must be disclosed. (2 points) **Candidate discussion:** This is a tricky question because GIPS states disclosure of calculation methodology changes are recommended, not required. However, that statement is in the context of the evolution of calculations required by GIPS over the years. The fact that material changes are not being disclosed is something completely different. Material changes would have to be disclosed. Failing to do so is a violation of the Standards of Professional Conduct and GIPS. The Standards of Professional Conduct. . . for example: Standard I(C): Misrepresentation Covered persons have an ethical obligation not to misstate facts or present information in a way that might mislead investors. Investment professionals violate the Standard when they know, or should know, that the presentation was biased or misleading. By violating the Standards, GIPS are also violated.

Question	Answer	Explanation
3. We will disclose the dispersion measure used in our performance presentations and report performance results gross of fees.	**Yes** (1 point) / No	
4. We will have our real estate investments valued every three months (and by a licensed appraiser every year).	**Yes** (1 point) / No	**Candidate discussion:** Current requirements are for RE valuation at the end of each quarter and for external valuation (a licensed appraiser) every 12 months (unless the client agrees to less frequent external valuation, in which case 36 months is the maximum). The statement is consistent with these requirements.
5. We will include all actual fee-paying portfolios (both discretionary and nondiscretionary) and all nonfee-paying discretionary portfolios in at least one composite.	Yes / **No** (1 point)	The firm must not include non-discretionary accounts in a composite. (2 points)
6. We will (based on our discretion) create a single asset portfolio out of a multiple asset class portfolio by allocating cash return to the carve-out portfolio in a consistent and timely manner.	Yes / **No** (1 point)	Alcor must set up separate accounts or sub accounts for each carve-out and hold the cash in each appropriate carve-out segment. (2 points) **Candidate discussion:** "Allocating" cash return was permitted prior to January 1, 2010. Carve outs are optional if the manager wishes to report carve out performance in addtition to total portfolio return.

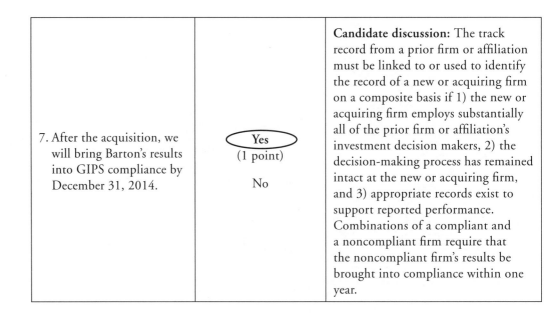

| 7. After the acquisition, we will bring Barton's results into GIPS compliance by December 31, 2014. | Yes (1 point) No | **Candidate discussion:** The track record from a prior firm or affiliation must be linked to or used to identify the record of a new or acquiring firm on a composite basis if 1) the new or acquiring firm employs substantially all of the prior firm or affiliation's investment decision makers, 2) the decision-making process has remained intact at the new or acquiring firm, and 3) appropriate records exist to support reported performance. Combinations of a compliant and a noncompliant firm require that the noncompliant firm's results be brought into compliance within one year. |

QUESTION 10

Source: Study Session 7, LOS 15.c
Study Session 8, LOS 17.b

A. $$E(R_d) = \frac{D}{P} - \Delta S + i + g + \Delta P / E$$

= 1.25% − (−1.5%) + 2.5% + 3.5% + 4.0% = 12.75%

(1 point)

The formula is a variation on the concept that estimated return is yield plus growth:

Dividend yield of 1.25% provides direct cash flow return to shareholders. (1 point)

Share repurchase is another way for companies to return cash to shareholders –(−1.5%) indicates additional return to shareholders. (1 point)

Inflation of 2.5% is one component of nominal growth. (1 point)

Real earnings growth of 3.5% is the other component of nominal growth. (1 point)

Repricing of 4% indicates the initial P/E is too low, and, as it rises, it will add to investor return. (1 point)

B.   Strategic asset allocation creates the portfolio's general asset (allocation) mix under "normal" conditions. To determine a strategic asset allocation, expected capital market conditions and investors' objectives and constraints, are analyzed over a long-term time horizon.

(2 points)

Tactical asset allocation exploits a perceived capital market opportunity by temporarily deviating from a portfolio's long-term strategic allocation. The analysis of short-term capital market forecasts is more critical for implementing a tactical asset allocation strategy.

(2 points)

C.   Price is SAA. The model output is only as good as the estimates used as inputs.

Adrienne is TAA. Time series are subject to all of the assumptions of linear regression. If those are violated, the analysis may be invalid.

Candidate discussion: One point each for the four required items. This question synthesizes much of what you know about capital market inputs, SAA, and TAA.
- Price's approach relies on long-term economic relationships and expectations for those relationships. His approach ignores short-term capital market conditions and focuses on an investment time horizon long enough for transitory conditions to smooth out into long-term trends. Price's methodology is best suited to establishing CIA's *strategic* asset allocation.
- Adrienne's approach uses autoregressive time series models that base future estimates for a variable on the variable's prior value (called a lagged variable). These models

usually provide better short-term than long-term forecasts because they fail to consider changes in underlying structural relationships. Such forecasts become less useful when short-term relationships change. These models are better suited to *tactical* asset allocation decisions.

QUESTION 11

Source: Study Session 9, LOS 18.f, g
Study Session 15, LOS 27.e

A.   Any of the three strategies can be recommended.

Hedging with futures contracts:

Because the mutual fund manager is only interested in hedging translation risk, the optimal hedge ratio is 1.0. The potential for the euro to depreciate against the dollar is the risk that must be hedged. Therefore, the number of euro contracts to short (sell) is equal to:

$$\frac{\text{Exposure to be hedged}}{\text{Contract size}} = \frac{1,000,000,000}{125,000} = 8,000$$

or

Insuring with options:

Insuring with options takes advantage of the asymmetrical payout patterns of puts and calls. These contracts offer downside protection, while retaining upside potential. The risk the fund is facing is that the euro will depreciate against the dollar. To initiate this hedge, the manager should *buy* the following number of *puts* on the euro.

$$\frac{\text{Exposure to be hedged}}{\text{Contract size}} = \frac{1,000,000,000}{125,000} = 8,000$$

or

Delta hedging with options:

Delta hedging recognizes that the relationship between the option value and the underlying exchange rate does not move in lockstep before expiration. The goal of delta hedging is to continually eliminate the risk exposure by constantly adjusting the options position in response to changes in the relationship between the option value and the exchange rate. To initiate the hedge, the manager could *buy* the following number of

$1.30/€ *put* contracts:

$$N = \frac{\text{Exposure to be hedged}}{(\text{Option delta} \times \text{Contract size})} = \frac{1,000,000,000}{0.5 \times 125,000} = 16,000$$

Candidate discussion: Option delta (from Exhibit 3) is required to calculate delta hedging, therefore you must select one of the options to answer the question. Normally the most liquid option would be used and that is most likely the at-the-money option with a strike price of $1.30/€, which matches the current spot exchange rate. Because the question was not specific, selecting one of the other strikes would be acceptable as long as the correct delta is used in the calculations and state what you are using.

(4 points total)

Answer for Question 11-B (6 points total)

Recommended strategy (choose only one)	Justification
Hedging with futures	• Currency futures contracts typically offer greater liquidity than options. • Futures contracts cost nothing to enter versus paying option premiums for other strategies. • Futures hedges do not require frequent adjusting. (2 points for any one reason)
Insuring with options	Offers upside gain while hedging downside losses. (2 points)
Delta hedging with options	• Offers the opportunity to capture upside gains, if they occur. • Will more closely hedge the exposure than the option insurance strategy. (2 points for any one reason)

Strategies not recommended (choose only two)	Explanation
Hedging with futures	• Forgoes any potential appreciation in hedged currency. • More distant contracts increase basis risk. • More distant contracts are less liquid. (2 points for any one reason)
Insuring with options	• Requires initial outlay of option premium. • Option premium creates an imperfect hedge. (2 points for any one reason)
Delta hedging with options	• Requires constant rebalancing to maintain hedge. • Transaction costs can be expensive because of frequent rebalancing. (2 points for any one reason)

PRACTICE EXAM 2
AFTERNOON SESSION ANSWERS

To get detailed answer explanations with references to specific LOS and SchweserNotes[TM] content, and to get valuable feedback on how your score compares to those of other Level III candidates, use your Username and Password to gain Online Access at schweser.com and choose the left-hand menu item "Practice Exams Vol. 1."

1.	B	21.	C	41.	B
2.	B	22.	B	42.	B
3.	C	23.	A	43.	B
4.	B	24.	A	44.	C
5.	C	25.	C	45.	A
6.	B	26.	C	46.	B
7.	C	27.	B	47.	B
8.	C	28.	B	48.	C
9.	B	29.	A	49.	C
10.	C	30.	C	50.	C
11.	C	31.	A	51.	B
12.	A	32.	B	52.	A
13.	A	33.	C	53.	C
14.	A	34.	C	54.	B
15.	B	35.	B	55.	A
16.	C	36.	B	56.	C
17.	C	37.	B	57.	C
18.	C	38.	C	58.	A
19.	A	39.	A	59.	B
20.	A	40.	A	60.	C

PRACTICE EXAM 2
AFTERNOON SESSION ANSWERS

QUESTIONS 1–6

Source: Study Session 1

1. **B** Information found on a website (even in error) is deemed to be "public." If Brigand maintains records and has made reasonable and diligent efforts to avoid misrepresentations then he may use the data that he found. (Study Session 1, LOS 2.a)

    However, he is in breach of Standard V(A): Investment Analysis, Recommendations, and Actions – Diligence and Reasonable Basis since he created a regression model from just six monthly data points. It is implausible to assume that such a small quantity of data could lead to meaningful results. (Study Session 1, LOS 2.a)

2. **B** Standard III(A): Duties to Clients – Loyalty, Prudence, and Care permits the use of client commissions to pay for research used in the management of client accounts. The process of "paying up" in order to obtain soft dollars that benefit the manager and not the client is in breach of the standard but research for the benefit of clients is permitted. This practice is also in compliance with CFA Institute's Soft Dollar Standards, which are not compulsory. (Study Session 1, LOS 2.a)

3. **C** Brigand has breached all three quoted Standards.

    Standard I(B): Professionalism – Independence and Objectivity: In placing compensating trades, Brigand may be perceived as putting his needs ahead of those of his clients.

    Standard III(A): Duties to Clients – Loyalty, Prudence, and Care: Brigand is effectively transferring client assets to Scarpers in the form of higher commissions, which is a clear violation of the Standard.

    Standard III(B): Duties to Clients – Fair Dealing: Directing future trades to Scarpers is using client business to cover Brigand's mistake. It would also be likely that other clients' trades will be used to cover the mistake made in the erroneous transaction.
    (Study Session 1, LOS 2.a)

4. **B** Stuart made it clear from the outset that she did not want to invest in derivatives of any kind (including warrants!)—hence Brigand would have breached Standard III(C): Duties to Clients – Suitability by buying the warrants for Stuart's portfolio. Brigand may have breached Standard III(B): Duties to Clients – Fair Dealing regarding some other clients, but in this instance Stuart has been treated fairly. (Study Session 1, LOS 2.a)

5. **C** The CEO has breached a duty of confidentiality, and indeed acted illegally under US law, and Brigand acted correctly in his behavior.

    Brigand does not have an obligation under the standards to expose the CEO's behavior to the CFA Institute (or to the legal authorities). Under Standard I(A) Knowledge of the Law, Bernard should notify legal counsel if he thinks he has witnessed a violation of the law within his own firm or if he has witnessed some other securities related crime. The firm's legal counsel would then determine whether or not legal authorities should be notified. (Study Session 1, LOS 2.a)

6. **B** Although A is also technically correct, it isn't enough in itself—it must also be in the client's interests. Irrespective of the merits of A, B is a better answer—look out for this trick in the CFA Institute's exams, if two answers both seem right, go for the more comprehensive.

    Answer C is a red herring—it is perfectly acceptable to determine a standing policy towards voting, however it must be a clause the client can reasonably be expected to have seen. (Study Session 1, LOS 2.a)

QUESTIONS 7–12

Source: Study Session 1

7. C   Standard II(B) Market Manipulation. Transaction 1 is simply an attempt to exploit a market mispricing through a legitimate arbitrage strategy. Transaction 1 does not violate Standard II(B). (Study Session 1, LOS 2.a)

8. C   Standard II(A) Material Nonpublic Information. Stirr violated Standard II(A) by using material nonpublic information in his decision to take a short forward position on the ONB Corporation bonds (Transaction 2). Stirr would have known about any publicly announced plans by ONB to offer more debt since the company's bonds were already a holding in the Fixed Income Fund at the time of the forward transaction. Stirr obviously knew that the unannounced bond offering by ONB would affect the price of the firm's existing bonds since he acted on the information shortly after overhearing the conversation between the investment bankers. Standard II(A) prohibits such trades. It does not matter that the trade utilized a derivative security rather than the actual underlying security or that the trade prevented losses for his investors. Stirr should have waited for the information to become public before making any trades on ONB securities. Transaction 3 is not in violation of the Standards. Transaction 3 reflects a trading advantage that Stirr has discovered. He is not using material nonpublic information to complete the trade. Rather, he is simply processing news and information faster than other market participants to make profitable trades. Transaction 3 also is not intended to manipulate market prices or information and is therefore a legitimate trade. (Study Session 1, LOS 2.a)

9. B   Standard IV(B) Additional Compensation Arrangements. According to the Standard, Chang must obtain written consent from all parties involved before agreeing to accept additional compensation that could be reasonably expected to create a conflict of interest with his employer. Chang's arrangement with Cherry Creek involves providing investment advice in exchange for additional shares to be added to his account with Cherry Creek. Such compensation could affect Chang's loyalty to WMG or affect his independence and objectivity. Therefore, Chang must obtain written consent from WMG before accepting the arrangement with Cherry Creek. (Study Session 1, LOS 2.a)

10. C   Standard VI(C) Referral Fees. According to the Standard, Stirr must disclose referral arrangements to his employer, clients, and prospective clients before entering into an agreement to provide services. Stirr's agreement with Cherry Creek constitutes a referral relationship whereby he has agreed to provide professional investment advice in exchange for referrals of Cherry Creek customers seeking traditional asset management services. Stirr's employer, clients, and prospects must be informed of this arrangement so that any partiality in the recommendation and the true cost of the services being provided by Stirr can be assessed. (Study Session 1, LOS 2.a)

11. C   Standard V(B) Communication with Clients and Prospective Clients. Standard V(B) requires members to disclose the basic format of the investment processes used to analyze and select securities, the processes used to construct portfolios, and any changes to these processes. In addition, members are required to use reasonable judgment in selecting the factors relevant to their investment analysis or actions when communicating with their clients and prospects. Chang's first statement is correct; all of the items mentioned must be disclosed in the newsletter. His second statement is incorrect. Chang is not required to disclose every detail of every factor used to make decisions for the last quarter. It is possible that such disclosure may be appropriate, but there is no blanket requirement to include every piece of information in a report to clients and prospects. (Study Session 1, LOS 2.a)

12. **A** Standard V(B) Communication with Clients and Prospective Clients. In addition to the requirements of Standard V(B) listed in the previous answer, members are required to clearly distinguish between fact and opinion in the presentation of investment analysis and recommendations. Stirr is correct in his first statement that the newsletter must indicate that projections are not factual, but based on the opinion of the report's author. Stirr is also correct in stating that an abbreviated report may be used to communicate with clients as long as a full report providing more detailed information is maintained and made available to any clients or prospects requesting additional information. Best practice would be to note in the abbreviated report that more information is available upon request. (Study Session 1, LOS 2.a)

QUESTIONS 13–18

Source: Study Session 16

13. **A** Comment 1 is correct. The success of a calendar rebalancing strategy will depend in large part on whether the rebalancing frequency is appropriate to the volatility of the component asset classes. If volatility is high (or rebalancing infrequent), the asset mix can drift to the point where rebalancing could create a market impact, thus increasing the cost of rebalancing dramatically. If volatility is low (or rebalancing too frequent), the portfolio could incur numerous costly small trades to achieve minor adjustments in the asset mix.

    Comment 2 is incorrect. Annual rebalancing is most likely too infrequent. The asset mix may well drift far enough over a year's time to necessitate large trades to rebalance. These trades would increase market impact. Market impact will be lower with more frequent rebalancing. (Study Session 16, LOS 30.e)

14. **A** A higher risk tolerance for tracking error provides more flexibility for the asset allocation relative to the target mix, and therefore a wider rebalancing corridor. If the volatility of other asset classes is high, then large differences from the target asset mix are more likely. Lower volatility reduces the likelihood of large differences, and allows for a wider corridor. (Study Session 16, LOS 30.f)

15. **B** Factors indicating a narrower corridor width are low transaction costs, low correlation with the rest of the portfolio, and high volatility. Emerging market stocks have the lowest correlation with the rest of the portfolio, as well as the highest standard deviation. Their transaction costs are only slightly higher than U.S. small cap stocks. The narrow corridor means that small changes in value may necessitate rebalancing. The low correlation and high volatility increase the likelihood of increasing divergence from the target asset mix. The low transaction costs reduce the cost of rebalancing back to the target mix. (Study Session 16, LOS 30.f)

16. **C** The constant mix strategy will be optimal for Client C, an investor whose absolute risk tolerance varies proportionately with wealth, and who expects a choppy stock market with frequent reversals. Client A has a floor value which limits his willingness to take risk if his portfolio declines below that value. Further, Client A appears to have a risk tolerance that varies by more than any change in his wealth (his multiplier is greater than 1). Client B has risk tolerance that varies proportionately with her wealth, as evidenced by the fact that she wants to hold stocks regardless of her wealth level. However, Client B expects a trending market with few reversals, in which a constant mix strategy would perform poorly. (Study Session 16, LOS 30.h, j)

17. **C** A buy and hold strategy has a linear payoff curve. The constant mix strategy is a concave strategy that supplies liquidity to the market, in effect "selling insurance" by taking the less popular side of trades when the market is trending up or down. A buy and hold strategy would not be an appropriate strategy for Client C, whose risk tolerance varies in proportion to her wealth, and who expects a volatile stock market. (Study Session 16, LOS 30.i)

18. **C** The constant mix strategy has a concave payoff curve and a multiplier between 0 and 1. The return on the portfolio using this strategy will increase at a declining rate when stocks go up, and decrease at an increasing rate when stocks go down. The constant proportion strategy has a convex payoff curve and a multiplier greater than 1. The return on a constant proportion portfolio will increase at an increasing rate when stocks go up, and decrease at a declining rate when stocks go down. (Study Session 16, LOS 30.i)

QUESTIONS 19–24

Source: Study Session 12

19. **A** Highwings is using a multi-manager, core-satellite approach. This is evident from its approach whereby half of the portfolio is being indexed and the remaining half is being divided equally between two additional managers. These two additional managers will hopefully be able to generate positive active returns relative to their respective benchmark indexes. A completeness fund is a sub-portfolio of stocks added to align the overall equity portfolio more closely with the benchmark while simultaneously retaining the potential alpha-generating capacity of the active managers. With alpha and beta separation, the core and overall market exposure (beta) is obtained with lower cost index-type portfolios and active management is then used to add value (alpha). Had Highwings specifically referenced using the Russell 1000 for beta and then the other managers for value added, then alpha and beta separation would be the best choice. (Study Session 12, LOS 23.r)

20. **A** The active returns, tracking risk, and information ratios of Eagle, Hawk, and Osprey are:

	Eagle	Hawk	Osprey
Active return	2.2%	1.7%	2.4%
Tracking risk	4.2%	2.0%	5.7%
Information ratio (Mean active return/ Mean active risk)	0.52 (2.2%/4.2%)	0.85 (1.7%/2.0%)	0.42 (2.4%/5.7%)

Eagle's 2.2% active return and 4.2% tracking risk and Osprey's 2.4% active return and 5.7% tracking risk indicate that neither are indexing but both are engaging in active management. In contrast, Hawk has lower active return and much lower tracking risk, which would indicate that Hawk is most likely an enhanced indexer (eliminating it as an answer choice). Because Eagle has a higher information ratio than Osprey, it is considered the best active manager. (Study Session 12, LOS 23.b)

21. **C** Statement 1 is inaccurate. The benchmarks used in returns-based style analysis must be mutually exclusive. Adding the Russell 1000 Index would violate this rule, as the Russell 1000 Index is a large-cap index that includes both growth and value stocks. The analysis already includes a large-cap growth index (S&P/Citigroup 500 Growth Index) and a large-cap value index (S&P/Citigroup 500 Value Index). Statement 2 is also inaccurate because it is overstating what a return-based analysis can identify. The analysis does not focus on or reveal the actual underlying stocks owned or asset classes held. The purpose of returns-based style analysis is to describe the past returns of portfolios relative to passive benchmarks, which involves fitting a regression to numbers (the different benchmarks). If a manager's return series looks like that of a particular asset class, even if it was actually generated by a different asset class, then the process allocates a factor weight accordingly. As a result, it is possible that Osprey, Eagle, and Hawk hold fewer mid-cap stocks and T-bills than stated in the analysis. Further investigation by the Committee, possibly including a holdings-based analysis, is necessary to determine whether these managers stray significantly from the large-capitalization investment mandate. (Study Session 12, LOS 23.i)

22. **B** The R-squared in Exhibit A indicates that 94.30% of the variation in returns of Osprey can be explained by the S&P/Citigroup 500 Growth Index. The high R-squared also indicates simply owning that index could have passively replicated the past return data. However, that by itself does not indicate it is the best normal benchmark for Osprey. The data in Exhibit B regressed the past return data versus seven indices (including the S&P/Citigroup 500 Growth Index) and found the best replication is a blend of four indices. Therefore, this blend of four must have a higher R-squared and be a better normal benchmark. If one index alone had been better, that would have been the result of the regression in Exhibit B. The regression of return data does not consider the actual holdings in the portfolio and cannot determine if the portfolio actually held cash equivalents or the actual weighting on average or at any moment in time in cash equivalents. (Study Session 12, LOS 23.i)

23. **A** Hawk purports to be a large-cap value manager as indicated by its stated index benchmark, the S&P 500/Citigroup 500 Value Index. However, it appears unlikely that Hawk is a pure large-cap value manager given the large weightings to mid-cap (both growth and value) stocks. Hawk appears to be exhibiting style drift. The regression's style fit (R^2) measure provides no information as to the approach used to achieve the active returns, such as market timing. The R^2 indicates the percentage of the variation in the manager's returns that is explained by the analysis. Given the regression's large weightings to mid-cap (both growth and value) stocks, it is unlikely that the S&P 500 Value Index is the most appropriate index benchmark for Hawk. (Study Session 12, LOS 23.k)

24. **A** An important property of a valid benchmark used for manager evaluation is that the manager be aware in advance of that benchmark. Without this information, any value added by the manager versus that benchmark would be pure random luck. The managers must be informed of their respective style benchmarks but have no need to know what overall benchmark is used by Highwings. The overall benchmark determines misfit active return and risk added by Highwings's decisions (not manager decisions). The overall benchmark does not affect determination of manager value added. (Study Session 9, LOS 19.a, b, c and Study Session 12, LOS 23.s)

QUESTIONS 25–30

Source: Study Sessions 10

25. **C** Interest rate risk is generally the most important risk in a fixed-income portfolio and that is the case here. For a defined benefit plan, the most relevant duration factor is to compare asset to liability duration (i.e., liability framework risk). Credit risk and income (cash flow risk) would be only subsidiary considerations. (Study Session 10, LOS 20.c)

26. **C** For a pension plan, the most important issue is generally the duration and other characteristics of the liabilities. Strategic asset allocation (SAA) should focus on an asset benchmark that most closely replicates the liabilities (asset-liability matching). Both benchmarks 3 and 4 match the liability duration. Tactical asset allocation (TAA) focuses on deviating away from the SAA to exploit perceived shorter term opportunities. With the trustees and Kompella expecting interest rates to rise and credit spreads to fall, Benchmark 2 with shorter duration and more corporate credit exposure best reflects these short-term views. (Study Session 10, LOS 20.c)

27. **B** The coupon interest on the bond is $90 per year or $45 per semiannual period. The facts assume that coupons received can be reinvested at 8% annually during the two-year investment horizon. The future value of an annuity of $45 per period for four periods at an assumed reinvestment rate of 4% per period is:

n = 4; i = 4; PMT = 45; solve for FV = $191.09

At the investment horizon (in two years), the bond is expected to be a 5-year, 9% coupon bond, priced to yield 10% (5% per period). The price of the bond at the investment horizon is, therefore, expected to be $961.39. This future bond price and the expected return are calculated as follows:

n = 10; i = 5; PMT = 45; FV = 1,000; solve for PV = –961.39

Total future value = $191.09 + $961.39 = $1,152.48

Using financial calculator, solve for semiannual return:

n = 4; FV = 1,152.48; PV = –1,000; PMT = 0; solve for i = 3.61

Annualized total return = 2 × 3.61% = 7.22%. (Study Session 10, LOS 20.f)

28. **B** To maintain the portfolio dollar duration at the initial level, all portfolio positions must be rebalanced by the ratio of original dollar duration to new dollar duration:

$$\frac{\text{rebalancing}}{\text{ratio}} = \frac{\text{original dollar duration}}{\text{new dollar duration}} = \frac{\$4.5 \text{ million}}{\$4.7 \text{ million}} = 0.9574$$

Subtracting 1 from 0.9574 provides the percentage change for each portfolio position required to restore dollar duration to $4.5 million:

0.9574 – 1 = –0.0426 or decrease 4.26%.

Because dollar duration has risen as the result of a 100 bp decrease in the interest rate environment, Kompella has to decrease the position size to restore the portfolio's dollar duration. (Study Session 10, LOS 20.h)

29. **A** To fund payouts on multiple dates using coupon bearing bonds, the longest payout must be matched first and then work back to earlier payout dates.

    Step 1, buy a sufficient amount of three-year eurobonds to fund the last liability from the principal and last coupon the three-year bond will pay. The three-year bond pays an annual coupon of 6%, so each $1 of par will pay $1.06 in three years. To pay $8,000,000: 8,000,000 / 1.06 = 7,547,170 is the par to purchase. At a price of par, this will cost $7,547,170.

    Step 2, the three year-bond will make a coupon payment of 7,547,170 (0.06) = 452,830 in two years, which will be applied to the $5,000,000 required in two years. This leaves 5,000,000 − 452,830 = $4,547,170 to be covered by principal and coupon from the two-year bond.

    The two-year bond also pays an annual coupon of 6%, so each $1 of par will pay $1.06 in two years. To pay $4,547,170: 4,547,170 / 1.06 = 4,289,783 is the par to purchase. At a price of par, this will cost $4,289,783.

    Step 3, no other steps are required to answer the question. The amount of one-year bond to purchase is not relevant but could be found by extending the same process. The three- and two-year bonds will make coupon payments of $452,830 and $257,387, respectively. This leaves $5,289,783 of the $6,000,000 required to be funded by principal and coupon payment on the one-year bond. The principal and coupon per $1 par is 1.06 for the one-year bond and par is also the price, for a par amount and cost in the one-year bond of $5,289,783 / 1.06 = $4,990,361. (Study Session 10, LOS 20.n)

30. **C** Return maximization allows a trade-off between risk and return such that immunization risk measures can be relaxed if the additional return warrants additional risk. The strategy then maximizes a lower bound on portfolio return. The lower bound is determined as the lower confidence interval limit on the expected return required to immunize the portfolio. A return-maximized immunized portfolio is at risk of ceasing to be immunized when the yield curve changes shape. This is especially true if the yield curve change is large. Thus, this is not a primary difference between the two methods. It is important to remember that while a return-maximized immunized portfolio does maintain immunization in the classical sense, it trades off some risk of not remaining fully immunized in exchange for additional return. Duration matching is commonly done in minimizing immunization risk and maximizing return subject to immunization constraints. Thus, this too is not a primary difference between the two methods. (Study Session 10, LOS 20.m)

QUESTIONS 31–36

Source: Study Session 11

31. **A** The additional portfolio return equals the leveraged portfolio return less the unleveraged portfolio return of 5.75%. The leveraged return is:

$$Rp = \frac{(\text{return on borrowed funds } + \text{ return on equity funds})}{\text{equity}} = \frac{B(R_i - c) + E(R_i)}{E}$$

$$= \frac{\$32(0.0575 - 0.0550) + \$64(0.0575)}{\$64} = 5.875\%$$

where: B = the amount leverage
R_i = return on invested assets
c = cost of borrowed funds
E = amount of equity invested

or $R_p = R_i + [(B / E) \times (R_i - C)]$

= 0.0575 + [(32 / 64) × (0.0575 − 0.055)] = 5.875%

The incremental return is 0.125% (5.875% − 5.750%). (Study Session 11, LOS 22.a)

32. **B** Having no provision for physical delivery of the Treasury, security collateral would result in the highest repo rate of the choices listed. Borrowers receive a lower rate when lenders have greater control over the collateral. The other two answer choices would result in a lower, not higher, repo rate. If the buyer/lender wanted the securities for a short sale, they would charge a lower rate. If interest rates fall, repo rates generally follow suit and fall. (Study Session 11, LOS 22.b)

33. **C** Each of the derivatives provides some form of credit protection to meet Bowers's credit exposure reduction needs. However, only the credit spread forward meets his desire to not expend any capital at initiation or during its life. The credit default option would require Bowers to pay a premium to buy the option. For protection, the credit default swap would require Bowers to make a one-time up-front payment or make periodic payouts. (Study Session 11, LOS 22.g)

34. **C** Bowers should sell futures contracts to reduce portfolio duration, as evidenced by the negative sign on the calculation for the number of contracts required for the hedge:

$$\# \text{ of contracts} = \frac{(D_T - D_0)P_0}{D_{CTD}P_{CTD}} \times CF_{CTD}$$

$$= \frac{(4.0 - 7.0)67,500,000}{6.5 \times 100,000} \times 1.09 = -339.58 \cong -340$$

(Study Session 11, LOS 22.e)

35. **B** Given the foreign bond's duration of 3.8, the percentage change in value should be:

$$\%\Delta V_F = -D \times \beta \Delta y_D = -3.8 \times 0.36(0.0075) = -0.01026 \cong -1.03\%$$

Converted to basis points, the −1.03% is closest to −100 bps. (Study Session 11, LOS 22.i)

36. **B**   Investing in the foreign market (China bonds) exposes Bowers to two sources of return: the R_{FC} of the bonds and the change in the CNY, the R_{FX}. Bowers is now assuming the nominal spread in the bonds will not change (i.e., the yield of both bonds will increase 75 basis points). (He is now assuming a yield beta of 1.00.) The assumption in this type of analysis is the two bonds have equivalent duration. Thus, both will decline equally in price and will have equal R_{FC}. The R_{FX} of the U.S. bond is zero, so there is no currency exposure. For the China bond, the expected decline in the USD of 2% is equivalent to an approximate 2% appreciation of the CNY. This means a purchase of the China bond will be superior to the U.S. bond for Bowers. However, he must also consider any premium or discount currency hedging will earn to determine if an unhedged or hedged currency exposure is optimal. The forward premium or discount depends on the differential in short term interest rates. The U.S. short term rate is 3% higher, which means the CNY will sell at a forward premium of 3%. Selling the CNY forward (buy the USD) will earn 3% and is superior to not hedging the currency and earning an expected 2% in a later, unhedged spot sale of the CNY. (Study Session 11, LOS 22.j)

QUESTIONS 37–42

Source: Study Sessions 9 and 15

37. **B** The currency overlay approach follows the IPS guidelines, but the portfolio manager is not responsible for currency exposure. Instead, a separate manager, who is considered an expert in foreign currency management, is hired to manage the currency exposure within the guidelines of the IPS. A strategic hedge ratio probably refers to a long-term percentage of currency risk to be hedged. In a separate asset allocation approach, there are two separate managers much like the currency overlay approach, but the managers use separate guidelines. (Study Session 9, LOS 18.i)

38. **C** Since the question is concerned with eliminating basis risk and not with mitigating transactions costs, statement C is the best choice. The only way to avoid basis risk is to enter a contact with a maturity equal to the desired holding period. Continually adjusting the hedge would likely create significant trading costs, but is the best method for reducing basis risk. When the futures contract is longer than the desired holding period, the investor must reverse at the end of the holding period at the existing futures price. If the futures contract is shorter than the desired holding period, the investor must close the first contract and then enter another. Both the shorter-term and longer-term contracts will create basis risk for Wulf's portfolio. (Study Session 9, LOS 18.d)

39. **A** Candidate discussion: The CFA text discusses delta hedging of an option position by using the underlying. Because delta is the change in value of an option for change in value of the underlying, delta determines the number of shares of the underlying to hedge an option position. This question is the reciprocal situation: hedging the underlying with options on the underlying. As the reciprocal situation, the hedge ratio is based on the reciprocal of delta. It makes the question tricky and fair but fortunately there are generally not a lot of questions that are this tough.

    First calculate the appropriate number of yen put options to purchase for the initial delta hedge. The appropriate number of options to purchase is equal to $(-1/\delta)$ times the negative value of the portfolio in foreign currency units.

    $$\text{yen put options} = \frac{-1}{0.85} \times \frac{-25,000,000}{1,000,000} = 29.41$$

    Given the change in delta, the number of yen put options needed reduces to:

    $$\text{yen put options} = \frac{-1}{0.92} \times \frac{-25,000,000}{1,000,000} = 27.17$$

    The difference is 29.41 − 27.17 = 2.24 yen options. So in order to remain delta-neutral, two put options need to be sold to accommodate the decrease in delta. (Study Session 15, LOS 27.e)

40. **A** Futures remove translation risk by protecting the investor against losses on the amount hedged, but they also eliminate any chance of a gain from favorable movements. They are, however, very liquid and are less expensive to use. Options require a premium in order to provide insurance against unfavorable exchange rate movements. (Study Session 9, LOS 18.g)

41. **B** Wulf invests a total of 6,410,256 euros (= £5,000,000 / 0.78£/€) in the British asset. After 180 days, the value of the asset has increased to €6,800,000 (= £5,100,000 / 0.75£/€). Therefore, the unhedged return on the asset in euros = [(€6,800,000 − €6,410,256) / €6,410,256] = 6.08%.

The next step is to calculate the return on the futures contract:

Wulf originally sold the £5,000,000 in futures for 0.79£/€, = (£5,000,000) × (€ / 0.79£) = €6,329,114.

Since the pound has strengthened relative to the Euro (the futures exchange rate has dropped to 0.785£/€), he has lost [(£5,000,000) × (€ / 0.785£) =] €6,369,427 − €6,329,114 = −€40,313, which translates to a loss on the futures transaction of −€40,313 / €6,410,256 = −0.63% return. The total return from hedging the principal is 6.08% − 0.63% = 5.45%. (Study Session 9, LOS 18.a)

42. **B** If Bauer shorts the appropriate amount of the index and the short position is perfectly correlated with the investment, the return must be the foreign risk-free rate. If Bauer then chooses to hedge the currency risk, he knows the exact value of the foreign currency to hedge and that the return to the (double) hedging strategy must be the domestic risk-free rate. (Study Session 15, LOS 26.g)

QUESTIONS 43–48

Source: Study Session 15

43. **B** Worth should assume the receive fixed/pay floating arm of the swap, since they are currently paying a fixed interest rate on its outstanding debt. If interest rates decline, Worth would like to take advantage of the lower rates. In order to do so, it must either reissue long-term debt (which can be an expensive process) or enter into a swap to convert its fixed payments into floating payments. Thus, Worth will receive fixed and pay floating in the swap. The net interest payment that Worth will pay is calculated as follows:

interest rate on existing debt − fixed rate received from swap + floating rate paid to swap

7.2% − 5.8% + EURIBOR = 1.4% + EURIBOR = 140 basis points + EURIBOR

(Study Session 15, LOS 28.a)

44. **C** The MIA analysts are correct, both with regard to the swap duration and to the balance sheet effects of entering into the swap. Worth will enter into the swap as the fixed rate receiver/floating rate payer. Since pay floating on the swap is equivalent to having a floating rate liability, the swap duration from this perspective is:

$$D_{pay\ floating} = D_{fixed} - D_{floating}$$

The duration of the floating rate side is a minimum of zero and maximum of 0.5 since the swap is semiannual settlement. Thus, the average duration of the floating side is 0.25. The duration of the fixed side is given as 1.2. Therefore, the duration of the swap from Worth's perspective is:

1.2 − 0.25 = 0.95

Currently, Worth is "matching" its balance sheet asset/liability durations by funding long-term fixed assets with fixed liabilities. This minimizes equity volatility. Entering a receive fixed/pay floating swap will reduce the absolute duration of the net liabilities on the balance sheet by creating synthetic floating rate debt. If interest rates decline as expected, the economic value of assets will rise faster than that of liabilities, raising the economic value of balance sheet equity. The equity is becoming more sensitive to changes in rates. (Study Session 15, LOS 28.b, c)

45. **A** In a long interest rate collar, the firm purchases an interest rate cap and sells an interest rate floor, locking in a range of interest rates that the firm will pay. This position is frequently taken by borrowers with floating rate debt. The firm can manage its cash flow risk within the effective range of interest rates defined by the collar. If the underlying interest rate rises above the cap strike rate, the cap payoff to the borrower (purchaser of the cap) will mitigate the higher interest payments on the firm's debt. If the underlying interest rate falls below the floor strike, the borrower (seller of the floor) will make a payment which will offset the decrease in interest payments on the firm's debt. The payoff is made in arrears, so for Enertech's collar, the caplet and floorlet that expire in 18 months would payoff (if they were in the money at 18 months) in 24 months. Thus, to determine the payoff from the collar that occurs in 24 months, we must determine whether the cap or the floor is in the money at the 18th month. In the vignette, LIBOR

is expected to be 4.1% in 18 months. This is below the floor strike of 4.5%. Therefore, Enertech will need to make a payment calculated as follows:

$$\text{floor payoff} = \text{notional principal} \times \left[\max\left(\text{strike rate} - \text{actual rate}, 0\right) \left(\frac{\text{days in period}}{360}\right) \right]$$

$$= \text{notional principal} \times \left[\max\left(0.045 - 0.041, 0\right) \left(\frac{180}{360}\right) \right]$$

$$= \text{notional principal} \times \left[0.002 \right]$$

Enertech will need to make a payment equal to $0.002 per dollar of notional principal.

(Study Session 15, LOS 27.d)

46. **B** In 18 months, Enertech will be required to make an interest payment on its loan equal to:

(LIBOR at 12 months + 150bp) / 2 = (6.1% + 1.5%) = 7.6% / 2 = 3.8%

This interest payment will be partially offset by the payoff from the interest rate cap. Because LIBOR at 12 months is above the cap strike rate of 5.5%, the cap is in the money and will have a payoff equal to:

$$\text{cap payoff} = \text{notional principal} \times \left[\max\left(\text{actual rate} - \text{strike rate}, 0\right) \left(\frac{\text{days in period}}{360}\right) \right]$$

$$= \text{notional principal} \times \left[\max\left(0.061 - 0.055, 0\right) \left(\frac{180}{360}\right) \right]$$

$$= \text{notional principal} \times \left[0.003 \right]$$

Thus, assuming the notional principal is set equal to the face value of the loan, the effective interest rate is equal to:

0.038 – 0.003 = 0.035 = 3.5%

(Study Session 15, LOS 27.d)

47. **B** Prior to the swaption, SBK had fixed-rate debt and swaps to receive fixed versus pay floating. This created net floating rate debt.

Recall that payer and receiver refer to the fixed rate on the swap from the swaption buyer's perspective. Let fl stand for the floating rate and F for fixed rate. Before the swaption, SBK is net paying fl.

As the seller of the payer swaption, SBK will receive fixed (F) and pay floating (fl) if the swaption buyer chooses to exercise. The buyer of the payer swaption will pay F and receive fl. In simple terms, the buyer will exercise if fl increases and exceeds F.

Direction of rate change:	Buyer of payer swaption will pay fixed versus receive floating.	SBK will receive fixed versus pay floating if swaption buyer chooses to exercise.
Rates decrease fl < F	Receive floating is unattractive; buyer will not exercise.	SBK continues to net pay floating on its debt, which is decreasing cash outflows.
Rates increase fl > F	Receive floating is attractive; buyer will exercise.	SBK still pays net *fl* on the initial debt and on the exercised swaption is now also paying *fl* versus receive *F*. Net net this is pay 2fl – F. Recall *fl* is now above *F*, so cash outflows increase.

Selling options (swaptions) gives the right to decide to the counterparty. This will increase risk for SBK, which is why the sale was a mistake. SBK was correct that they have cash flow risk if rates increase. SBK should have bought a payer swaption giving it the right to pay fixed and receive floating, which would produce offsetting inflows if rates increase. They made a mistake. (Study Session 15, LOS 28.c, h)

48. C   MIA will own a floating rate debt and will experience decreasing cash flow if rates decline. Buying an interest rate put would generate receipts if rates fall below the strike rate. An 8% strike rate on the put would provide immediate protection, but 7% is all that is offered. Selling calls is not an acceptable answer because the cash premium received is in no way linked to that actual future decline in rates. (Study Session 15, LOS 27.c)

QUESTIONS 49–54

Source: Study Session 18

49. **C**   The Moss account should not be added to the Aggressive composite. Moss's portfolio is all equity, not balanced. The Bateman account should be added to the conservative composite. CCM does not use options or futures to manage any of their portfolios, so Bateman's request that CCM not use options or futures is immaterial. (Study Session 18, LOS 32.g)

50. **C**   Composites can be delineated using equity and bond exposures, as long as the ranges are tightly defined. GIPS do not mandate what type of composites or the number of composites to create. (Study Session 18, LOS 32.g)

51. **B**   CCM should move North's account from the aggressive composite to the conservative composite. However, the historical performance of North's account must stay with the aggressive composite. (Study Session 18, LOS 32.h)

52. **A**   Currently, GIPS verification is not required, only recommended. The verification process is central to the reliability of the GIPS. Normally, CCM must include the number of accounts in each composite. However, if the composite has five or fewer accounts, CCM is not required to disclose the number of accounts. The cash returns must be included in the total account return. (Study Session 18, LOS 32.s)

53. **C**   Beginning January 1, 2010, he may not report a bond result from the balanced accounts unless he had first separated each account into bond and equity subaccounts and allocated the actual cash to equity or bonds based on the strategic asset mix of the accounts. Based on Exhibit 1 data, we can determine what that result would have been, but because he did not meet GIPS requirements, he may not report the number. The result would have been 4.8%.

The accounts hold only 56% in bonds ($182 / 325); cash would have been held in each account bond segment sufficient to reach 70% of $325,000,000. The return this would have produced is:

$(56 / 70)5.2\% + (14 / 70)3.4\% = 4.8\%$

(Study Session 18, LOS 32.i)

54. **B** Current GIPS requirements specify that a portfolio market value on the date of all large external cash flows is needed, resulting in a true time weighted rate of return being calculated with each cash flow defining a subperiod. The subperiod returns are then chain-linked for the quarterly return. While GIPS does not define what constitutes a large external cash flow, it is likely the $300,000 versus beginning market value of $2,500,000 would be considered a large external cash flow. The Modified Dietz is not a true time weighted rate of return but is instead an estimate of the true time weighted rate of return. Unless Moss can document that the Modified Ditz calculation of 11.1% does not deviate materially from the current requirements, it may not be used. While unneeded to answer this question, Modified Dietz is calculated as:

$$r_{ModDietz} = \frac{MV_1 - MV_0 - CF}{MV_0 + \sum (CF_i \times w_i)}$$

Moss portfolio: inflows for 61 days of the total 91 days

$$\left(\frac{3,100,000 - 2,500,000 - 300,000}{2,500,000 + \left[300,000 \times \left(\frac{61}{91} \right) \right]} \right) = 11.1\%$$

(Study Session 18, LOS 32.e)

QUESTIONS 55–60

Source: Study Session 4

55. **A**   This is a trivial question, but the reading does point out that flat heavy tax regimes often include provisions for tax exemption of some types of bond interest. (Study Session 4, LOS 9.a)

56. **C**   Since she lives under a flat tax regime, one does not have a benefit over the other. (Study Session 4, LOS 9.a, e)

57. **C**   Increasing the investment horizon will increase tax drag because the number of compounding periods increases. Lowering returns will reduce tax drag because the aggregate amount taxed is reduced. Since the two effects are opposite, we would need to know the increase in the investment horizon as well as the decrease in return to be able to estimate their combined effect on tax drag. (Study Session 4, LOS 9.b)

58. **A**   Typically, a heavy capital gain tax regime does not have a favorable treatment for capital gains, but it does have a favorable treatment for both dividend and interest income. (Study Session 4, LOS 9.a)

59. **B**   The most recently acquired shares will have the highest basis and the lowest tax consequences. (Study Session 4, LOS 9.h)

60. **C**   There must be a weight for the allocation of each asset to each type of account. (Study Session 4, LOS 9.d)

PRACTICE EXAM 3
MORNING SESSION ANSWERS

QUESTION 1

Source: Study Session 16, LOS 29.l

A.   (2 points each for any two of the following)
1. Automated trading according to set rules.
2. Minimizes trading costs and risk.
3. Breaks large orders into several smaller orders.
4. Minimizes market impact.

Candidate discussion:
In algorithmic trading, a computer uses quantitative rules to determine the optimal sizes of trades to minimize costs and risk. Larger trades are often broken into several smaller trades so as to blend into the typical market flow of orders. Algorithmic trading strategies can be classified as logical participation strategies, opportunistic strategies, and specialized strategies.

Candidate discussion: Maximum 4 points.

Source: Study Session 16, LOS 29.m

Answer for Question 1-B

Stock	Appropriate trading strategy	Justification
1. Star	Implementation shortfall strategy	High urgency level **Candidate discussion:** Although the Star trade is a small percentage of daily volume and has a narrow spread as a percentage of the last price, the urgency level is high thus the implementation shortfall algorithmic trading strategy is appropriate. $\text{narrow spread} = \dfrac{39.76 - 39.74}{39.75} = 0.0005$ $\text{small \% of daily volume} = \dfrac{700,000}{11,500,000} = 6.1\%$

Stock	Appropriate trading strategy	Justification
2. Moon	Use a broker or crossing system	Large relative average daily volume and large spreads. **Candidate discussion:** The Moon trade's wide spread and large percentage of daily volume suggests a broker or crossing system should be used. In addition, the trade has a low urgency level. $$\text{wide spread} = \frac{150.37 - 149.62}{150.00} = 0.005$$ $$\text{large \% of daily volume} = \frac{500,000}{2,200,000} = 22.7\%$$ *Note: Using a broker is NOT an algorithmic trading strategy.*
3. Sun	Simple participation strategy based on VWAP, TWAP, or another benchmark	Narrow spread, low urgency, and small relative average daily volume **Candidate discussion:** The Sun trade has a narrow spread as percentage of last price, low urgency level, and trades at a small percentage of daily volume which makes the simple participation *algorithmic* trading strategy best suited for this trade. $$\text{narrow spread} = \frac{80.02 - 79.98}{80.00} = 0.0005$$ $$\text{small \% of daily volume} = \frac{500,000}{6,000,000} = 8.3\%$$

Candidate discussion: Maximum 6 points. 1 point for each algorithmic trading strategy. 1 point for each justification.

Source: Study Session 16, LOS 29.1

Answer for Question 1-C

Circle one	Defend Your Selection
Incorrect (1 point)	(2 points) • Traders needed to monitor automatic trading process and manage more complicated trades. • Role of trader has changed with greater emphasis on thinking strategically and tactically rather than managing broker relationships. **Candidate discussion:** Rather than eliminating traders, algorithmic trading strategies will make them more productive by increasing the amount that can be traded at a lower cost with less error. The role of a trader has changed under algorithmic trading as greater emphasis is placed on strategic and tactical decision making rather than managing broker relationships. The automated trading process needs to be monitored thus the role of a trader would not be eliminated.

Candidate discussion: Maximum 3 points. 1 point for incorrect. 2 points for one correct statement.

QUESTION 2

Source: Study Session 18, LOS 32.h, k

Answer for Question 2-A

Comment	Is the comment consistent with the requirements of GIPS? (circle one)	If not, recommend the change that will bring the firm into GIPS compliance
"We have not reported the performance for our real estate composite because we only have eight portfolios in it, which is less than the minimum number of portfolios required to form a composite. Once we have the required ten portfolios necessary for composite creation, we will begin reporting performance for the real estate composite."	No	Firm required to report performance of composite regardless of how many portfolios are in it. **Candidate discussion:** There is no minimum required number of portfolios necessary for composite creation. Richardson may have been thinking of the requirement for reporting the number of portfolios in a composite. To be GIPS compliant firms must report the number of portfolios in a composite and a measure of internal dispersion unless there are five or less portfolios in the composite.
"We have different policies for when portfolios are added to a composite. The time period for inclusion of new portfolios is longer for the private equity composite than it is for the small cap equity composite."	Yes	**Candidate discussion:** This policy is consistent with the GIPS standards. Depending on the type of asset, it can take several months to find a suitable investment for an investor's funds. Finding an investment in the private equity world can often take longer than in the case of publicly traded equity.

Candidate discussion: Maximum 6 points. 1 point each for correctly identifying whether the comment is inconsistent with the GIPS standards. 2 points for recommending the change necessary to bring the firm into compliance with the GIPS standards. 0 points possible if the yes/no decision is wrong. 3 points for correctly identifying whether a comment is consistent with GIPS.

©2016 Kaplan, Inc.

Source: Study Session 18, LOS 32.d, h, l, m, p

B. 1. Not a problem. Delray is following normal GIPS requirements of deducting only direct trading expense. It is common for wrap fee accounts to use a bundled fee where trading cannot be separated from other fees, in which case the entire fee must be deducted for GIPS.

2. Not a problem. GIPS only requires some internal dispersion measure be reported but specifies standard deviation for three years of monthly returns must be used for the external dispersion measure.

3. Agree with the recommendation. If the process continues substantially as before, with the same staff and Delray can document the past results, BJAM's past record must now be part of Delray's GIPS presentation. Because Jones had not been active in the investment process for the last five years, his retirement is not material for GIPS.

Candidate discussion:

1 point for each decision and 1 point for each explanation. Concern 1 is a direct test of the special issues associated with wrap fees. The question specified that Delray had not previously offered wrap fee accounts leading to a difference in how the two firms have reported. Concern 2 tests the distinction between internal and external dispersion reporting requirements. GIPS requires an internal dispersion measure but does not specify what to use. It does specify that standard deviation for three years of monthly returns be used for the external dispersion. Concern 3 deals with the apparent exception to the normal GIPS prohibition of retroactively changing the past GIPS record. It is not really an exception because the GIPS principle is that the record belongs to the firm and not the individuals involved in the management process. BJAM is now Delray; this was an acquisition of BJAM. If Jones had been material to the investment process, that would have been a material change that might prohibit reporting the past record but it is not an issue here.

QUESTION 3

Source: Study Session 6, LOS 13.i, k

Answer for Question 3-A

Objectives	Comments
1. Return (3 points)	$(1.045)(1.04)(1.0035) - 1 = 9.06\%$ desired $(1.04)(1.04)(1.0035) - 1 = 8.54\%$ minimum return **Candidate discussion:** 1 point for showing the three components of return. 1 point for 9.06% with the desired 4.5% distribution. 1 point for 8.54% with the minimum 4.0% distribution. No points for calculating with addition because the question specified compounded.
2. Risk tolerance (3 points)	Above average due to the perpetual nature of the foundation, the ability to reduce distributions by 0.5%, and the use of a smoothing distribution rule. **Candidate discussion:** 1 point for above average and 1 point each for two relevant supporting reasons.

Constraints	Comments
1. Time horizon (2 points)	Long term, perpetual.
2. Liquidity (2 points)	Hold 6 months of annual return distribution as emergency cash reserve, approximately $\frac{1}{2} \times 4\% \times \$(500 - 2.5)$ million. Distribute in 6 months: $2.6 million / 1.04 = $2.5 million for capital expenditure. **Candidate discussion:** 1 point for each specific need. The PV of the 2.6 must be specified for credit because the needed data was provided.
3. Legal (2 points)	No specific requirements beyond normal professional standards.
4. Taxes (2 points)	Tax exempt. (1 point) Must distribute 4% annually to maintain tax exempt status. (1 point) **Candidate discussion:** The 4% distribution could have been shown under legal.
5. Unique (2 points)	The college has significant nondomestic (USD) revenue, and this should be considered in the portfolio asset allocation.

Candidate discussion: Maximum 16 points.

Source: Study Session 6, LOS 13.i,k; Study Session 8, LOS 17.s

Answer for Question 3-B

Recommended Change	Explanation (For the exam)
1. Decrease cash	With no specified need for this much, it only creates cash drag.
2. Increase corporate bonds	Less risk than equity and would provide diversification.
3. Reduce venture capital	Too high considering 60% allocation to higher risk assets (small caps, hedge funds, venture capital)

1 point for a correct direction of change, and 1 point for a correct explanation of the change.

Source: Study Session 9, LOS 18.c

Answer for Question 3-C

More likely to hedge foreign currency exposure. The college already has foreign currency revenue, so foreign stock is increasing the exposure to foreign currency.

> **Candidate discussion:** 1 point each for correct decision and then supporting it.

QUESTION 4

Source: Study Session 12, LOS 23.b, d, i

Comment	Circle one	Supporting statement
"Large-cap stocks are the most appropriate place for active management because managers can take big enough positions to capitalize on pockets of inefficiency."	Incorrect	More public information available on large caps makes efficient pricing more likely and generating excess return less likely.
"Because the S&P 500 Index is price-weighted, out-performing stocks tend to have more and more influence on its value."	Incorrect	S&P is market-value weighted.
"The Shailor College endowment should employ a passive index vehicle, such as a Russell 2000 index fund, for our small-cap stock portfolio. The market for small-cap stocks tends to be more efficient than the market for large-cap stocks and would provide more opportunities for us to benefit from active management."	Incorrect	Small cap stocks tend to receive less research and be less efficient, making it easier to generate alpha with small caps.

Candidate discussion: Maximum 9 points. 1 point for each correct/incorrect decision that is correct. 2 points for each supporting statement as long as the correct/incorrect decision is correct.

QUESTION 5

Source: Study Session 17, LOS 31.f

Comment	Agree or Disagree (circle one)	If you disagree, support your decision with one reason related to the characteristics of valid benchmarks
"For a benchmark to be considered valid, it must be investable. To be investable, I should be able to recreate and hold the benchmark as a portfolio."	Agree	
"Although I agree with you that market value-weighted benchmarks are generally considered the most valid, the benchmark you have applied in my performance appraisal is not truly market value-weighted because you have not included the total market capitalization of all the benchmark firms."	Disagree	It is typical and appropriate to float-adjust the benchmark by removing shares that do not trade and cannot be purchased.
"Perhaps as an alternative we could use a multi-factor model-based benchmark. Factor model-based benchmarks are considered valid benchmarks and, since they are based on sound statistical methods, their results are irrefutable."	Disagree	Multifactor models can be appropriate but they are not unambiguous. There are different models based on different factors that lead to different results.
"If you do not like the idea of multi-factor-based benchmarks, we can always go back to comparing my performance to the average equity manager. At least that way I know exactly who I'm up against."	Disagree	Comparing to the average manager is common but not a valid benchmark. It cannot be specified in advance and is not an investable alternative to active management.

Candidate discussion: Maximum 12 points. 3 points for agreeing with first statement. 1 point each for disagreeing with remaining three statements. 2 points for each correct explanation *only if* agree/disagree decision is correct.

QUESTION 6

Source: Study Session 11, LOS 22.e

A.   To lower duration, contracts will be sold:

$$\text{\# contracts} = \left(\frac{D_T - D_P}{D_f}\right)\left(\frac{V_P}{P_f\,(\text{multiplier})}\right) \times CF$$

$$\text{\# contracts} = \left(\frac{5 - 6.8}{6.5}\right)\left(\frac{250{,}000{,}000}{100{,}000}\right) \times 1.3 = -900$$

sell 900 contracts at $100,000

Candidate discussion:
Show your work. If you make a calculation error you may get partial credit for having the correct equation. The contracts should be sold, as indicated by the minus sign in the answer. However, be sure to clearly state buy or sell and round to the closest whole number.

Source: Study Session 11, LOS 22.d

B.   •   Futures offer greater liquidity. (1 point for any one of the following advantages: greater liquidity, lower transaction costs, efficiency, can achieve durations not possible with underlying assets.)

   •   Basis risk is the risk that the difference between the cash securities price and the futures price will change unexpectedly. Basis risk could cause the hedge to perform better or worse than expected. (1 point for defining and 1 point for the implication.)

Candidate discussion:
Compared to cash market instruments, futures are: more liquid, less expensive because transaction costs are less, and easier to short futures than the actual bond because there is greater depth in the futures market.

Since this is a cross-hedge (i.e., using Treasury futures to modify or fully hedge the risk of a corporate bond portfolio), the strategy is subject to basis risk. If the basis should unexpectedly widen or narrow significantly, the hedge will be valued incorrectly. Think in terms of the values used to determine the number of contracts. A significant change in the basis represents a change in the relative values of the portfolio and the futures position, and the resulting duration of the strategy could be more or less than desired.

Candidate discussion: Maximum 3 points.

Source: Study Session 11, LOS 22.g

Answer for Question 6-C

	Credit forward at a contract spread of 250bp
i. The maximum potential loss to Mulder.	• The maximum loss would occur if the spread declined to zero which is an unlikely event. • payoff $= \left(\text{spread at maturity} - \text{contract spread}\right) \times \text{notional principal} \times \text{risk factor}$ $= (0.0 - 0.025) \times \$10,000,000 \times 3 = -\$750,000$ (2 points) **Candidate discussion:** Mulder is worried about the quality of the bonds decreasing and is purchasing a credit spread forward which will pay off if the spread on the bond increases above the contract spread due to the price of the bond decreasing. The credit forward is a zero sum game because if the spread at maturity is less than the contract spread, the forward buyer will have to pay the forward seller.
ii. The payoff if the spread narrows to 200bp at the maturity of the derivative.	• payoff $= \left(\text{spread at maturity} - \text{contract spread}\right) \times \text{notional principal} \times \text{risk factor}$ $= (0.020 - 0.025) \times \$10,000,000 \times 3 = -\$150,000$ (1 point) • Mulder would have to pay \$150,000 (1 point) **Candidate discussion:** A spread of 200 bp means the price of the bond went up from the original 250 bp spread. The 200 bp spread is below the contract spread and knowing that credit spread forwards are zero sum games this means Mulder will owe the payoff amount to the seller of the credit spread option.

Candidate discussion: Maximum 4 points.

QUESTION 7

Source: Study Session 4, LOS 9.e

Answer for Question 7-A

Statement	Correct or incorrect	If the statement is incorrect, state why it is incorrect.
1. Both tax deferred and tax exempt accounts provide a tax advantage in allowing tax free compounding while funds are held in the account. However a tax deferred account is superior for after-tax wealth maximization because it provides an initial tax deduction.	Incorrect	Generally, the tax deferred account is only superior if initial tax rates are higher than tax rates at the end of the deferral period. **Candidate discussion:** If initial and end of period withdrawal tax rates are the same, the two account types produce the same after-tax ending value. The TEA pays taxes at the initial rate and the TDA at the ending rate. If initial rates are lower, the TEA is superior. If initial rates are higher, the TDA is superior.
2. The accrual equivalent after-tax return is the tax-free return that if compounded annually would produce the portfolio's after-tax ending value. Therefore it considers the impact of all the various tax rates and deferrals that may apply to a portfolio.	Correct	
3. Shorter-term trading strategies have an advantage when short tern gains and losses are taxed more heavily than long term gains and losses because the shorter-term trader will realize short term losses to shelter short term gains that would have been heavily taxed.	Incorrect	Higher short-term tax rates penalize short-term traders. **Candidate discussion:** The statement ignores that over time portfolios are expected to generate net positive returns, not losses. Even if there were short-term losses and a tax advantage to realizing those losses, both short- and long-term traders could realize the loss.
4. Maximizing after tax value will include optimizing asset location. Traditional mean-variance optimization can be modified to achieve this result or Monte Carlo simulation can be used.	Correct	

Candidate discussion: 2 points each for selecting correct for statement 2 and 4. 1 point each for selecting incorrect for statements 1 and 3 and 1 point each for a correct statement of why they are incorrect.

Source: Study Session 4, LOS 9.h

B.   Generally Korkov is correct and HIFO is best. Selling the highest cost basis lots will realize the largest loss and create the greatest tax sheltering of other taxable income or gains. Baltus could be right if tax rates are expected to rise. In that case it might be beneficial to defer the larger losses until after the higher rates go into effect.

QUESTION 8

Source: Study Session 5, LOS 11.a

A.   Wilson began as the entrepreneur and founder of Tides. As a start up private company and as the sole asset in the taxable portfolio, he had high company-specific risk. Entrepreneurs generally do not want diversification and accept high specific risk in the effort to create wealth.

When Wilson took the company public 10 years ago, he became an executive but still retained control of the company, functioning as an entrepreneur with relatively little desire for diversification. In both these first two stages, he had market and high specific risk. The specific risk of his portfolio was likely declining as he accumulated other portfolio assets and as the company matured and went public.

Post-sale Wilson will be an investor with no control over the company. While we do not know his total assets, he will receive 2 × $45 × 100,000 = $ 9,000,000 of pretax value. While this larger public company likely has lower specific risk, increasing diversification is appropriate for Wilson as an "investor." He can tailor his portfolio to his desired level of market risk.

Candidate discussion: Maximum 9 points. 3 points for describing how Wilson has progressed through the three different stages. 3 points for explaining how his risk exposure has changed in each stage. 3 points for explaining how his desire for diversification has changed during each stage.

Source: Study Session 5, LOS 11.h

B.   Total return equity swap, the return of Destiny stock could be swapped for the return on a desired index to provide diversification of return with no loan needed. Alternatively, the Destiny return could be swapped for LIBOR and then this hedged position in Destiny could be used to borrow and use the funds to purchase a diversified portfolio. Upside and downside exposure to Destiny is removed.

OTM protective put would limit downside risk in Destiny to the strike price. This hedge should facilitate a loan with a high LTV, providing funds for diversification. Upside potential in Destiny would remain.

Prepaid variable forward, no separate loan is needed because the PVF effectively packages the loan as part of the PVF. Cash is received and can be used for diversification. Downside risk is removed as the Destiny shares will be delivered to repay the loan. Some upside is retained as a smaller number of shares can be delivered if Destiny's stock price increases.

Candidate discussion: Maximum 9 points. 1 point each for describing how each strategy provides diversification. 1 point each for commenting on upside or downside risk exposure. 1 point each for discussing whether a loan is required.

QUESTION 9

Source: Study Session 4, LOS 8.g, i

A. *Generate return sufficient to provide law school tuition, pay his living expenses, pay his brother's care, and maintain purchasing power of portfolio.*

Portfolio value = 87,500 × 2 × $45 = $7,875,000

Required after-tax real return = [$45,000 + ($175,000)(1.03)] / $7,875,000 = 2.86%

Required after-tax nominal return = 2.86% + 3.00% = 5.86% (arithmetic)

or

Required after-tax nominal return = (1.0286)(1.03) − 1 = 5.95% (geometric)

Candidate discussion:

Formulate the return should be interpreted as listing or stating the objectives. That is not a calculation. This is good practice, even if not required, in order to determine what must be calculated. Thinking of a time line and clearly identifying when things will happen is often important. In this case the return period starts now, so the investable base is just the assets available (including the stock sale). The $175,000 is the past year and must be increased by inflation for the coming year needs. The $200,000 is needed in three years (see the case facts in question 7). It does not need to be earned this year nor is it being distributed, so it should not be removed from the investable base. The law school tuition is an ongoing expense for three years, so treating it as a return requirement is normal. Lastly, the future rate of inflation must be considered in order to maintain the real value of the portfolio. The question has more in it than many recent exam questions, but it tests your ability to read and organize the data to reach an expected solution. That is fair game for the exam.

Candidate discussion: Maximum 10 points. 2 points for correct portfolio value. 4 points for formulation of return requirement; 1 point for each component listed. 1 point for adjusting spending requirements for inflation. 2 points for correct real return. 1 point for adding inflation to the real return.

Source: Study Session 4, LOS 8.h, i

Answer for Question 9-B

Wilson's ability to tolerate risk would be considered: (circle one)	Support with two reasons
Above average	1. Significant flexibility as Wilson should have significant earning power after law school. 2. Large portfolio relative to spending needs. **Candidate discussion:** The two reasons given are fairly common. Always look for *flexibility* in the client. Flexibility refers to the client's ability to alter lifestyle and spending needs, which usually leads to an above average ability to tolerate risk. It is typically the result of age and personal circumstances. Wilson is quite young with a substantial portfolio, and that provides a plethora of alternatives. For example, he could choose not to work, he could start another business, he could finish law school and practice law, and so on. If you listed some of these alternatives without specifically writing *flexibility*, that would suffice as an answer.

Candidate discussion: Maximum 5 points. 1 point for correctly identifying above average ability to tolerate risk. 2 points each for any two reasons.

QUESTION 10

Source: Study Session 5, LOS 12.a

Answer for Question 10-A

The purpose of life insurance is to replace financial capital that would have been but is not accumulated from savings out of human capital, due to premature death. A less risky employment means a lower discount rate should be applied to expected future earnings. This increases estimated human capital today and the need for life insurance.

Candidate discussion: Maximum 4 points. The question is very specific: 1 point for each of the four items required by the question.

Source: Study Session 4, LOS 8.j and Study Session 5, LOS 12.c, d

Answer for Question 10-B

Asset Class	Recommended allocation (circle one)	Support with one reason
Cash	0% to 5%	Low liquidity needs indicate there is no reason to incur unnecessary cash drag. **Candidate discussion:** For SAA only, use cash for specific needs.
Bonds	36% to 45%	At 0.60 HC correlation to bonds, the HC is bond-like. Therefore, Wilson can select the lowest financial capital allocation to bonds. **Candidate discussion:** Another acceptable reason is that with an above-average risk objective, Wilson should allocate less than 40% to fixed income.
Stocks	61% to 70%	Stocks have the lowest correlation to Wilson's HC; therefore, a larger allocation to equity will provide diversification. **Candidate discussion:** An alternative answer is that with an above-average risk objective, Wilson should allocate more than 60% to equity.

Candidate discussion: Maximum 9 points. 1 point for each correct allocation. No other allocations are acceptable in this case. 2 points for each correct justification.

QUESTION 11

Source: Study Session 6, LOS 13.b

A.   The objective is to earn 1.75% above the minimum (5% discount rate) objective.

5% + 1.75% = 6.75%

Candidate discussion:
The committee wants to build a plan surplus by setting the return objective 175 basis points above the 5% minimum required rate of return set by the plan's actuary. The discount rate used by the actuary is a very common way for the question to provide you with the minimum required return. Based on assumptions employed by the actuary, if the portfolio produces that return, it will be able to meet pension obligations. A compounded return calculation is also acceptable but not required.

The minimum 10% return PHL's President Mauer mentioned is irrelevant. Since the plan should be run for the sole benefit of the beneficiaries, the president's comments should not affect the return objective set by the fund. This is a common distracter used by CFA Institute in this type of question and is aimed at making you think in terms of willingness to tolerate risk, which is typically of no consequence with institutional investors.

Candidate discussion: 1 point each for stating and for calculating the correct return objective.

Source: Study Session 6, LOS 13.c

Answer for Question 11-B

Risk factor	Select whether PHLP has below-average, average, or above average ability to tolerate risk compared with the average for the corporate helicopter leasing industry (circle one)	Justify each response with *one* reason
i. Sponsor financial status and profitability	**Above average**	Financially sound; lower D/E and higher ROE than industry. **Candidate discussion:** PHL is currently in a good position to make contributions to PHLP if needed. This gives PHLP an above average ability to take risk compared with the industry average.
ii. Workforce age	**Above average**	Workforce younger than industry; longer time horizon. **Candidate discussion:** Although 12% of the workforce is more than 50 years old, this is less than the 16% industry average. PHLP has an above-average ability to take risk compared to the average for PHL's industry because the younger age of its employees increases the duration of PHLP's liabilities.
iii. Retired employees	**Below average**	PHL has a lower ratio of active to retired lives than the industry average. **Candidate discussion:** A lower ratio of active to retired employees usually indicates a shorter time horizon and an aging active employee group. This reduces the relative duration of the PHLP's liabilities and increases the likelihood of PHL having to make special contributions to the fund. These give PHLP a below average ability to take risk compared to the average for PHL's industry.

Candidate discussion: Maximum 9 points. 1 point each for correctly selecting the risk tolerance level. 2 points for each correct justification.

Candidate discussion: While the answers given may be sufficient, it is easier to make them better by including some specific numeric data, for example, average age of 36 versus industry average of 43.

©2016 Kaplan, Inc.

Source: Study Session 6, LOS 13.c

Answer for Question 11-C

Factor	Identify whether the factor increases, does not affect, or decreases PHLP's ability to tolerate risk (circle one)	Justify *each* response with *one* reason
i. Sponsor (PHL) and pension fund (PHLP) common risk exposures	**Decreases**	Reduces PHL's ability to provide funds if drop in pension fund earnings. **Candidate discussion:** Unless McCormick can persuade the Investment Committee to reduce PHLP's 15% exposure to these securities, this factor decreases PHLP's ability to take risk. The desire to increase exposure should not be considered.
ii. Retirement plan features	**Decreases**	Early retirement options shorten plan liability duration. **Candidate discussion:** 12% of PHL's workforce qualify for early retirement. We are not given any indication of how many will elect to retire, but since the option is newly implemented, PKLP must be ready to meet increased liquidity needs. Liquidity requirements associated with this potential increase in payouts reduce PHLP's ability to take risk.

Candidate discussion: Maximum 6 points. 1 point each for correctly identifying how the factor will affect risk tolerance. 2 points for each correct justification.

Source: Study Session 6, LOS 13.b

Answer for Question 11-D

	Constraint	Formulate *each* of the constraints in PHLP's investment policy statement and justify *each* response with *one* reason.
i.	Liquidity requirement	Low liquidity needs: • Long time horizon relative to the industry. **Candidate discussion:** PHL has a relatively young and stable workforce compared to the industry averages. The plan is unlikely to need to make large payouts in the near future given the average duration of 17 years for PHLP's liabilities. PHLP may want to set aside a reserve, however, to deal with the possibility of employees taking advantage of PHLP's early retirement option at some time in the future.
ii.	Time horizon	Long, single-stage time horizon. • Average employee younger than industry. **Candidate discussion:** With a stable workforce with an average age less than the industry average, PHLP's time horizon is longer than average. When dealing with pension plans, always look at workforce characteristics for indications of the plan's time horizon, liquidity needs, risk tolerance, and unique circumstances. Taxes are not typically a concern since pension plans are tax exempt.

Candidate discussion: Be careful about drawing superficial comparisons from answers to other case facts and questions. There are often situations when reducing time horizon and increasing liquidity needs are connected. In this case, 11-C-ii asked directly about how plan features affect the plan's ability to take risk. The new early retirement option lowers ability because it may shorten time horizon and increase liquidity needs. In contrast, 11-D asks directly about the plan's liquidity and time horizon. Liquidity needs are overall low and time horizon is longer, given the comparison data to other companies and the facts regarding the lack of usage of the early retirement option and the low proportion of employees who are over 50 years old.

Candidate discussion: Maximum 4 points. 1 point for each correctly formulated constraint. 1 point for each correct justification.

QUESTION 12

Source: Study Session 13 LOS 24.s

Answer for Question 12-A

Hedge Fund Style	Description
Convertible arbitrage	Capitalize on mispricing between convertible securities and the underlying equity. Short the overvalued position and possibly earn interest on the proceeds of the short sale. Go long the undervalued position to hedge the risk of the short side. Leverage is often used to earn positive interest spread if the borrowing cost is less than the reinvestment rate. **Candidate discussion:** Capitalizing on mispriced securities is a common feature of all arbitrage. Beyond that, the specifics of the sources of return depend on the specifics of the arbitrage. A common convertible arbitrage strategy is to buy undervalued convertible bonds and short the stock to hedge the option to convert to stock that is embedded in the convertible bond. The cash received on the short position earns interest. The trade is also vulnerable to changes in volatility and the impact on option values. Rising volatility increases option values and the value of the convertible bond (because it includes an option to receive stock). Falling volatility would harm the value of the convertible bond.
Equity market neutral	Achieve a zero beta with long and short positions; gain by holding undervalued, shorting overvalued securities. Earn interest on the cash collected. **Candidate discussion:** Managers might pair together stocks with equal betas, one long and one short, to eliminate systematic risk. They gain from the ability to identify over- and under-valued securities while facing no systematic risk.
Hedged equity	Gain from holding short and long positions in over-valued and under-valued securities. Correctly tilting the portfolio to net long or short can benefit return if the market increases or decreases. **Candidate discussion:** Hedged equity managers gain from long and short positions without the specific goal of attaining zero systematic risk. Net portfolio position can be anywhere from net long to short, depending on the manager's forecasts.
Global macro	Take positions (either long or short) in financial and non-financial assets to take advantage of systematic (market) swings rather than changes in individual security prices. **Candidate discussion:** Managed futures are sometimes classified as a global macro strategy. GM managers sometimes use derivatives to increase their exposures.

Candidate discussion: Maximum 12 points. 3 points for each correctly described strategy. Description must include the basic strategy as well as how profits are generated.

Candidate discussion: This terminology is not always mutually exclusive. The terms hedged equity and market neutral can overlap. If long and short equity positions are set up to exactly offset each other, the strategy is both hedged equity and market neutral. If an equity portfolio is 130% long and 30% short, it is hedged equity of a sort but it is not market neutral. Know the basic terminology and apply it in the way that best fits the case.

Source: Study Session 13 LOS 24.c

Answer for Question 12-B

	Alternative investments special issues
1	Tax issues; frequently must deal with partnerships and other ownership forms with unique tax structures.
2	Suitability; holding periods might not be suitable to client.
3	Decision risk; extreme returns can make client want to change strategy quickly at disadvantageous point.

Candidate discussion: In addition to the due diligence necessary for any investment, alternative investments present several unique special issues. These include tax issues, suitability, communication with the client, decision risk, and the size of the position needed. Many private wealth clients have large positions in closely held equities. When this is the case, the alternative will probably not have the necessary liquidity. Also, the amount that must be invested in most alternatives is considerable. If it will take up too large a portion of the portfolio, the alternative is again unsuited for the client. Many times investing in alternatives involves buying into a partnership or other private investing relationship. These investment vehicles often have peculiar tax issues that might not be suitable for the client. Communication with the client is required, meaning the manager must thoroughly describe the return and risk of the alternative. Often times, clients are unable to comprehend the true nature of the investment, and this can lead to their wanting to liquidate the position at an inopportune time after a large positive or negative return.

Candidate discussion: Maximum 6 points. 2 points each for any three correctly described alternative investment special issues.

PRACTICE EXAM 3
AFTERNOON SESSION ANSWERS

To get detailed answer explanations with references to specific LOS and SchweserNotes™ content, and to get valuable feedback on how your score compares to those of other Level III candidates, use your Username and Password to gain Online Access at schweser.com and choose the left-hand menu item "Practice Exams Vol. 1."

1. C	21. A	41. C
2. B	22. B	42. B
3. C	23. B	43. B
4. B	24. A	44. B
5. C	25. C	45. B
6. C	26. B	46. C
7. A	27. A	47. B
8. A	28. C	48. A
9. C	29. B	49. B
10. A	30. C	50. B
11. B	31. A	51. B
12. A	32. A	52. A
13. B	33. B	53. C
14. B	34. C	54. C
15. C	35. A	55. B
16. C	36. B	56. B
17. B	37. C	57. C
18. B	38. C	58. C
19. C	39. A	59. C
20. C	40. C	60. C

PRACTICE EXAM 3
AFTERNOON SESSION ANSWERS

QUESTIONS 1–6

Source: Study Session 1

1. **C** Diligence and thoroughness shall be exercised when making investment recommendations, which should be supported by appropriate research and investigation while avoiding any material misrepresentations (Standards V(A) and V(B)). The information obtained from his friend would need to be verified for accuracy before it can be used. The information gathered from the CEO of IMI is material non-public and therefore cannot be used. Verde was unable to collect information and facts in sufficient quantity and quality to complete a reasonable investigation and analysis. The lack of information related to the quality of local market inputs and labor, as well as uncertainty surrounding foreign accounting systems and future elections, suggests that there is insufficient information to form a reasonably informed recommendation at present. (Study Session 1, LOS 2.a)

2. **B** There is no violation of the use of material nonpublic information standard per Standard II(A) as Verde's friend is not an official of the foreign government, holds no official title, and is not acting in any official capacity representing his government. However, Verde still has a duty to diligently seek to validate all information used in his report and to avoid any misrepresentations or omissions when disseminating his report. Thus, Verde has a duty to determine whether the information is accurate, whether it was obtained through a breach of duty, and whether it is material to his conclusion and recommendation. (Study Session 1, LOS 2.a)

3. **C** According to Standard II(A), material nonpublic information cannot be used to trade, or cause others to trade, in the associated security. Using the information obtained from IMI's CFO is a violation of the use of material nonpublic information standard. The CFO indicated that the information was not yet public when he revealed it to Verde. Thus, Verde is not at liberty to use it in his analysis or in his report unless he is able to find the same information through public and nonmaterial nonpublic sources. He is also prohibited from revealing it to his colleagues at New World. There is no need for Verde to encourage the firm to release the information in a timely manner because the firm is already prepared to reveal the information soon. (Study Session 1, LOS 2.a)

4. **B** A firm establishes policies and procedures for review to assure that others in the firm do not act improperly on information prior to client dissemination. This also applies to coworkers. Regardless of his intent Verde should not violate procedures. He could have gone to the boss's boss or to his compliance officer if unsure what to do. (Study Session 1, LOS 2.a)

5. **C** According to Standard V(B), known limitations of the analysis and conclusions should be documented in research reports. Material misrepresentations should also be avoided by including all pertinent information and by distinguishing between opinion and fact in the analysis and conclusions of a report. Verde may have violated the standards related to known limitations in his analysis by rushing to provide a recommendation. Verde felt somewhat unable to perform an analysis given the lack of essential data, but completed a report where the conclusions are largely driven by information derived from conversations that were not included or referenced in the report. These missing facts may also be construed as material misrepresentation. However, at no time should material nonpublic information be used for, or reported in, recommendations that are produced by Verde or New World. (Study Session 1, LOS 2.a)

6. **C** The report should not be disseminated because the information obtained from the CFO of IMI is non-public and material. In addition, the information received from the friend cannot be verified as accurate. Coupled with the overall lack of information essential to the analysis and the uncertainty related to accounting policies and political risk, the report should not be published at this time. Once these difficulties are overcome, suitable recommendations for individual firms should include an analysis of the prospects of the entire firm rather than narrow comments on the outcome of the joint venture bidding and attendant investments. (Study Session 1, LOS 2.a)

QUESTIONS 7–12

Source: Study Session 2

7. **A** David Lee only allocates Star Tech IPO to the employee benefit plans and not to his individual clients. This violates the Asset Manager Code of Professional Conduct where managers must establish policies to ensure fair and equitable trade allocation among client accounts. There is insufficient evidence to indicate that David Lee's investment action deviates from the employee benefit plans mandate. (Study Session 2, LOS 4.c)

8. **A** KIC's compensation scheme may result in managers putting their own interests (i.e., bonuses) before client's interests as given by the case scenario of David Lee. David Lee could be allocating shares to the employee benefit plans so as to boost the plans performance and hence his bonuses to the detriment of his other clients. (Study Session 2, LOS 4.c)

9. **C** Smith is wrong to suggest that it is possible to always apply only one method. The Asset Manager Code does not specify that only one pricing method should be used, thus, Haywood is correct in his remarks. Haywood is correct that multiple methods may be necessary and that client disclosure is appropriate. (Study Session 2, LOS 4.c)

10. **A** Under the Asset Manager Code of Professional Conduct, Armstrong is required to take investment action that is appropriate to the client's financial situation. Hence, Armstrong's action in allocating a high risk IPO to only the capital gains group of clients would be consistent with the requirements of the Asset Manager Code of Professional Conduct. Armstrong also has a reasonable basis (i.e., using assets size under management) in allocating the IPO shares among the capital gains group of clients. Therefore, there is no violation in terms of ensuring a fair and equitable trade allocation among client accounts. (Study Session 2, LOS 4.c)

11. **B** The IPO program is a conflict of interest as a manager who wants to get a hold of particular IPO shares would purchase shares in that IPO for client accounts regardless of its suitability to the client accounts. For the other staff, the IPO purchase scheme must ensure that clients' trades take priority, which KIC has ensured in this case. (Study Session 2, LOS 4.c)

12. **A** Haywood has no reasonable basis to execute client trades just to get a value. His firm has the obligation and bears the cost of obtaining this information. This might also be market manipulation if the intent is to manipulate price and volume. That intent is unclear and the effect is to push up the price not down. "A" is the best answer choice. (Study Session 2, LOS 4.c)

QUESTIONS 13–18

Source: Study Session 7

13. **B** For an equity long-short hedge fund, the bottom-up approach is the most appropriate forecasting approach. Individual security investments are determined by identifying over- or under-valued securities. Thus, managers will start at the "bottom" by analyzing individual securities and probably not move upward (broader) in the analysis. The net market exposure of the fund is not determined through an economy-wide analysis, as in top-down analysis. Rather it will vary based on the amount of long and short exposures. (Study Session 7, LOS 16.e)

14. **B** An increase in retirement age increases the labor force growth rate and leads to increased GDP growth. A decrease in the savings rate means less capital is available meaning higher interest rates, decreased investment in capital stock, and a decrease in economic growth. An increase in pollution controls increases costs of production and decreases economic growth. The reduction in economic output due to increased pollution controls could be only short term (Study Session 7, LOS 16.b)

15. **C** Real GDP growth can be estimated as follows:

$$\%\Delta Y \cong \%\Delta A + \alpha\left(\%\Delta K\right) + \left(1-\alpha\right)\left(\%\Delta L\right)$$

where:
$\%\Delta A$ = percentage change in total factor productivity
$\%\Delta K$ = percentage change in capital
$\%\Delta L$ = percentage change in labor

$$\%\Delta Y \cong 1.25\% + 0.6\left(-0.50\%\right) + \left(1-0.6\right)\left(2.50\%\right)$$
$$\%\Delta Y \cong 1.25\% + -0.30\% + 1.00\% = 1.95\%$$

For the period 1991–2000, growth in total factor productivity contributed more to real GDP growth than the growth in labor or the growth in capital. (Study Session 7, LOS 16.b)

16. **C** The first step is to estimate real GDP growth.

$$\%\Delta Y \cong \%\Delta A + \alpha\left(\%\Delta K\right) + \left(1-\alpha\right)\left(\%\Delta L\right)$$
$$\cong 2.35\% + 0.6\left(1.25\%\right) + \left(1-0.6\right)\left(0.42\%\right) = 3.27\%$$

Next, the intrinsic value of the market index can be estimated using the Gordon growth model.

$$P_0 = \frac{D_0\left(1+g\right)}{r-g} = \frac{75\times\left(1+0.0327\right)}{0.08-0.0327} = \frac{77.45}{0.047} = 1637.42$$

(Study Session 7, LOS 16.c)

17. **B** Comment 2 is correct. Comment 1 is incorrect. When the earnings yield for the S&P 500 is greater than the yield on Treasuries, the level of the index is low relative to expected earnings, making the earnings yield too high. Thus, equities would be considered under-valued. Comment 3 is incorrect because earnings and prices are restating according to CPI in the 10-year average price/earnings ratio model, so the model does account for inflation. (Study Session 7, LOS 16.f)

18. **B** The equity q ratio is computed as:

$$\text{equity q} = \frac{\text{market value of equity}}{\text{mv of assets} - \text{mv of liabilities}} = \frac{20}{50 - 26} = 0.8333$$

The ratio is less than one, so the equity index is considered to be undervalued. (Study Session 7, LOS 16.g)

QUESTIONS 19–24

Source: Study Session 12

19. **C** The way a long-only portfolio earns a positive alpha is through the selection of undervalued securities. Stock selection is how Kiley generates his performance. Kiley's portfolio is potentially exposed to both systematic and unsystematic risk. (Study Session 12, LOS 23.m)

20. **C** The change in allocations in Exhibits 1 and 2 indicate large changes in investment style. Allocations moved from a growth-oriented style in the first 5-year period to a value-oriented style in the second 5-year period. The returns based analysis confirms these findings—the slopes changed markedly for LCV (large increase in the second 5-year period) and LCG (large decrease in the second 5-year period). (Study Session 12, LOS 23.i, k)

21. **A** The most extreme negative decision that a long-only manager can make is to drop the allocation to the sector to zero. The active weight is the difference between the manager's allocation and the benchmark allocation: $0 - 3\% = -3\%$. (Study Session 12, LOS 23.m)

22. **B** In an alpha and beta separation approach, the investor gains systematic risk exposure by allocating funds to (low-cost) passive index managers, while separately adding alpha via allocation of funds to market-neutral long-short managers. (Study Session 12, LOS 23.t)

23. **B** The information coefficient (IC) measures manager skill. The information coefficient will be high, because the correlation between alpha forecasts and alpha realizations is expected to remain high. The investor breadth (IB) measures the number of independent investment decisions made within the investor's portfolio. The investor breadth will be low, because GenM employs a small number of active managers (the satellites managers), who, in turn, are mandated to consider only a small number of securities. The Information ratio = IC × (IB)$^{1/2}$. The information ratio could be higher or lower, depending on the level reached for each of the variables. (Study Session 12, LOS 23.p)

24. **A** Advantage 1 is correct. A Completeness Fund compliments or "completes" the actively managed portfolio so that the investor's portfolio has risk exposure similar to that of the benchmark. The advantage of the Completeness Fund approach is capturing the stock selecting ability of active managers, while making the overall portfolio risk profile similar to its benchmark.

    Advantage 2 is incorrect. Misfit risk is defined as the standard deviation of the differences between the returns on the managers' normal portfolio and the investor's benchmark. Although the completeness fund approach in its purest form would eliminate misfit risk, the elimination of misfit risk would prevent the fund from receiving the benefit of active management. If the Completeness Fund eliminates misfit risk, it will also eliminate the additional returns associated with the stock selecting ability of active managers. (Study Session 12, LOS 23.r)

QUESTIONS 25–30

Source: Study Session 3

25. **C**   The decision to deposit the money into a safe, low interest paying account is not irrational. It is not totally rational behavior, however, since McGriff did not seek out and evaluate all possible alternatives that might meet his requirements. The decision to deposit the money into an interest-bearing checking account moves McGriff toward his ultimate goal, so it is reasonable, but it probably represents satisficing rather than optimization. (Study Session 3, LOS 5.c)

26. **B**   The tendency to sell winners too soon and hold losers to long is a symptom of the disposition effect. It could also be thought of as indicating loss aversion, where investors are reluctant to accept losses. Bounded rationality, however, implies a reasonable, though not optimal, decision that generally moves the investor toward the ultimate goal. The disposition effect can actually produce the opposite effect, since the investor sells winners, effectively eliminating any further upside potential from them, while holding losers. This limits the portfolio's upside potential while increasing risk. (Study Session 3, LOS 7.f)

27. **A**   Although confirmation bias can lead an investor to ignore or place too little weight on new information, in this case McGriff's actions are more indicative of seeing too great a cognitive cost. He doesn't want to take the time or expend the energy necessary to analyze the information. If McGriff applied a Bayesian framework in making investment decisions, he would evaluate new information on its own to apply the proper base rate weighting. (Study Session 3, LOS 6.d)

28. **C**   Independent individualists:

    Are active, Robert has taken almost total control of the portfolio.

    Have medium to high risk tolerance, he buys and sells stocks.

    Mainly have cognitive biases, he does seek information and evidence (even if he does not use it very well and does not incorporate new information, these are still cognitive issues).

    (Study Session 3, LOS 7.a)

29. **B**   Independent individualists tend to be independent thinkers who have confidence in their own decisions, making them difficult to advise. Since their biases are mostly cognitive they will listen to sound reasoning, so education and sound investment analysis are recommended. Pointing out McGriff's failures would be counter-productive. First, it would tend to produce an adversarial relationship between McGriff and Little, and second, McGriff would have a tendency to explain away the failures by placing blame elsewhere. (Study Session 3, LOS 7.a)

30. **C**   Even when plan participants eliminate some of the alternative funds in a defined contribution pension plan, allocating evenly across the remaining funds is seen as an indication of 1/n diversification bias. By ignoring the pension portfolio, McGriff is exhibiting status quo bias. This is when plan participants make an initial allocation and do nothing after that. McGriff obviously intentionally over-weighted the one fund because it contains his employer's stock. Due to their familiarity with the employer, plan participants are likely to be over-confident about the future for their employers' stock and over-weight it in the portfolio. (Study Session 3, LOS 7.c)

QUESTIONS 31–36

Source: Study Session 11

31. **A** Higgins describes a cross hedge strategy. The investor sells the first foreign currency forward for a second foreign currency that is expected to appreciate to a greater degree than the currency of the bond. When the bond is sold or matures, the investor sells the second foreign currency for the domestic currency at the spot rate.

     Tyler is describing a proxy hedge strategy. The investor uses a second foreign currency to hedge the first foreign currency. Here the investor would use a forward contract where dollars would be bought and euros would be sold (remember the Bergen Petroleum bond is denominated in Norwegian NKr). If the NKr and euro are positively correlated, the movement of the NKr and euro will offset one another. The short euro position in the forward contract and the long NKr position from the liquidation of the bonds would offset so that the net return from the two positions would be zero. The dollar-euro forward contract provides the currency hedge. (Study Session 11, LOS 22.j)

32. **A** The returns for the unhedged and hedged positions are calculated as follows. Assume the U.S. dollar is currency d and the Norwegian NKr is currency f. The forward rate is denoted as F, and risk-free rates in each currency are denoted as i.

     The unhedged return is the return on the bond plus the expected change in the NKr:

     $$= 7.00 - 0.40 = 6.60$$

     To obtain the hedged return, we first calculate the approximate forward discount for the Norwegian NKr relative to the domestic currency:

     $$F_{d,f} = i_d - i_f = 2.50 - 4.80 = -2.30$$

     The hedged return is the return on the bond plus the forward discount for the NKr:

     $$= 7.00 - 2.30 = 4.70$$

     The highest return is from the unhedged position. Assuming the investor is risk-neutral (i.e., is only concerned with return), the unhedged position should be taken. (Study Session 11, LOS 22.j)

33. **B** Neither knows what he is talking about. IRP determines in free markets the difference between the current spot currency exchange rate and forward exchange rate (S_0 versus F_0). There is no valid evidence that F_0 is a predictor of what will happen to the spot exchange rate in the future. F_0 does not predict S_t, so Higgins is wrong.

     Tyler is doubly wrong, because he tried to use the forward quote to predict what will happen to the currency if it is unhedged, and he got the sign (–) for the forward premium wrong. The lower yen interest rate means it will trade at a +3.2% forward premium. If the yen currency risk were hedged, selling the yen forward versus buying the USD would earn +3.2%. The unhedged return will depend on how the market exchange rate changes. (Study Session 11, LOS 22.j)

34. **C**   Higgins is incorrect. He is correct that emerging country debt is usually denominated in a hard currency and that emerging country currency crises sometimes spread from one country to another (i.e., contagion does occur). However, the quality in emerging market sovereign bonds has increased over time. In addition, emerging market governments can implement fiscal and/or monetary policies to offset potentially negative events and they have access to major wide-world lenders (e.g., World Bank, International Monetary Fund).

    Tyler is correct because investing outside the emerging market bond index does provide the potential for excess returns. The major emerging market bond index, the Emerging Markets Bond Index Plus (EMBI+), is concentrated in Latin American debt (e.g., Brazil, Mexico). The portfolio manager can earn an alpha by investing in emerging country bonds outside of this region. (Study Session 11, LOS 22.l)

35. **A**   In breakeven spread analysis, the analyst determines the yield change that makes the returns on bonds equivalent. To determine the breakeven yield change at which the investor would be indifferent between purchasing two bonds, we must first compare the bonds' yields over the holding period. Over the one-year time horizon, the Horgen bond has a yield advantage of 1% (9% – 8%). For the returns to be equivalent over the one-year time horizon (once the investor has purchased the bonds), the price for the Horgen bond must fall by 1%. For its price to fall, its yield must increase. The breakeven change in price of the Horgen bond will be:

    change in price = duration × change in yield

    In this case, the change in yield is the widening of spread that must occur to make the investor indifferent between the two bonds. You can solve for the widening (W) by:

    1.0% = 7.25 × W   (7.25 is the duration of the Horgen bond)

    0.1379% = W = 13.79 basis points

    Therefore, if the Horgen bond's yield rises by more than 13.79 basis points, the value of the bond would decline by an amount that would offset the yield advantage, making the Midlothian bond more attractive. If the Horgen yield decreases, the price appreciation would add to the favorable yield differential of investing in the Horgen bond. Note that we calculated the breakeven yield change using the bond with the longer duration and that exchange rate and interest rate assumptions were ignored.
    (Study Session 11, LOS 22.k)

36. **B**   Breakeven spread analysis measures the change in price, resulting from yield spread widening, that would offset the favorable yield differential of one bond over another. Breakeven spreads do not provide any explicit measure of exchange rate risk. The calculation of the breakeven spread is based on duration. (Study Session 11, LOS 22.k)

QUESTIONS 37–42

Source: Study Session 15

37. **C** Number of futures = $V(1 + R_F)^T / P_f$ (multiplier)

    Number = $[3{,}000{,}000{,}000(1 + 0.03)^{5/12}] / (250)(1{,}058) = 11{,}482.71$ contracts; remember the S&P 500 futures quoted contract price is multiplied by 250 to get the contract size. (Study Session 15, LOS 26.c)

38. **C** payoff = # contracts$(250)(P_{f1} - P_{f0})$

    payoff = $-11{,}482(250)(1{,}125 - 1{,}058) = -192{,}323{,}500$ (Study Session 15, LOS 26.a)

39. **A** Current asset allocation is 88% bonds and 12% stocks; recommended asset allocation is 75% bonds and 25% stocks. Requires selling $3,250,000,000 (13% of $25 billion) in bonds and buying an equivalent amount of stocks.

    contract size = $250 \times \$1{,}058 = \$264{,}500$;

    number of equity futures = $[(\beta_T - \beta_p) / \beta_f] \times [V_p / (P_f)(\text{multiplier})]$

    $[(1 - 0) / 1] \times (3{,}250{,}000{,}000 / \$264{,}500) = 12{,}287.33 \approx 12{,}290$ equity futures contracts

    (Study Session 15, LOS 26.d)

40. **C** dollar value of portfolio = 162,225,000,000 yen / 108.15 = $1,500,000,000

    contract size = $(\text{multiplier})(P_f) = \$5.00 \times 10{,}337 = \$51{,}685$

    number futures = $[(\beta_T - \beta_p) / \beta_f] \times [V_p / (P_f)(\text{multiplier})]$

    $[(0 - 0.90) / 1.0] \times (\$1{,}500{,}000{,}000 / \$51{,}685) = -26{,}119.76$ contracts (short)

    (Study Session 15, LOS 26.f)

41. **C** Yield beta relates to bonds and the ratio of changes in interest rates. Hedging foreign currency risk from owning foreign securities requires selling the foreign currency forward. An equity position can be synthetically replicated, in this case, by buying futures on the foreign market and fully collateralizing the position with that market's risk-free bonds. (Study Session 15, LOS 26.b)

42. **B** Futures contracts on corporate bonds do not exist, therefore Choice A is incorrect. Forwards are the most frequently used method of hedging exchange rate risk in practice. Futures markets are used less frequently to manage exchange rate risk since they are relatively newer than the foreign exchange forward market and provide less liquidity. Choice C is incorrect since hedging the Japanese equity portfolio and the currency risk between the dollar and the yen would lock in the U.S. risk-free rate, not the Japanese risk-free rate. Also, management would have to know the exact future value of the equity to hedge. (Study Session 15, LOS 26.g)

QUESTIONS 43–48

Source: Study Session 15

43. **B** The duration of a pay fixed/receive floating swap for four years with quarterly payments would be equal to the duration of a 4-year floating rate bond with quarterly payments minus the duration of a 4-year fixed rate bond with quarterly payments. The duration of the 4-year floating rate bond would be approximately one-half of the payment interval, or $0.5 \times 1/4 = 0.125$. The duration of the 4-year fixed rate bond (based on the assumption given in the vignette) would be 75% of four years, or 3.0. Therefore, the swap duration is $0.125 - 3.0 = -2.875$. (Study Session 15, LOS 28.b)

 Professor's Note: The general rule is to assume the average duration of a floater is ½ the coupon reset period. Zero-coupon bonds have durations equal to their term to maturity. The duration of coupon-bearing bonds varies, and data will be provided in the question or case facts, as it was here.

44. **B** The duration of Swap B, a pay fixed/receive floating swap for five years with semiannual payments, would be equal to the duration of a 5-year floating rate bond with semiannual payments minus the duration of a 5-year fixed rate bond with semiannual payments. The duration of the 5-year floating rate bond would be one-half of the payment interval, or $0.5 \times 0.5 = 0.25$. The duration of the 5-year fixed rate bond would be 75% of five years, or 3.75. Therefore the swap duration will be $0.25 - 3.75 = -3.50$.

The required notional principal to achieve a portfolio duration of 4.5 using Swap B would be:

$$NP = V_p[(MD_T - MD_p) / MD_{swap}] = \$800M \times [(4.5 - 6.5) / -3.5] = \$457M$$

(Study Session 15, LOS 28.d)

45. **B** The dual currency bond creates JPY coupon inflows but no principal JPY exposure; therefore, Skinner cannot use a standard currency swap, which requires exchange of notionals. He needs the special swap to pay JPY versus receive USD on coupons only. (Study Session 15, LOS 28.f)

46. **C** Note that selling any type of swaption cannot work. Skinner would be giving the purchaser the right to decide what to do. Skinner must be the buyer, and he must receive fixed to replace the lost fixed coupons if his bonds are called. The terms *buyer* and *receiver* refer to the fixed rate from the swaption buyer's perspective. The portfolio is at risk if rates fall and the callable bonds are called. Funds would then have to be reinvested at lower rates. Skinner should buy a receiver (receive fixed) swaption. If rates fall, he will exercise the swaption and the fixed inflows will replace the lost fixed inflows on the called bonds. (Study Session 15, LOS 28.h)

47. **B** To increase the portfolio duration, enter a receive fixed swap. A received fixed swap has positive duration. It is equivalent to buying fixed-rate bonds, generating more fixed coupon inflows. (Study Session 15, LOS 28.b)

48. **A** The swap would reduce the cash flow risk, since Barter will have locked in a fixed payment by using the swap. However, the duration of the fixed rate payments will be much higher than the duration of the floating rate payments, thus increasing the market value risk of the debt. (Study Session 15, LOS 28.c)

QUESTIONS 49–54

Source: Study Sessions 8 and 13

49. **B** Direct investments in real estate have correlations of returns with both stocks and bonds that are very close to zero; this means that direct real estate investments may provide good diversification benefits with both stock and bonds. Therefore, McDonald's consultant is incorrect regarding his opinion on the lack of diversification benefits with bonds.

    Although not required to answer the question, the diversification benefits from direct investments in real estate tend to disappear when hedge funds and commodities are added to a portfolio of stocks and bonds. (Study Session 13, LOS 24.f)

50. **B** Choice B is an accurate difference. Venture capital returns are negative early in the fund's life because the firm spends a significant amount of cash, but may turn positive later when investments are exited. In contrast, buyout fund investors get their cash more quickly because investments are at a later stage.

    Choice A is inaccurate. Buyout funds are more leveraged, with generally 60-75 percent of capital needs raised through debt obligations. Debt is not used for venture capital investments.

    Choice C is incorrect. The first part of the statement is accurate because venture capital investments have more risk of downside (loss) but a higher upside when the investments actually succeed. The second part of the statement is inaccurate because estimates of venture capital returns have greater chance for error than estimates of buyout returns. (Study Session 8, LOS 17.i)

51. **B** Venture capitalists typically participate in formative-stage companies in either seed or early-stage financing, as well as in expansion-stage companies. They do not typically participate in expansion-stage companies as indicated in Statement 2. Statement 3 is correct; that is, buyout funds purchase private companies and participate in taking public companies private. (Study Session 13, LOS 24.f)

52. **A** Statement 4 is correct. The three sources of return are the return from changes in the spot price (spot or price return), the implied opportunity cost of investing in the futures contract rather than the risk-free asset (collateral return or yield), and the return from rolling long futures positions forward into a term structure in backwardation (roll return).

    Statement 5 is incorrect. In contango, more distant futures prices are higher than nearer-term futures prices; the roll return will be negative, not positive. Conversely, in backwardation, more distant futures prices are lower than nearer-term futures prices; the roll return would be positive, not negative. (Study Session 13, LOS 24.k, l)

53. **C** If McDonald's assessment of a downward-sloping term structure is accurate, a positive roll return should be earned as the commodity market is exhibiting backwardation. The roll yield occurs when rolling forward a futures into a lower cost futures position. This creates a positive roll return when the term structure for the futures slopes downward.

    Choice A is incorrect. While a negative return is earned with a market in contango, it is associated with an upward-sloping term structure. McDonald has identified a downward-sloping term structure.

    Choice B is incorrect. Increasing volatility will most likely increase roll return, but is not the primary reason for a positive roll return. The reason roll return could be positive would more likely be a function of a downward-sloping term structure for the commodity as determined by McDonald. (Study Session 13, LOS 24.p)

54. **C** Energy and precious metals tend to provide an effective hedge against unexpected inflation because their prices increase with inflation, while fixed-income instruments have expected inflation included in their price and will fall if expected inflation exceeds actual inflation.

    Choice A is incorrect. Markets in contango would indicate a negative roll yield, thus sending commodities in the same direction as bonds. This would not make them an effective hedge.

    Choice B is incorrect. Returns from agriculture or non-energy commodities tend to be positively correlated with returns from stocks and bonds. Returns from holding energy or precious metals, however, would be negatively correlated with returns from stocks and bonds during periods of unexpected inflation. (Study Session 13, LOS 24.s)

QUESTIONS 55–60

Source: Study Session 7

55. **B** Using the Grinold and Kroner model, the expected return on a stock market is its dividend yield plus the inflation rate plus the real earnings growth rate minus the change in stock outstanding plus changes in the P/E ratio:

$$\hat{R}_i = \frac{D_1}{P_0} + i + g - \Delta S + \Delta\left(\frac{P}{E}\right)$$

where:

$\hat{R}_i$ = expected return on stock market i

D_1 = dividend next period

P_0 = current stock price

i = expected inflation rate

g = real growth rate in total earnings

ΔS = change in number of shares outstanding

$\Delta\left(\frac{P}{E}\right)$ = change in P/E ratio

The highest expected return is for Bergamo. The expected equity market return calculations for Alzano (A), Bergamo (B), and Lombardo (L) are:

$$\hat{R}_A = 2.70\% + 2.80 + 4.80\% - (-0.20\%) + 0.70\% = 11.20\%$$
$$\hat{R}_B = 0.60\% + 5.30 + 5.70\% - 1.20\% + 1.10\% = 11.50\%$$
$$\hat{R}_L = 3.60\% + 1.90 + 2.20\% - (-0.80\%) + (-0.20\%) = 8.30\%$$

Note that when the change in stock outstanding decreases (i.e., stock is repurchased), this is to the investor's benefit (the repurchase yield is positive). Changes in the P/E ratio also affect the expected return. If investors think, for example, that stocks will be less risky in the future, the P/E ratio will increase, and the expected return on stocks increases. (Study Session 7, LOS 15.c)

56. **B** The data show that yields are declining as maturity increases, therefore the yield curve is inverted. The downward sloping yield curve indicates that the economy is likely to contract in the future. (Study Session 7, LOS 15.i)

57. **C** Given that the Linden economy is likely to contract in the future, Wieters should recommend that the Balduvi Endowment move toward government and investment grade bonds, because inflation and interest rates will decrease and economic growth will slow. Stocks, especially cyclical stocks, should be underweighted. High yield bonds should also be underweighted, because the default risk premium on them may grow as the economy slows. Therefore, Wieters should recommend Portfolio C for the Balduvi Endowment. (Study Session 7, LOS 15.f, g, o, p, r)

58. **C** Mora is likely susceptible to the confirming evidence trap. The confirming evidence trap is when analysts give too much credence to evidence that supports their existing or favored beliefs. Note that Mora's prior belief from her master's degree training was that the default risk premium has predictive power for stock returns. In the analysis, it appears that lagged changes in the stock market have a strong relationship with future stock returns. Mora's conclusions seem to focus solely on the default risk premium.

It could be argued that she is also susceptible to the anchoring trap because she puts too much weight on the first set of information she received (from her master's studies). (Study Session 7, LOS 15.b)

59. **C** Wieters is likely susceptible to the recallability trap. The recallability trap is when analysts let past disasters or dramatic events weigh too heavily in their forecasts. Although the 80-year history indicates that Lombardo stocks returns average 13.6%, Wieters projects returns much lower. He may be letting the credit crisis of 2007-2008 overly influence his predictions.

It might be argued that he is also susceptible to the status quo trap, because his prediction is influenced by recent events, but in this trap he would probably predict closer to the recent value of −12.6% in his forecasts. (Study Session 7, LOS 15.b)

60. **C** Statement 1: Mora's statements on emerging market debt are correct.

Statement 2: Mora is incorrect. It is true that emerging market debt is particularly susceptible to financial crises and that an emerging government must have foreign currency reserves to defend its currency in the foreign exchange markets. However, most emerging debt is denominated in a non-domestic currency. The currency of emerging bonds is usually a hard currency (e.g., dollars, euros, etc.) and an emerging government must have a hard currency to pay back the principal and interest. This can increase the default risk for emerging market debt. (Study Session 7, LOS 15.m, p)

Notes

Notes

Notes

Notes

Notes

Notes

Notes

Notes

Notes

Notes

Notes